PRAISE FOR *Mister Monkey*

"Expertly constructed, 'Mister Monkey' is so fresh and new it's almost giddy, almost impudent with originality. Tender and artful, Prose's fifteenth novel is a gently spiritual celebration of life. . . . Chekhovian. It's that good. It's that funny. It's that sad. It's that deceptive and deep."

—Cathleen Schine, *New York Times Book Review*
(front cover review)

"In this novel, the imminent end of the world feels as inevitable as the end of a particular life. *Mister Monkey* itself, though, is gripping and engaging all the way through, the characters' miseries as moving as their fierce attachments to hope and the possibility of unexpected mercies."

—*San Francisco Chronicle*

"Masterful. . . . A lovely tribute to the transformative value of imagination."

—*Washington Post*

"Beautifully crafted, incisively written. . . . Engaging and accessible. . . . What elevates this novel is Prose's ability to let us see into the heart of each character, to render each so vulnerably human, so achingly real in just a few short paragraphs."

—*Minneapolis Star Tribune*

"Prose hilariously nails the down-at-the-heels milieu while also evoking the magic even low-rent theater can inspire in the narratives of the show's costume designer (an underpaid NYU grad student), the moonlighting emergency room nurse who plays the villainess, and the director, whose closing monologue reveals someone much kinder than his prior treatment of Margot suggested. Wickedly funny and sharply observant, in the author's vintage manner, with a warmth that softens the satire just enough."

—*Kirkus Reviews* (starred review)

"Remarkable. . . . [Prose] is the Meryl Streep of literary fiction, convincingly shifting between multiple voices and points of view—not just from book to book, but within a single work." —NPR.org

"A comedy of manners for the digital age. . . . An astonishing tour de force." —*Brooklyn Eagle*

"Prose is at her consummate, canny best in this superbly incisive comedy of errors, a cleverly choreographed relay in which each character subtly passes the narrating baton on to the next, and what a beguiling and bedeviled cast this is! . . . Each character's inner soliloquy is saturated with yearning and profound spiritual inquiries as the silly play covertly evokes questions about truth and lies, evolution and extinction, and how we care for each other and the world. Prose is resplendent in this exceptionally keen, artistic, funny, empathic, and intricate dance of longing and coincidence." —*Booklist* (starred review)

"This novel promises to be madcap and profound in equal measure." —themillions.com

"It's always exhilarating when a serious novelist reveals her ridiculous, irreverent streak, when she isn't too self-consciously proper to jape and jeer at the ineptitudes of everyday living. Prose has always been an unafraid novelist with a thirst for the mordant and satirical." —barnesandnoble.com

MISTER MONKEY

MISTER MONKEY

A Novel

FRANCINE PROSE

HARPER ● PERENNIAL

NEW YORK ● LONDON ● TORONTO ● SYDNEY ● NEW DELHI ● AUCKLAND

HARPER ● PERENNIAL

A hardcover edition of this book was published in 2016
by HarperCollins Publishers.

HarperCollins books may be purchased for educational,
business, or sales promotional use. For information,
please e-mail the Special Markets Department at
SPsales@harpercollins.com.

FIRST HARPER PERENNIAL EDITION PUBLISHED 2017.

Designed by Fritz Metsch

The Library of Congress has cataloged the hardcover
edition as follows:

Names: Prose, Francine, 1947– author.
Title: Mister monkey : a novel / Francine Prose.
Description: New York : Harper, 2016.
Identifiers: LCCN 2016013864| ISBN 9780062397836
(hardcover) | ISBN 9780062397850 (ebook)
Subjects: LCSH: Musical theater—Fiction. | Interpersonal
relations—Fiction.
    | BISAC: FICTION / Literary. | FICTION / Humorous.
| FICTION / Coming of Age. | GSAFD: Black humor
(Literature) | Humorous fiction.
Classification: LCC PS3566.R68 M57 2016 | DDC
813/.54—dc23 LC record available at https://lccn.loc.gov
/2016013864

ISBN 978-0-06-239784-3 (pbk.)

17 18 19 20 21   LSC   10 9 8 7 6 5 4 3 2 1

For Emilia, Malena, and Jackson

MISTER MONKEY

A Page from Mister Monkey

ONCE UPON A TIME, not so long ago, a scientist (and loving mother) by the name of Mrs. Jimson said a tearful good-bye to her family in New York and went to study monkeys in Africa. There she became friends with a smart, friendly, playful, super-cute baby chimpanzee she named Mister Monkey.

She and Mister Monkey and Mister Monkey's chimpanzee mom and dad spent hours tossing coconuts back and forth in their lovely jungle home among the trees that smelled sweetly of tropical flowers and the brilliantly colored birds nesting in the vines.

All night the full moon lit up the jungle like a baseball field. Sometimes Mrs. Jimson wrote in her notebook. Sometimes she sent home letters telling her family how much she missed them, and how she had come to love little Mister Monkey.

One night evil hunters sneaked into the game preserve and shot Mister Monkey's parents. And when Mrs. Jimson tried to protect them, the hunters killed her too.

Poor Mister Monkey was an orphan! No one knew what to do. The game wardens put him in a cage for his own protection. Day and night, he sat in a corner of his big cage and cried. It was like being in a zoo! Every kid who has ever seen a monkey in the zoo will know what Mister Monkey was feeling.

Then one day the wardens got a letter from New York asking if Mister Monkey could come to the United States. The Jimson family wanted to adopt him!

Pretty soon Mister Monkey found himself on an airplane—and then in New York. The tall buildings scared him. What if they fell down? He couldn't get used to the noise of the traffic and the smoky air. Where were the birds and flowers? It was so different from his jungle home.

But Mister Monkey liked his new dad and sister and brother. He liked their big comfortable sunny apartment. He liked their smart friendly housekeeper, Carmen.

Mister Monkey learned to talk and taught himself tricks to entertain his new family. At parties, he'd scamper among the guests, picking pockets. When people discovered their wallets missing, he always gave them right back.

Life was perfect until Mr. Jimson's evil girlfriend,

Janice, accused Mister Monkey of stealing her wallet and not returning it.

Even when he was put in jail, Mister Monkey knew that everything would be all right. That was because he had magic monkey vision. He could see the past and the future. He knew what was going to happen to the humans he loved, and to the humans he didn't love. He had godly superpowers. He could read minds. He could see into souls.

Mister Monkey told Mr. Jimson not to worry. But just to be on the safe side, Mr. Jimson hired a lawyer named Portia McBailey. . . .

CHAPTER 1

MARGOT HOLDS THE MOMENT

WHO CARES IF it's children's theater? Margot is playing a criminal lawyer crusading for truth and justice! So would someone please tell her where, in what deranged fashion universe, a defense attorney would appear before a judge in a rainbow Harpo Marx wig and an obscenely short, hobblingly tight, iridescent purple suit? Margot arrives at the theater an hour early, since part of her preparation now involves a series of meditations designed to help her overcome the humiliation of squeezing into an outfit that her character—Portia McBailey—would never wear unless she'd quit being a lawyer and gone to work for an escort service, role-playing a slutty executive-secretary birthday clown.

Now, as she enters her dressing room before the Saturday matinee, she notices that the hem of the purple skirt has come entirely undone. The dimpled fringe of ragged cloth trailing clumps of thread will *hypnotize* the audience. *Mommy, Daddy, why is that funny lady's skirt so hairy?* Margot counts off ten deep breaths so as to repel any negative thoughts that might otherwise collect around Lakshmi, the overworked, underpaid NYU drama-department graduate student who runs—who *is*—the costume department.

Margot had volunteered a thrift shop treasure from the

back of her own closet, an '80s Armani pants suit from her brief marriage to Enrico; it would have been perfect for Portia. But Roger had insisted on indulging his fetishistic attachment to the sleazy synthetic that morphs from violet to scarlet when it catches the light.

Roger won. Roger is the director. Roger didn't threaten to have Margot replaced. Roger didn't *have* to threaten to have Margot replaced. Margot gave in to his blackmail, his mortifying demands: the fright wig and the hooker suit.

Not until the first time she walked out onstage—and the audience burst out laughing—did she understand what Roger intended. How many hours has Margot spent, in her career, practicing entrances and exits for a specific effect? Until now, mocking childish hysteria was not an effect she'd gone for.

But this is children's theater, not the freaking *Merchant of Venice*. *The quality of mercy is not strained, it droppeth as the gentle rain from heaven*. Margot memorized Portia's soliloquy when she was in high school. She thanks and blames her drama coach, Mr. Blake, for everything that happened since. How disengaged he was, so irresistibly bored that all the girls adored him. What was *that* poor bastard's story? Margot never thought to wonder, and now she doesn't want to know.

The quality of mercy is not strained—not even for a monkey.

Lakshmi has lowered the hem twice, as Margot requested. Begged. In return, Lakshmi persuaded Margot to tone down the fuchsia lipstick which, along with her newly flaming pelt of spiky orange hair, she favors these days. Margot imagines Portia going for that look: confident, self-sufficient but available, a brittle protective screw-you shell encasing a gooey caramel of longing.

"Really?" Lakshmi had scrutinized Margot's lips, which

the drugstore lipstick had turned a hypothermic purple. "For Portia?"

So this is what it's come to: a note on her lipstick means that Margot is *being taken seriously*. She'd traded her drugstore Night-Blooming Orchard for the Dior Dusky Pink that cost a chunk of that week's paycheck, the pathetic pittance for which, like the rest of the cast, she feels absurdly grateful.

They are in this together, everyone is happy to be here and disappointed to be here, glad to have a part in a play, glad to work for scale, but truthfully not all that overjoyed to be working in an off-off-off-off Broadway production of *Mister Monkey*, the umpteen-hundredth revival of the cheesy but mysteriously durable musical based on the classic children's novel.

The actors and the stagehands behave as if they've taken a blood oath not to complain, except for twelve-year-old Adam, who whines because his monkey suit smells and he can't breathe. His stage mom, Giselle, has told everyone that if Adam develops health issues from asthma-causing dust mites, she'll sue.

Only the interns are cheerful, as are Jason and Danielle, who have taken a break from their drama class to play the Jimson kids: the two motherless teenagers who have become Mister Monkey's de facto siblings. By the end of the play, their widowed father, Mr. Jimson, marries Portia the lawyer— played by Margot.

Jason and Danielle have *no idea* that *Mister Monkey the Musical* is not the beginning of something but rather the middle (Margot *hopes* it's the middle) of something, that *something* being the bewildering stall in which Margot's life is circling. And what did Jason and Danielle imagine beginning when they couldn't learn their characters' names and missed so many cues that Roger changed their

characters' names from whatever they were in the script to
Jason and Danielle?

Margot takes ten more breaths, counting backward, then
does her vocal exercises, which her therapist, Dr. Reid, says
is a form of Zazen meditation. The oxygen blast reminds her
of what she tells herself at moments like this: give everything. Self-doubt is lethal. Irony is poison. Every role you play
with your whole heart and soul can be Ophelia, Juliet, Portia.
Lady Macbeth. Well, maybe not Lady Macbeth.

The great Carola Lester, Margot's acting teacher at Yale,
used to say it was their *job* to be theatrical, on- and off-stage.
They must never forget that they are telling the stories of
the tribe. Margot was the star, the one for whom the drama
department had high hopes. And now she's Portia McBailey,
representing a monkey.

Margot prepared for *Mister Monkey* as if for a real play.
She'd worked out Portia's background, the successful legal
career that has enabled her to take on cases—an innocent
monkey!—for fun. But the purple suit had forced Margot to
reimagine Portia as a noble failure, lonely and slightly desperate but consequently happier to meet and fall in love with Mr.
Jimson, an attractive widower with two children.

It had seemed like a lucky sign when, on the first day of
rehearsal, Margot found, in the garbage near her third-floor
walk-up on Sixth Street and Avenue A, a ton of 1950s law books,
several of which she lugged to her dressing room. Carola had
instructed them to surround themselves with objects their
characters might collect. What will Margot do with the law
books when *Mister Monkey* closes? And what were they a
lucky sign *of*? Some doddering lawyer retired or died in his
storefront office in Alphabet City. Best case: a renovation.

In a moment she'll go find Lakshmi. But for now Margot

closes her eyes and runs through the great soliloquies, in her head. *Out, damned spot. Romeo, Romeo.* The speech that most calms and inspires her, the 10 mg. Xanax of art, is the heartbroken aria with which Sonya wraps up the tragic misdirected love duets of *Uncle Vanya*.

We shall go on living, Uncle Vanya. We shall live through a long chain of days and endless evenings, we will work for the happiness of others, now and in our old age, without rest, and we will die submissively, as we have lived. Beyond the grave, God will know that we have suffered and wept, and He will pity us, and we will see a bright beautiful life, and rejoice and look back on our hard lives with tenderness—and smile.

Brave, disappointed, resigned to her fate, Sonya would know what it's like to play a lady lawyer in a musical for children, aged five to twelve, and their parents, grandparents, birthday party and bar mitzvah guests, and on selected weekday afternoons, for school groups offered tickets at a steep discount. That Margot's character is named Portia is one of the little jokes thrown in to keep the parents from poking their eyes out from boredom.

Portia is the only lawyer willing to represent a beloved pet chimpanzee whose party trick is picking pockets. Mister Monkey has been falsely accused of stealing the wallet from the Hermès (another mom and dad joke) bag of Mr. Jimson's evil girlfriend, Janice, who sees Mister Monkey not only as a rival and threat but also as a banana-eating lower life-form with filthy personal habits. Eleanor, who plays Janice, gets the Hermès, a plain black dress, long scarlet press-on nails, and her own (naturally) auburn hair.

Eleanor's day job as an emergency room nurse has made it tricky to schedule rehearsals. An inconvenience that Roger has seemed, inexplicably, not to mind.

Mr. Jimson is being played by a young actor named Eric on whom Margot has a tiny hopeless crush. Much too hopeless and tiny to hurt, as others have in the past. *My unhappy love affair.* Margot used to like describing men as *my unhappy love affair.* She only used it in the past tense. Alec or Jim, or Enrico, he was my unhappy love affair. But hadn't that presumed the existence of a *happy* love affair that made the others seem unimportant? What if unhappy is the only kind that Margot ever has?

Mr. Jimson's two teenage children love Mister Monkey. Their mom—Mr. Jimson's martyred wife, Mrs. Jimson—willed them the baby chimp whose parents were shot by poachers. She'd grown close to the chimpanzee couple before she too was killed in Africa, where she'd studied and defended endangered primates.

After one rehearsal Roger showed the cast a documentary about heroic scientists and gamekeepers fending off poachers and mercenaries hired by the oil company, which wants to destroy the wildlife and exploit the rich resources of the national parks. The film, which featured heartrending footage of murdered animals, was supposed to inspire them, but it only depressed Margot more. Shouldn't they be doing something about that instead of acting in *Mister Monkey*?

Mrs. Jimson (who is dead before the play begins) saw herself as Mister Monkey's godmother. So to her widower and kids, Mister Monkey is more than a pet, more like an adopted son or brother. The "children" know that Dad's girlfriend, Janice, is trying to frame their goofy monkey sibling. Janice is pressing charges, and Mister Monkey is being tried for larceny, at taxpayers' expense.

Roger told the cast that the premise wasn't actually so farfetched. Only a hundred years ago, a dog was found guilty by a British court for having bitten a child—and sentenced to be hung by the neck until dead. Dogs were executed on the gallows at the Salem witch trials.

Danielle burst into tears, and Giselle, who came to every rehearsal, put her hands over Adam's ears and said, "At least the poor creatures got trials. Now the world's so crowded, they euthanize innocent puppies just for taking up space."

Margot has prepared for her role by concentrating on the affection that the Jimson family, and Carmen, their maid, have for Mister Monkey. She has had to imagine a different monkey, an enchanting creature. Unlike Adam, a grumpy child actor in the monkey suit that Lakshmi sewed from a nubbly, brown chenille bedspread.

At another rehearsal Roger showed them a video about companion animals, dogs and monkeys and even goats that live and work with the blind, the elderly, the quadriplegic. Margot tries to focus on those admirable primates and, she's learned from Dr. Reid, to avoid calculating her own chances of winding up dependent on a chimpanzee to bring her the TV remote. She has been given her mantra: this is not about me!

Animals frightened Margot's mother, so Margot never had a pet, except for the contraband turtle her mother made Margot's father flush down the toilet when he stopped by. A child's love for a kitten or puppy is one of the positive emotional memories that Margot will never be able to draw on, so she substitutes a sense memory of how angry she was when Dad took Yertle into the bathroom and emerged empty-handed. He never apologized. It makes it harder for Margot to feel compassion for Mister Monkey's worried family but easier to work herself into a snit over a mistreated pet. So that's how she's playing Portia: fired by indignation.

The hem has *got* to be fixed. Margot opens her dressing room door and, propping one elbow against the edge of the doorway, warbles, "Has anyone seen Lakshmi?"

Bad timing. She should have looked both ways. Roger is shambling down the hall, mumbling. As he passes Margot, she hears him say, "How the fuck can someone fire a person who's hardly getting paid in the first place?"

"Hi, Roger," Margot says. Why did she do *that*? Does some infantile part of her still crave Daddy's attention?

Roger stops, turns around, walks back. There's a stutter in his gait that Margot finds alarming. Roger's eyes look milky. It's selfish and small of Margot to resent him just because of her ugly costume.

Roger is a suffering human. As they all are, God help them.

Roger takes a crumpled letter from his pocket, hands it to Margot, and says, "A gentleman left this for you at the box office. Fan mail from a flounder."

JUST YESTERDAY, ERIC came to Margot's dressing room and asked if she'd noticed anything strange about Roger. Maybe something about the show or about *them* (Eric smiled) had driven Roger over the edge. Could their director have suffered one of those teensy transient strokes?

That Eric is shy, tall, with a beautiful smile, and ten years younger than Margot is not Eric's fault. Nor is Eric to blame for the fact that he is not terribly bright.

To feel grief and shame because Eric was asking her the way a kid might ask his older sister's opinion was a waste of the precious time that Margot is paying a fortune in therapy bills to learn to appreciate and value.

No one in the cast tells Margot anything. No gossip, no

rumors, nothing. But a week or so into the run, she ran into Eric and Rita in the hall. Rita plays Carmen, the passionate Latina housekeeper who refuses to accept the injustice being done to the monkey so beloved by the children she's cared for since their mother died.

In the dimly lit, cramped, fire-safety-code-violating corridor, Eric and Rita leaned over a sheet of paper. They were eager to show Margot the news item that Eric had found online and printed out, a story from South Africa about a chimpanzee that turned against its owner and ripped his face off because the guy refused to share the birthday cake he'd bought for another chimp. Eric and Rita were including Margot in a select club whose members would think this was hilarious: a cult that began when they'd watched Roger's film of the home-assistance monkeys doing everything for their owners but programming the DVR.

If Margot didn't think that the murder-monkey story was as funny as Eric and Rita did, it wasn't because she was a more sensitive compassionate person, but because it was suddenly clear to her that they were sleeping together. Their laughter was so private they could have been laughing at her. Margot needs to remember Rita's laugh in case she ever again in this lifetime gets cast as someone having sex with another human being.

Margot couldn't answer Eric's question about Roger behaving strangely. She has forgiven Roger for her costume by telling herself that his brain's been destroyed by a lifetime of dinner theater and summer stock. *Mister Monkey* was a step up for him. But there's no point in Eric thinking about steps up or down. He would know what step *Mister Monkey* was for a woman Margot's age.

It would have been unfair to Eric too. How old is he?

Thirty? His best friend from drama school might be star-ring on Broadway right now. A Yale classmate of Margot's is playing the mother in a revival of *The Glass Menagerie* at Lincoln Center. Margot doesn't know what's worse: her un-talented classmate's success or the fact that a woman her age is playing the mother. Nothing can disarm the angel with the fiery sword guarding the gate to the garden where the ingenues frolic, the pretty young girls unaware of the outer darkness.

Margot will never play Sonya again, not unless she can find her way out from behind the disguise of the forty-four-year-old woman and reveal her true face, the unlined, hope-ful face of a girl who has mischievously chosen to wear the mask of middle age.

All that Margot could say was, "Roger? Roger's . . . always been weird."

Later, during "Speed Dial," the duet in which she and Eric fall in love while singing into their cell phones, she saw something in Eric's eyes. Rather she saw something *missing*: basic friendliness, maybe. Surely his turning against her must be about something more than her reluctance to discuss Roger's mental health.

Fan mail from a flounder. What *had* Roger meant? It's not every day that Margot gets letters from a mysterious gentle-man. Not *any* day. The biographies of iconic stage actresses and movie stars, which Margot used to read when she felt stronger, described receiving diamond bracelets and invita-tions to weekends in Paris and parties on luxury yachts, notes tucked into bouquets of red roses.

Margot's fan letter arrives in a plain business envelope, sealed. Nothing is written on the outside. Was Roger sure it was meant for her? Why didn't she ask him what the flounder looked like?

She is about to open the letter when someone knocks on the door.

"Come in," Margot says.

"You looking for me?" asks Lakshmi.

AT THE START of the production, Lakshmi wore funny outfits, vintage items from costume shops. Striped tights, green tutus, tuxedo jackets, flowered straw hats. But lately she's given all that up for the baggy navy shirt and the belted blue pants in which she plays the cop who first arrests Mister Monkey and then Janice.

"Are you ready for 'Monkey Tango?'" she asks Margot.

"Do I look ready?" Margot replies. "Sorry, I didn't mean to sound—"

"I've got this," Lakshmi says.

Margot has to be onstage for the opening number, "Monkey Tango," a musical extravaganza featuring the entire cast and referencing King Kong, Cheetah, Mighty Joe Young, the monkey murderer in Poe, the Hindu monkey god Hanuman, every good and bad ape the lyricist could think of, all culminating in Mister Monkey, the smartest, cutest, nicest, strongest, most powerful chimp of all.

After that Margot is off for twenty minutes, during which time the audience meets Mister Monkey, Mr. Jimson and his kids, the housekeeper Carmen, and Mr. Jimson's girlfriend, Janice. No wonder everyone hates Janice. Everyone hates Eleanor, who seems to take an extreme (even for an actress) delight in playing the wicked, scheming Janice.

Margot has made a mental note never to wind up in the

ER where Eleanor works. Eleanor is one of the biggest bitches Margot has ever acted with, and the bar for *that* has been set very high indeed.

Margot gave Eleanor a chance. During rehearsals she invited her out for coffee. When Margot tried to talk about Chekhov, Eleanor had been unpleasant. But after Margot overheard Eleanor telling Roger about her drama school experience, it occurred to her that Eleanor's bitchiness might mean she is staying in character, which would make Eleanor the most committed actor in the cast.

Margot used to spend her downtime hanging out with Lakshmi, a well-meaning person with an interesting background: two dads, one Hindu, one Muslim, both big fans of musical theater, and a Web-designer boyfriend, Mal, whom everyone but Lakshmi thinks is possibly sinister and definitely sexually confused. Given her family history, it's odd that Lakshmi's gaydar should be so weak, but Margot has had her own troubles with that form of myopia: her second husband and one boyfriend. If there is one thing Margot has learned, it's to resist the temptation to give advice or tell strangers about her professional and romantic disappointments.

According to Lakshmi, her dads gave her the wrong name: Lakshmi is the Hindu goddess of wealth.

Margot said, "You never know. You might get rich." And Lakshmi giggled, because she secretly thinks she might. Most young people do.

Lakshmi has mentioned that she's writing a one-act play with a part in it for Margot. But when Margot failed to ask even one polite, follow-up, fake-interested question about Lakshmi's play, she sensed her disappointment. When Margot asked Dr. Reid why her heart is so hard, he advised her to be more forgiving to herself. Lakshmi will be fine.

Margot's burden is heavy enough without her taking on the weight of the world.

By this point in the production Margot and Lakshmi have run out of conversation. Lakshmi has quit stopping by Margot's dressing room, except on business. Margot can work on her voice, or better yet, disappear into the Empty Space, as first Carola Lester, then her former acting coach Maureen, and now Dr. Reid have all suggested, though each with a different name for it and for a different reason.

LAKSHMI SAYS THEY have just enough time before "Monkey Tango." She can pin Margot's hem. Then in the twenty minutes between "Monkey Tango" and Margot's next cue, Lakshmi can mend the purple skirt. Wrinkling her nose at the skirt is Lakshmi's sign that she is on Margot's side. She knows the skirt is a travesty, and that it's Roger's fault. Why should *that* hurt Margot's feelings too?

Margot glances regretfully at the envelope containing her mystery fan letter, then puts it on the counter and climbs onto a chair. She'd rather not read it with Lakshmi watching. Lakshmi spaces two large safety pins around the hem, which puckers and droops. Dreamily she fastens the third pin outside the skirt instead of inside, so that now the pin, instead of the hairy threads, will grab the spotlight and distract the audience from whatever Margot is trying to do.

"Punk lady lawyer," says Lakshmi. "Own it."

"I'll take that note," Margot says icily as Lakshmi hurries out.

Margot tucks the letter into her book, a paperback of *Just Kids*. Why do people only want to hear the story of how a future celebrity got all mixed up and knocked around in the big martini shaker of youth, until something—ambition, re-

silience, a lucky break, a dear friend's death—poured out a
famous person, alchemically mixologized into a perfect cock-
tail, refreshing and delicious?

THE JACKED-UP SMILEY intensity with which they per-
form "Monkey Tango" always makes Margot think, and try
not to think, about an Evangelical youth group she saw once
in a Birmingham mall when she was touring Alabama with
a road company of *Wicked*. And like it or not, it always reminds her (as it is supposed to) of yet another of Roger's ha-
rangues:

"The parents slave at their jobs all week, the kids work
hard in school, and they come to the theater to watch us work
harder than they do. The more energy we put out, the more
of ourselves we give, the more the audience will like the play,
and the longer the show will run."

He'd asked how many of them had heard of Raymond
Ortiz. No one had. Apparently Ortiz was a Vietnam vet from
the Bronx who wrote what he'd intended to be a novel for
grown-ups, but the god of children's theater had other plans
for *Mister Monkey*. When the book was adapted for the stage,
the contract contained a clause prohibiting *one word*, one
joke, one reference to the theory that man descended from
the apes. Don't even *think evolution*.

Giselle had asked if this Ortiz was some kind of Christian
fanatic, and Roger said no. It was a savvy business decision
made by Gavin Leaming, who adapted the musical from the
novel. That clause has allowed the musical to be performed
all over the South and even (with some modifications and the
actresses costumed differently) in the United Arab Emirates.
In fact the book said nothing about humans and chimpanzees being biologically related, so why introduce a controver-

sial and freighted topic, so distracting and extraneous to this charming and deeply touching story?

During rehearsals, Roger had pushed the cast, yelling in his pebbly cigarette voice, "Faster! Higher! Reach for the stars! Monkey Tango for the Fat Lady!"

"What Fat Lady?" Danielle asked the group. She was afraid to ask Roger. Eric explained that it was a quote from J. D. Salinger, from *The Catcher in the Rye*. Margot knew he was wrong. She couldn't remember the right book, but she wasn't going to ask Roger and reveal that she didn't know. *And* make Eric look bad.

"Idiot," Roger had mumbled. No one knew if he meant Eric or Danielle. No one knew which of them not to look at, so no one looked at anyone else.

Roger needn't have worried. At every performance they monkey-tango as if their heads are about to explode from sheer simian joy. And the audience enjoys the snappy rhythms and the breakneck Cole-Porteresque rhyming of the names of every monkey in literature, stage, and screen, every heroic deed and petty crime that a primate has ever committed.

> *Monkey Tango.*
> *Orangutang-o.*
> *You rang? Oh tango.*
> *King-King Kong-o. Mighty Joe Young-o.*
> *Monkey tango. Into the jungle. With me.*

The tango is more like a square dance and just about as sexy. The cast form couples and slide-step across the stage with stiff tango arms, then switch partners and tango back, then line up facing the audience and do The Monkey, 1970s style, which amuses the grandparents and the older parents.

It isn't so much a performance as a final warning for the kids to quit wriggling in their booster seats; for the grandparents to unwrap the cough drops; for the tourist couples to check one last time that their cell phones are off; and for the parents to wonder if they can take a nap and still find their kids there when they wake up.

No one—no one but Margot—is thinking about Margot's skirt.

The song marks time. The applause is like a parting slap, reflexive and halfhearted, an afterthought as Portia and Carmen, lawyer and maid, skip together offstage.

BACK IN HER dressing room Margot steps out of her skirt and hands it to Lakshmi, who goes off to fix it. Then Margot puts on the jeans she wore to the theater, sinks into the grimy corduroy recliner, and opens the letter.

Somehow she'd known that it would be anonymous, just as she'd known that it wouldn't be a death threat or a psychotic rant. The sheet of plain white paper is neatly folded, in thirds.

The typeface is soft, slightly blurred. The letter seems to have been typed on something like the hand-me-down IBM she used in middle school. She thinks of those (antique!) detective stories in which forensic experts track the letter writer through the wear on the typewriter keys. Ancient history! Gone forever!

On the page are four lines, single-spaced:

"Failures and disappointments make time go by so fast that you fail to notice your real life, and the past when I was so free seems to belong to someone else, not myself."

—Anton Chekhov, from a letter to Maxim Gorky, January 3, 1899

It's the saddest sentence ever! The melancholic sweetness of it, oh, the wrenching grief! And what an amazing coincidence: Margot was just thinking about *Uncle Vanya*. Though of course, as every artist—every human being—knows: there are no coincidences, but rather a river of mystical connections into which, from time to time, we are allowed to dip our big toe. Who knows how and when we are suddenly enabled to draw from that stream flowing constantly around us? And when two people, or two events, enter that stream together, we—simple, unenlightened creatures who have no idea what else to call it, or what it really means—we call it a coincidence.

Margot rereads the letter. My God. Those lines were written by the theater's greatest genius, or anyway one of the top three. Even Chekhov, even *he* believed that he had let his life, his real life, slip by in a fog of failure and disappointment. Does everyone feel that way?

We are alive for such a short time, and we spend it so unsatisfied, longing for what we can never have. Trying so hard. For what? We'll all die, and what will it matter, the Tony or the Obie or the Oscar or the dusty, badly lit dressing rooms in the recently renamed High Line Theater where they are doing *Mister Monkey*?

Maybe there *is* another life, less painful and lonely, its details better worked out, a life in which Margot and Chekhov will share angelic contentment, or at least acceptance. Chekhov was forty-four when he died: Margot's age. Perhaps they would have been friends and helped each other endure the failures and disappointments.

Margot's eyes fill with tears. How maddeningly counterproductive! Portia the high-powered lawyer isn't blubbering over *her* vanished youth. Portia's too busy preparing the defense that will save Mister Monkey.

Margot cannot use her grief right now. And she'll have to redo her makeup.

A voice from the hall says, "Five minutes, Margot." She finds a cotton ball and dabs at the raccoon mask and black rivulets that the tears and mascara have applied to her face

Though she has no basis for believing this, she feels certain that the letter writer knows her. He knows where she has come from, what she's been through, what she's suffered, who she is.

UNCLE VANYA WAS their class senior-thesis project in the graduate program at Yale. The fact that Margot got the part of Sonya proves that she hasn't imagined or invented the promising girl she used to be.

She hardly even had to act. She *was* Sonya, madly in love with the melancholy doctor Astrov, who loves Yelena, whom Vanya also loves, and who loves Astrov but who refuses to leave her elderly professor husband. And so on and so on, like Popeye and Olive Oyl, like Krazy Kat and Ignatz, everyone wanting the one person they can never have.

How can Sonya not love Astrov, so handsome and kind, so modest—and so far ahead of his time? So worried about the planet! The Russian forests are groaning under the ax, birds and forest creatures are being smoked out of their houses, rivers are drying up, landscapes vanish, never to return . . .

This work-ravaged, burned-out hero shows up at Vanya's farm, straight from treating a typhus epidemic. Will the future thank him?

God will remember, says Nanny.

Alec was playing Astrov, so playing opposite him had been easy. Yearning, pure yearning had poured out of Margot. How thrilling it was to escape the prison of her self and become the brainchild of a genius, fueled by pieces of her soul, burning like the plumes of fire, the cast-off carapaces of a rocket. What had she wanted so badly? What was *so important?*

Oh, the sad, sad, *sadness* of their puny ambitions. Chekhov got that right. Because the truth is: some part of her still wants the world to know that she is a talented actress.

The road from Sonya to Mister Monkey's lawyer has been paved with concessions, good manners, and graceful acceptance. Below a certain level of fame, a diva is just a pain in the ass. After a point Margot had done what came easily, automatically, what someone else wanted, all the time thinking that it didn't count, that she would have her life to do over, to get right. She has changed from a girl showing the world what it is like to love someone who will never love you into a woman having a daily shit fit because of the ridiculous costume some sadistic half-mad children's theater director is making her wear.

If only she had listened to Carola, who, the week classes ended at Yale, invited Margot to dinner at a New Haven address. The address was all she gave Margot, who imagined how chic and elegant—how Carola—the dinner would be. How intensely she had looked forward to that celebratory banquet!

The address turned out to be a take-out Chinese food joint. Carola wore a perfect Chanel suit. Over their plastic trays of General Tsao's chicken and fried rice, at a Formica table under a buzzing fluorescent light, Carola told Margot that if she wanted to be happy in life, she needed to lower her expectations. Starting now. Margot has eaten in plenty of greasy spoons since then—there's a Cuban-Chinese place, La Isla des Perlas, right near the theater—and it's done nothing for her happiness level.

There is no single moment that Margot can point to and say, This is where things took a turn. If the weather had been sunny, if only she'd missed that flight. No Broadway spectacle shuttered in a week. No train wreck ended her career. More no's than yes's. A few unanswered prayers. Two marriages and several love affairs torched, each by its own demonic arsonist.

She could have been a *great* Sonya if she'd known what she knows now. That the thankless servitude Sonya describes, the life of lowered eyes and expectations, of unrelenting hard work, no love, no romance, no children, no reward, old age, then death—*it is a real possibility*! That life could happen to anyone! More than likely it will. Sonya doesn't believe it. She can't. She's too young. The irony is that you don't believe it until you're too old to play Sonya.

Who sent Margot the letter? Was it one of the actors who wanted to date her at Yale, who took her out for a drink and asked why her heart was set on Alec, a sociopath in the midst of a lifelong love affair with his insane twin sister? Could the letter have come from her therapist? Dr. Reid might own an old typewriter; that would be his style. But it wouldn't be his style to quote someone else. He's been very helpful, but sometimes Margot notices that he is only interested in his own opinions. When she'd asked him to please *not* come to see her in *Mister Monkey*, he was insultingly eager to respect her wishes.

If she were smarter, more imaginative, more talented, if she had any of the qualities that would mean she'd be playing the mother in *The Glass Menagerie* instead of Portia in *Mister Monkey*, she'd know who sent the letter.

A dozen men from her past scurry through her memory en route to where they belong. No, not that one. Wait. No. Not that one, either.

Who knows Margot well enough to know how moved she would be, how saddened but heartened by the Chekhov quote? Like a note in a fortune cookie baked for her by God, a kindly reminder that she is concerned with—obsessed by—the wrong things, with age and fame and success, when, as Chekhov and Dr. Reid say, she must remember that each moment of life is a gift.

Did the man who left the letter stay to watch the show? Could he be a stranger who has followed her career? Does he see every production she's in, even *Mister Monkey*? Will he be in the audience this afternoon?

Fairy godmother Lakshmi reappears with the skirt. Margot takes off her jeans. The skirt fits. The purple suit seems almost stylish, coolly retro and ironic. Even the Harpo wig isn't as disfiguring as usual. Margot thinks of Lucille Ball. A female comic genius!

"Great look," Lakshmi says.

Margot has gone from being not dressed for the party to being dressed for the party.

THE KIDS PUSH the revolving scenery around, and the lights come up on Margot, at a desk. More lights, more slappy applause. Carmen enters and sings a rumba about poor Mister Monkey, wrongly accused by Janice. By the final chorus, Portia and Carmen are singing to a modified salsa beat, "The monkey didn't do it. He didn't, no, no, no . . ."

Margot knows the scene so well she could do it with half her brain missing, which is helpful, because she's still distracted by memories of playing Sonya to Alec's Astrov. She'd poured her entire soul out, believing that she could make Alec love her and stop wishing that he was having sex with his twin sister in a stall in the men's room of the Beinecke

Library. *We shall go on living, Uncle Vanya. Beyond the grave, God will know that we have suffered and wept, and He will pity us, and we will see a bright beautiful life.*

Margot's pain had been awful. But it seemed preferable to her current state, this hamstering back and forth between panic and numbness. Once more she lets feeling pour through her, this time directed at the man who sent the letter, somewhere in the darkened rows among the yellow-and-black booster seats donated by the Yellow Pages. She feels a taste of the excitement she used to feel when she thought that someone in the audience might offer her a part.

By the time Margot and Rita sing the final verse, the most anxious child in the theater has stopped worrying. Mister Monkey will be fine!

The letter writer knows that Margot is capable of putting her whole self into the role of a righteous lawyer, like Spencer Tracy as Clarence Darrow in that film about . . . Oops. Evolution. The *E* word. It throws Margot off, and she's a heartbeat slow in getting out her lines. The others look at her. Even Jason and Danielle are wondering what's wrong.

Nothing is wrong. Unlike the others, except Roger, Margot has been doing this long enough to know that it happens. Actors go up, they forget their lines, blow their cues. It's just a pity that it's happening when the man who sent her the letter might be out there, in the dark.

Things improve during the courtroom scene. Margot/ Portia is cross-examining Eleanor/Janice, when Carmen, Danielle, and Jason dance onstage with Janice's wallet, the one she's accused Mister Monkey of stealing. Not only have Carmen and the kids found the wallet, but—this is a crucial plot point—they have found two of the outrageously long scarlet fingernails that Janice has worn since the start of the play.

And now it turns out that Janice (will the witness please hold up her hands?) is missing two of her talons. Somehow this proves that Janice hid the wallet and that it wasn't stolen by Mister Monkey.

In rehearsal, Roger admitted that this was a plot hole. But they had to go with it, even if they wondered—as anyone might—why Janice hadn't simply gotten her nails replaced during the time between the alleged theft and the trial. It was a problem in the book, but generations of *Mister Monkey* lovers and their parents haven't complained.

Roger said that the burden of making this unlikely plot-turn work was on Eleanor, who is playing Janice, and Eleanor said, "I can handle it, guys," in a tough, gum-cracking tone. Maybe she was being Janice. Lucky Eleanor, with her other life, her outside life as a nurse. Acting's a hobby for her, not a vocation, not a heartbreak and a torment.

Anyhow, the kids in the audience aren't wondering why Janice has been walking around missing two nails ever since she hid her own wallet and pretended it was stolen. They are too busy loving the jaunty, hilarious gross-out raucousness of the song that Janice/Eleanor is singing about fingernails. How she loves fingernails, how she likes to eat them, chew them, swallow them, bake them into cookies, brew them into tea. But now her beloved fingernails, her darling fingernails have betrayed her. She peels off the rest of her press-on nails, and flings them into the front rows, like a stripper. The children shriek with horror and delight and scramble to catch the nails. The parents think it's a little weird, but the kids are having fun.

Lakshmi, in her police hat and blue shirt and pants, her

authority considerably compromised by her giant yellow clown shoes and red golf-ball nose, marches out and perp-walks Janice offstage, just as she did to Mister Monkey.

The judge—Roger in a barrister's wig—tears up the charges against Mister Monkey. Jason and Danielle fling the scraps into the audience, and the kids leap out of their seats like baseball fans trying to catch a pop fly.

Mr. Jimson thanks Portia, and Portia says, "Mister Monkey is innocent! The quality of mercy is not strained—not even for a monkey."

The kids burst into applause. The parents are clapping too, so are the out-of-town couples. Justice has been served. Everyone likes the triumph of innocence, especially the parents, who think it's a good lesson, well worth the (very reasonable) price of the tickets. They would have paid ten times more to see *The Lion King*, and the kids wouldn't have gotten half as much.

For the moment, it's working. Brushing off the scraps of "legal document" confetti lodged in her wig, Portia believes in what she's done, Margot believes in what she's done, and through Portia, Margot has reached the audience via the glorious medium of theater.

Art is art, theater is magic, no matter how humble the venue. Together they have transformed a house full of strangers into a group of people all rooting for Mister Monkey! Portia is their heroine. If the letter writer is out there, let him accept this *thank you* from Margot: a reminder that the muse chooses her own time and place to make an entrance.

Right on cue, Mister Monkey bounds onstage and races across the courtroom. In a burst of high spirits, he leaps into his lawyer's arms and clamps his legs around her. Adam is small, but in the weeks since rehearsals began, he has grown taller and heavier, making this "spontaneous" lift and hug more of a challenge for Margot.

This afternoon, just when Margot least expects it, just after her moment of spiritual connection, of quasi-transcendence, that's when she realizes that Adam is pressing his groin into her hip, grinding hard, and—can this be true?— she feels the hummock of a hard-on under his fuzzy monkey suit.

That filthy little pervert! What does he think he's doing?

She drops him. Boom. Adam's a gymnast. He bounces onto his feet. He looks up at her. A glint of triumph flashes inside the frayed eyeholes of his costume.

Margot has been molested by a boy in a monkey suit! And she kept on acting right through it. Somehow she stayed in character. How professional is *that*? Or is she just another female victim, putting up with anything that any male of any age thinks he can get away with?

Margot needs to do something. But what? She knows better than to accuse Adam. No one will believe her. What if it happens again? She'll take the little perv aside. Let the lunatic stage mom sue her.

Margot's concentration lapses once more, this time descending into a spiral from which she can't retrieve it, even during the low-effort, audience-pleasing cell phone duet with Eric. Mr. Jimson is trying to call Portia, to thank her for saving Mister Monkey. His cell phone keeps cutting out: another crumb of reality tossed to the grown-ups.

Finally, frustrated and desperate, he pockets his phone and sings out loud for all to hear: He loves her! I love you, Portia! I love Mister Monkey's lawyer!

Poor Eric hasn't done this long enough to know how contagious another actor's off night can be. He goes flat on a high note, misses another, forgets a lyric and then a line.

Margot can hardly get out the four words required of her: *I love you too.*

Normally, it doesn't matter what she and Eric say. While they are belting out their love, the overjoyed chimp is climbing the walls, the kids in the audience are whooping and yelling, thrilled by Adam's super-monkey leaps from rope to pole. And the parents are figuring out that their imprisonment in these uncomfortable seats is almost over.

Adam knows what he's done to Margot. He stands there, frozen, staring at her. In the second row, where she always sits, Giselle must be losing what's left of her mind.

Eric is supposed to say *"Will* you be Mrs. Monkey, dear Portia? I mean, Mrs. Jimson."

Instead he says, "I mean, will you be my Mrs. Monkey, Mrs. Jimson?"

The children giggle. Eric is sorry he's blown the line, but also liberated from the challenge of pretending to fall in love with his monkey's tacky, middle-aged lawyer.

So what if they've made mistakes? They are artists. Professionals. The show must go on. Margot and Eric run toward each other and meet in a body-slam embrace. In unison, or near unison, they sing out, "Calling my soul mate! Coming in clear! I'm never losing you again!"

Just then Margot's cell phone flies out of her hand, clatters onto the stage, and lands not far from her feet, where it spins and then stops.

Everyone is watching. Should she pick it up? Would Portia? Portia would bend over in a flash, even if it made her skirt ride up and show the audience her ass.

A couple of parents laugh nervously.

Margot holds the moment. She has the audience in her power. How long can she let it go on? She thinks of all the great silences in the history of the theater. The echoing silence in *Macbeth* after the knock at the gate. The two-minute silence that followed Isabella's plea to Angelo in the Peter Brook *Measure for Measure*. Krapp's silence as he shuffles through the Beckett play. The silence that is the only answer when the stage manager in *Our Town* asks about the dead sitting in their straight-backed chairs, waiting, waiting . . . *What are they waiting for?*

What are they waiting for?

Focused on Portia's dropped cell phone, this silence lacks the profundity and intensity of those great theatrical silences. On the other hand, it is silence. The audience waits to see what will happen. It's Margot's silence, hers to end or prolong for as long as she wants.

It is then that she hears a child in the second or third row say, very loud and clear, "*Grandpa, are you interested in this?*"

Grandpa, are you interested in this? What a rude little freak! Any child who could put those words together is old enough to know better. Old enough to know that if you talk that loudly during a silence in a tiny theater with weird acoustics, chances are pretty good that everyone can hear you, even the actors on stage.

Grandpa, are you interested in *what*? In this blood, these tears? In these lives, the only lives that these actors will ever have, in the point which they have reached in their lives and from which they can only hope and pray to ascend?

At least no one laughs. Maybe the audience is too embarrassed. They are probably thinking that the kid is saying what they would say if they had the nerve. Like Jesus in the temple. Grandpa, are you interested in the emperor's new clothes? Does *anyone* really care whether a monkey's owner and his defense lawyer decide that they are soul mates, or whether a lady lawyer in a rainbow wig picks up her cell phone?

What is the letter writer thinking? Margot can't bear to imagine *his* compassion, the loving kindness curdling into pity, or worse, the knowledge that she is beyond his help, too low in this circle of children's-theater hell to be saved by a message from Chekhov.

The cell phone remains where it landed. No one moves to retrieve it. The audience listens for Grandpa's reply. The cast is bewitched. The silence continues, but now the audience is straining to hear Grandpa's answer.

Unlike the child, he will whisper. He will say yes. He wants the grandchild to be happy. Margot cannot see the old man in the dark, but she feels sure that he is a loving grandfather, protective, the kind of grandpa Margot never had, either of the grandfathers who died before she was born. How different things would be if Grandpa, the kid, the cast, and the audience knew that the boy playing Mister Monkey has just tried to jerk off against Margot's hip.

Grandpa will say, Yes, I'm interested. Then maybe he will ask the child, Are *you* interested in this?

The child loves the grandfather. So the child will also lie and say, Yes, Grandpa, I am.

Margot doesn't think. She acts. It is a drama-class exercise, repeated over and over, never to be forgotten. Act. React. Don't think. She acts without thinking and kicks her cell phone as hard as she can. Blam. It shoots behind the curtain. Later she will be sorry. But right now it feels great!

The audience applauds. Hooray! We're free! Let's all kick our cell phones straight to hell! Three cheers for gutsy Portia!

The child squeezes his grandfather's arm and scoots forward. The lady kicked her cell phone! Is she going to get into trouble?

The child's first sign of genuine interest lifts the grandfather's spirits, even though he worries that if the child goes home and kicks his mom or dad's cell phone, just lightly, just to see what will happen, and the parents ask the child why, he will say that he saw a lady do it, in the play he saw with Grandpa. The grandfather knows that this worry is needless. Unlike the actress, the child is too smart and mature to kick a phone. But children learn by testing, observation, and imitation.

Though the child's parents are too kind and polite to mention it to the grandfather, they will blame him if their son kicks a phone. They will laugh about it when they wake in the darkness and talk the way couples do when they are trying to shorten the night or lull themselves back to sleep. They will agree it's hilarious, the bad behavior their son learned when his loving, well-meaning grandfather took him to the theater.

DANIELLE ASKS, "DON'T you ever miss the jungle, Mister Monkey?"

The lights go down, and a full moon, pale as lemon ice, rises over the stage. Adam puts his paws over his eyes, inhales swarms of monkey-costume dust mites, and, trying not to gag, sings the first notes of his solo, "Monkey Moon"—a ballad about longing to be a baby chimp again, back in his lost tropical paradise, tossing coconuts back and forth with his murdered monkey mom and dad.

But that's not what Adam wants. He wants to forget the sad film Roger made them watch about the dead wild animals in Africa. He wants his voice not to crack before he finishes the song. He wants to grow taller so he can play something cooler—and hotter—than a shrimpy orphan chimp. But none of those desires will help him call up the feeling that his mom says he needs for this song. Yearning, she'd said. *Yearning. What the hell does that even mean?* There's a girl in his building Adam thinks about sometimes. But Mister Monkey doesn't—and wouldn't. And the next eighty minutes are supposed to be about what Mister Monkey wants. Mister Monkey wants to be tossing a coconut with his parents.

Mother, can you hear me? Adam raises his arms over his head and steps into the spotlight so that the fuzzy Y of his silhouette falls across the moon. On the Internet and in books and newspapers, he's read that the moon is approaching Earth, exerting its unstoppable, ever-strengthening tidal pull on the waves and winds and weather. So here come the tsunamis, the blizzards, the tornadoes, the Katrinas and Sandys. And they still call it *extreme weather?* It's mild compared to what's coming, so what will they call *that?* Adam imagines his favorite weather girl, the one with the tight shiny blouses and the cascade of blow-dried curls. Another catastrophe by late in the week, folks, and brace for a wind and water disaster during the morning commute . . .

Maybe by then it will be possible to leave the planet and start over somewhere else. Soon people will be able to travel to the moon on a shuttle rocket. Adam wants to be the first gymnast-child-actor-skateboarder in outer space. He wants to ride the lunar craters.

Here is something else he wants, something that makes it even harder to touch the audience's heart with his monkey yearning. He wants to spit or sneeze into his paw so that, at the end of the song, when Jason and Danielle skip out onto the stage and dance his sorrows away in a fruitcake jitterbug, each of them will grab his paw and get a slimy surprise. Adam knows it's a terrible thing to want. Does it make him a terrible person?

In one of the monkey books he read, a baboon saved up water and dirt to make mud to fling at a colonial gentleman who'd been tormenting him. Adam doesn't have mud but only his own available fluids. And it's not that Jason and Danielle are tormenting him; everyone and everything is.

Let "the kids" complain to Roger. Who is Roger going to

fire? A twelve-year-old actor and gymnast and singer the size of an eight-year-old who can take direction like a grown-up and do triple flips? Or two college students who can't even remember their characters' names?

Adam cracked up laughing when Roger got so annoyed that he renamed the characters Jason and Danielle. Was Roger allowed to change things in the play? Adam's mom said no, but Adam knows that plenty of things from the book have been changed. For example, cell phones. No cell phones in the novel.

In the book, which is from the 1970s, Portia and Mr. Jimson keep leaving messages on each other's answering machines. No one has those anymore. No one but Adam, who has saved the machine on which his dad says, "Wait for the sound of the beep and leave a message for baby Adam—or his mom and dad." Adam keeps it in the back of his closet and every so often plays it when his mother's not home.

The point is that sneezing or spitting on Jason and Danielle would be a seriously monkey thing to do. That would be taking Adam's character to a whole other level.

Ever since Adam got the part of Mister Monkey, it's been monkey 24/7 at his house, where Adam is being home-schooled by his mom after he and his best friend, Derek, got kicked out of private school for setting a trash can on fire in the hall behind the gym.

Adam's dad was secretly proud of him. Dad said the school had no sense of humor. Dad was also relieved. He'd been paying Adam's tuition. Dad's supporting two households now: Adam and Mom downtown, and Pushy Heidi and baby Arturo in Park Slope.

Adam's life hasn't changed all that much since he stopped going to school. Derek is still his only friend. Adam just sees him less often. And now Adam gets to sit at the kitchen table in their uncool Battery Park City apartment with its view of New York harbor, its unobstructed front-row seat at the coming sci-fi apocalypse film that plays in Adam's head when he can't sleep, which is practically every night. In fact that's how he puts himself to sleep, imagining the wind and waves, the lips of water frothing with spit as they rise to swallow the pavement, the lobbies, the little dogs whose owners thought they'd take them out for one last poop, and now there's no need to pick it up with those plastic gloves, cold salt water's pouring into the first-floor windows, the second floor, the third, it's hypnotic and almost comforting now that it's finally happening, until a flash of green lightning jolts Adam awake and he has to run to the window and make sure that his nightmare isn't real. Yet.

The main difference between school and no school is that now Adam has to listen to his mom talk about *whole learning*, which in Adam's case means that if he's going to play a monkey, he has to study monkey biology, primate behavior, monkey literature, monkey myths, jungle climate, flora and fauna. He has always liked going deep into subjects, finding out everything—every trivial and even sometimes annoying fact—that he can. For a while he was obsessed with dinosaurs, then spiders, then the Reverend Martin Luther King Jr., then the 1970s punk rock scene.

Now the bookshelf beside his bed is his personal monkey library. For a while his favorite book was a graphic novel called *Journey to the West*, about a Chinese superhero who travels with his helpers, among them a monkey whose name—Adam loves this—means "awakened to emptiness," and who is so aggressive that the only way to calm him down is to put a gold ring around his head. But the first prize for monkey violence goes to the orangutan in Edgar Allan Poe's "Murders in the Rue Morgue." That monkey slits an old lady's throat with a straight razor (he's pretending to be a barber and screws it up) and then strangles her daughter and stuffs the daughter's battered corpse up the chimney, upside down. Adam loves it that his mom told him to read this. How hilarious that (Mom's phrase) "an American classic" should be so totally gory and sick.

Does his mom have any idea what's *in* these monkey books that she's so happy he's willing to read? Actually he likes them a lot, he's read Jane Goodall and Dian Fossey and a new book whose title he keeps forgetting, all about bonobo sex. It's always the same story, the scientist getting down with the monkeys, overjoyed to make friends with them and be accepted in their gang. And then things start to go south . . . A mother and daughter monkey turn into psycho serial cannibal killers, kidnapping and murdering monkey children. The chimpanzees in one habitat divide themselves into groups based on bloodlines or kinship or whatever, and start bloody wars that involve killing and eating each other's babies. When Adam read that, he'd wanted to give up. What was the point? The really bad shit that people do is still there, always there, deep in our brains, from way back when we used to be monkeys.

Maybe just because he's not supposed to think about it on-stage, evolution has become Adam's favorite subject. He Googled it, and then, just for fun, hit NEWS. He found some photos of brain fossils, then returned to the Web and dug harder and found a series of articles about legal trials to determine the content of public-school science textbooks.

At least he doesn't have to read *those crap books*! He was, however, interested in the stories of how those decisions were made, how those battles worked out, how in 2005 a case reached the Pennsylvania courts because some parents wanted their kids' schoolbooks to say: evolution is only one of many theories about the origin of mankind.

Evolution is not a theory! What part of science do they not get? Humans evolved, they are still evolving. Adam just hopes it happens fast. Fast enough to save him, to include him among the humans who breathe greenhouse gases and surf the tsunamis.

At bedtime, Adam has been reading *On the Origin of Species*. He hasn't gotten very far. He reads pages without understanding one word and then has to read them all over again. He likes how the book begins: "When on board HMS *Beagle* as a naturalist, I was much struck with certain facts in the distribution of the inhabitants of South America, and in the geological relations of the present to the past inhabitants of that continent. These facts seemed to me to throw some light on the origin of species—that mystery of mysteries, as it has been called by one of our greatest philosophers."

That mystery of mysteries! Seriously? What's the mysterious part? Look at a monkey for five minutes and you know we used to be them. There's a sentence from Darwin that Adam loves, something about how humans would never have been classified as a separate species if humans hadn't been the ones doing the classification. The only thing that's supposed to make us superior to the animals is our moral conscience, and from what Adam has seen and read about his fellow humans, he's not so sure we have that. Although Roger told them they're not supposed to think about evolution, that's how Adam plays Mister Monkey—as an intelligent animal a few generations away from becoming human.

In one of Adam's dreams, a worm crawled out of the mud and turned into a baby. A cute little baby boy!

The first time Derek saw Adam's monkey costume, he'd closed his eyes and said that he was receiving a communication from beyond the grave: an old lady had died of bowel cancer under the same shit-brown bedspread from which Adam's costume was made. Derek's just jealous; he'd read for *Mister Monkey* and didn't get the part. Adam wishes his mom hadn't mentioned the dust mites inside the monkey suit, which, unlike Derek's psychic message from the afterlife, probably *is* true.

Adam sings, "Mother, I threw you a coconut and you threw me back the moon." He doesn't mean *his* mom, Giselle, but the beautiful monkey mother who was so sweet to him, who fed him delicious bananas, and who loved him with a perfect love until she was killed (like the gorillas in the documentary Roger showed) by poachers, right in front of his eyes.

Adam shuffles across the stage with a sad-funny old-man walk he learned from the gorilla at the Bronx Zoo. When Adam got the part in *Mister Monkey*, his mom let him go to the zoo with Derek if he promised to call home every forty-five minutes and write a one-page paper about what he saw.

For almost an hour they watched a gorilla masturbate and sulk. Darwin used to spend hours at the zoo, giving monkeys snuff to see if they closed their eyes when they sneezed, giving other monkeys a doll and a mirror to find out what they'd do with that. In one of Darwin's books there's a story about a mandrill in the zoo trying to seduce the youngest and prettiest girls on the other side of the bars; Darwin thought it was so scandalous he put it in a footnote—in Latin!

*   *   *

ADAM CALLED HIS mom in the middle of the solo gorilla
jerk and said that he and Derek were fine and having loads
of fun. The monkey kept pulling on his dick until Adam and
Derek were beginning to get a little bored. More surpris-
ing than the gorilla's lack of interest in privacy was the fact
that none of the other zoo-goers seemed to notice what it was
doing. Look at the funny monkey! One dad wondered aloud
if he could get a DVD of *King Kong*. He wanted the kids to
see it. Adam sensed a lesson—but about what? People see and
don't see what they want and don't want to see. If only he
knew how to use that, playing Mister Monkey.

Adam and Derek finally left when a well-dressed, middle-
aged Latin guy in a hipster fedora came and stood in front
of the monkey cage, his body wracked by spasms that at first
made Adam think that he was masturbating too, until Adam
looked more closely and saw that the guy was weeping. A
masturbating, sulking three-hundred-pound gorilla was one
thing, but the crying guy creeped them out, and they quickly
moved on.

What Adam would *really* like to do onstage would be to
go all the way monkey, deep monkey, and show the audience
that Mister Monkey has a penis. The smelly monkey costume doesn't have a penis. But Adam does; it's growing hair,
like the masturbating gorilla. Isn't that what monkeys do?
Monkeys wank and spit. And sulk, when they're in captivity.
Except for bonobos. Why couldn't Mister Monkey be a hot
sexy bonobo instead of a stupid, people-pleasing chimpanzee?

"Father, you watched me climb the tree, your arms outstretched to catch me if I fell. But when you fell I couldn't
catch you." Adam stretches out his arms toward his lost
monkey dad.

The audience isn't feeling it. Adam can sense their remove, their restlessness, the children's itchy boredom. He doesn't blame them. He moonwalks backward across the stage and does a double flip. His mom has told him to play Mister Monkey like a cross between a Romanian gymnast and Michael Jackson in *Thriller.* She showed him the clip on YouTube.

In the essay for his mom, Adam wrote that at the zoo he saw a baby chimpanzee sleeping, and he wondered if the monkey was dreaming and what he was dreaming about.

"I love this," his mom had said, rattling the paper near his head, almost whispering, as if she and Adam were sharing some intense private communication. His mom gave him an A plus. What could be more pathetic than being graded by your mother on an essay that (a) is totally made-up and (b) you wrote in twenty minutes, late, in your bedroom, while watching porn on your computer?

Adam sings, "Mother, are you up there, can you see me?"

Obviously she can see him. Giselle is sitting in the second row, where she sits every night. How can she stand to watch the play so often? Adam can hardly bear it, and he gets to do somersaults and climb the scenery.

Despite himself, pity for his real mom, not his monkey mom, plucks lightly at something taut and ropey deep down in his chest. Are heartstrings actual body parts? Anatomy is another subject his mom never gets around to.

Poor Mom! Underneath the flowing scarves and skirts, she's just this side of a serious weight problem. It will only make things worse if he mentions it, so Adam confines himself to glaring furiously at the little snacks—cupcakes the color of dried blood dusted with rainbow sprinkles—with which she comforts herself. As if it's the cupcakes' fault for jumping into her mouth! What if his mom has a heart attack?

What will happen then? Someday Mom is going to die, definitely before his dad.

Then Adam will have to live with Dad and Pushy Heidi—who wants him dead, though she'd never admit that, not even to herself—and with his baby half-brother Arturo, whom he's not allowed to hold. Heidi is scared that Adam will give the baby a monkey disease or drop him, which he would never do. Heidi is a lesson sent to teach Adam that you have to be careful about people, especially women.

On opening night, Dad and Heidi elbowed their way backstage before anyone else. Heidi knelt and hugged Adam so hard that it hurt, even as he was still struggling out of his monkey suit. When his mom showed up seconds later, she said to Heidi, "*Really*? Do you have to get down on your knees in front of *every* male in my family?" And everything stopped. Just stopped. The cast and crew quit laughing and high-fiving each other, and everyone stared at the picture they made: Adam, his parents, and Pushy Heidi, kneeling, glaring up at his mom.

As Adam sings the final notes, he tastes, at the back of his throat, the vinegar bite of loss and, all right, *yearning* he's supposed to pour into the song. He thinks about Mom drowning in the science-fiction flood. He thinks about how she can't stop herself from mentioning all the famous child stars who flamed out and died young and how important it is that Adam not wind up like that. He tries to think about the time when his parents were still together, but he can't remember one thing from when they were a family. He can't imagine his mom and dad happy and in the same room.

Now he really *is* sad. He's singing Mister Monkey's song *as if it happened to him.*

So he's unprepared when he finishes on a big note, a *huge*

note, and the applause is thin and sad. Well, fine, it *should* be sad. It's weird to sing a tragic song and have everyone clapping their heads off, loud and fast and . . . happy!

Jason and Danielle skip out onstage, grinning like shrunken heads, unaware of how narrowly they missed getting the gift of monkey spit and snot. They grab Adam's hands and half-dance, half-pull him around, so he can pretend to be cheered up until their wannabe stepmother, Janice, accuses him of stealing her wallet, and Lakshmi, in her police clown outfit, escorts him offstage. Janice is a little like Pushy Heidi. Why did Adam never notice that before? The difference is, Adam sort of likes Eleanor, who in real life is nothing like Janice. Eleanor is a nurse.

Lakshmi's only pretending to drag him as Adam fakes being dragged. Lakshmi is a nice hardworking person, yet everyone's always dumping on her, including Adam's mom, when really it's Roger, not Lakshmi, who makes them wear disgusting uncomfortable costumes: a purple suit, a rainbow wig, a dying grandma's mite-infested bedspread. Lakshmi is Roger's bad cop, so it makes sense that she plays one.

Adam remembers one rehearsal at which his mom raised her hand and said in her scared little rabbit voice, which gets even smaller out in the world, "Wouldn't the police department send *two* officers to arrest a monkey?" And Roger had talked right over Mom as if she hadn't spoken.

Adam gets a break while Portia and Carmen, his lawyer and the family maid, do their sexy rumba duet. Rita is younger and prettier, Adam knows. But weirdly, he thinks Margot, the older one, is the hot one.

He likes the tight sleazy purple suit, though he knows it's supposed to be tacky. Both Rita and Margot have tried to be friendly to him in that robotic way adults talk to kids. But his mom had frightened them off, just by looking at them. Eleanor is the only one who actually talks to Mom or even acknowledges her existence.

Rita and Margot are actors, Adam's coworkers. They have come to respect him for hitting his marks and not upstaging them (too much!) and being professional. Portia and Carmen are on his side. But it's Margot—Portia—who saves him from chimpanzee prison, which probably doesn't exist. No one admits that what Mister Monkey's facing is probably euthanasia. The thought has definitely occurred to Adam, and he uses the queasy feeling it gives him to make Mister Monkey even more frantic when he fears that he is in danger. Lots of times, real monkeys shit when they are afraid.

Adam's got a few minutes before he has to go on. You'd think he would be present at his own trial, but here in Mister Monkeyland, animals aren't entitled to due process. His mom has made him read a boring book and some online articles about courts and legal procedures, all of which he already knew about from TV.

When Giselle first told him that the play was holding open auditions, he'd hoped that it wasn't based on the *Mister Monkey* book he read in his fourth grade class. It had practically made him sick, the way Miss Julia said certain things about the book and made the class repeat those things, either because she believed them or because she had to.

What is a stereotype, class? Mister Monkey shows us that the stereotypes aren't true. The brave Latina housekeeper. The crusading woman lawyer. Animal rights. The high point of Adam's educational career was asking Miss Julia, in front of the whole class: If the writer cared so much about animal rights, why didn't Mister Monkey get to testify at his own trial? Even Miss Julia had to agree that Adam had a point.

Adam would still like to know the answer to that one and a lot of other things in the plot, like the detail about Janice's missing fingernails that Roger has told them to ignore.

Adam waits for his cue: "Mister Monkey is innocent!" Then he's supposed to run onstage and, after shooting rapid crazy-monkey looks at his human dad, his siblings, and the maid, to jump into his lawyer's waiting arms. He's read that when chimpanzees are happy, their eyes sparkle, like human eyes, so he has worked hard to make his eyes extra shiny even inside his monkey suit.

Adam scampers on stage. When Margot's purple skirt rides up, it nearly drives him nuts.

This is weird: he's got a hard-on. He hopes it will subside as he takes a flying leap at Margot. But it doesn't. Margot catches him and holds him. He's way too heavy for her, and he tries to make himself lighter.

He rubs his penis against her hip. Does the audience notice? People see and don't see what they want and don't want to see.

How did he get from there to here, from not doing this to doing this? It was as if some force picked him up and threw him into her arms. Against her. But now that he's here, with his crotch touching some part of Margot's body that is maybe her hip, maybe somewhere *near* her hip, he can't believe how good it feels, even with the woolly monkey suit and the polyester skirt between them. Maybe that makes it better. How can anything wrong feel this right? He is in danger of floating off in some warm delicious broth of pleasure and bliss when Margot drops him as if she wants to smash him flat against the stage.

Adam lands on his feet. He tries to smile an apology at her through the ragged holes in his monkey face. He's sorry, deeply sorry. And yet he would have done anything, risked everything, to feel what he just felt. A sensation rising up from his toes tells him it was worth it. How can these happy sensations be bad, even though Margot's pinched little face has gone white with shock?

What Adam did was wrong. Forgive him. Was that . . . was that *rape*? Could he be arrested? Margot looks flash-frozen, her dark eyes turned to marbles and her pretty teeth to icicles.

Maybe she'll snap out of it when dorky Eric—who's always trying to act young and hip, calling Adam "bro" and "homes"—sings, into his pretend cell phone, that he loves Portia. One afternoon, before a show, Eric showed Adam a newspaper clipping about a crazed chimpanzee that ripped his owner's face off because the guy wouldn't give him a slice of birthday cake. From the way Eric laughed, Adam could tell that Eric thought it was super cool to be showing something like that to a kid. Adam had been pretty sure he'd smelled alcohol on Eric's breath.

Maybe Eric's drunk now, because from the way he's blowing his lines, you'd think that Adam had just jumped into *his* arms and humped *him*. Why is *Eric* falling apart? Mr. Jimson reaches, like a drowning person, for Carmen's hand. That is not in the script *at all*. Wait till Roger sees *that*.

Margot's supposed to say, "Now we can all live together!" Instead they stand around watching her try to unthaw her brain. This is all Adam's fault. He is so, so sorry. Something outside him made him do it. Or maybe something inside him . . .

Margot finally mumbles, "Now we can all live together."

By now Adam should be climbing the scenery and flipping around the ceiling. But he stands there, paralyzed, watching.

It throws Margot and Eric even further off, like some evil chain reaction.

Mr. Jimson asks Portia if she will be Mrs. Monkey. *Will she be Mrs. Monkey?* Eric must be high! Could this be more awkward? Especially after that hug between Adam and Margot: that is, between Mister Monkey and his lawyer. Adam has to remember: everyone doesn't know about that. Only Adam and Margot know. So far.

Will she be Mrs. Monkey? Would she by any chance like to marry the trashy perv chimpanzee who just sexually aggressed her?

Adam wants to be back in kindergarten. Meaning: before the divorce? Brilliant insight, doctor. Adam's mom says it's indecent, how Margot is in love with her therapist, obviously a quack who should be brought up on charges. Margot will have plenty to tell Dr. Quack-Quack now. Mister Monkey humped me. Adam likes the idea of them discussing how Margot felt when she finally noticed that Mister Monkey has a penis. Oh, what has he done? They will be talking about *him*. He imagines the doctor saying, Really? Mister Monkey has a penis? And he feels himself getting hard again. God, he hates being his age.

Adam wants to be back in kindergarten. Miss Linda had shown the class a video of elephants and told them all to line up and clasp their hands and swing their trunks as they walked their elephant walk. He was no longer Adam with the fighting parents, the Adam who knew, in nursery school, that he would never be the kid whom the other kids wanted to be friends with. No, he was Adam the Elephant, trumpeting his confidence and pride as he and his elephant posse dominated the jungle. Fuck with an elephant and he will stomp you flat, no questions asked.

Adam says good-bye to his happy kindergarten memories and hello to the scary reality of Mr. Jimson and Portia, motionless and mute, unable to work their way back from Eric asking Margot to be Mrs. Monkey.

Derek is always talking about how great things are going to be when he gets older and gets a girlfriend and they have sex. Adam used to believe him, but based on what just happened with Margot, he's no longer sure. Maybe the first time he has sex won't be as much fun as the first time he became an elephant.

His kindergarten teacher saw something in him. He was the best elephant in the class. The kids took another look. His teacher told his parents that Adam had a gift. That summer he started theater day camp, where he began his rise to stardom by playing one of the orphans in a scene from *Oliver.* Who would buy their beautiful morning, their beautiful day? Orphan child, orphan monkey, Adam's career has come full circle and wound up one step down the evolutionary ladder he's not supposed to think about.

Adam would like to think about that instead of doing what he's supposed to do, which is: grab the rope that Lakshmi is lowering from the ceiling, then scramble up a pole and climb around the set, so the audience can watch his monkey high jinks and be spared the full douchiness of Mister Jimson and Portia falling in love.

Normally Adam's glad he doesn't have to observe that pitiful spectacle, but this afternoon, Eric and Margot are so *bad* he can't stop looking. So it's a standoff, as they try to get a grip, and Adam fantasizes about kindergarten and keeps being yanked back to watch Portia and Mr. Jimson wreck the play. Meanwhile the rope just dangles there with Lakshmi on the other end.

A shaming twinge of jealousy makes Adam shiver inside his stifling costume. A few times he's gotten the feeling that Margot sort of *likes* Eric. And now some demented part of him is hoping that the reason why Portia is having trouble declaring her love for Mister Jimson is that Margot has feelings for Adam. Maybe she didn't completely hate it when he jumped her. Adam knows it's not the coolest way to get a girl, to leap into her arms and press your monkey dick into her innocent flesh. But it made Margot pay attention! Adam wants to grow up, get it over with. He's sick and tired of his childhood.

He's drifted so far out that when he hears a crash, it takes him a while to figure out that Margot has dropped her phone. This is cool. What now?

What would Mister Monkey do? Mister Monkey would run and pick up the phone and hand it to his lawyer. He would make it into an adorable chimpanzee move. But Adam can't. It's no longer simple, Portia and Mister Monkey, the heroic lawyer and her grateful client. Now it's Margot and Adam. The victim and her . . . what? Margot forced him into it, not knowing how smokin' hot she looked in that purple suit. What would Adam's mom say if she knew *he even thought that*?

Could he make it up to Margot by picking up her phone? Would he be doing her a favor? Or would she hate him even more: the pushy child actor spoiling the scene that she imagines is going to win her an Obie.

Mister Monkey waits and watches. He wonders: What would Charles Darwin do?

Then, all of a sudden, some little preschool turd in the audience yells, "Grandpa, are you interested in this?" The kid's waited for the most dramatic moment—when Margot's phone is lying on the stage—to ask his retarded question.

Adam should have picked up the phone. Mister Monkey should be doing triple flips. He should have had Margot's back. It would have made her hate him less.

But the kid's question interests Adam. It's as if the kid's asking *him*.

Is Adam interested in this? Not really. But now— finally!—he knows what he wants. Not to travel to the moon, or to hand Jason and Danielle a wad of snot, or to be back in kindergarten, or to show the world that Mister Monkey has a penis.

He wants the theater to turn into a real jungle. He wants to become a real monkey, a chimp who knows how to swing from vine to vine with flocks of bright parrots screeching around him and the air damp and heavy with the perfume of tropical flowers. He wants to swing through the lights and the pulleys and ropes until he escapes through a window.

He wants to land on his feet, on the sidewalk outside. He wants to take off his Mister Monkey face. Then he will figure it out.

It's just at that moment that Margot kicks her phone. Margot aims and punts it. Hard. Slam-dunks it into the wings.

Adam loves her. He always will. And he's ruined it forever.

ADAM LOITERS OUTSIDE the theater, which is too crappy even to have a stage door, not that they need a secret exit to help them avoid the mob of adoring fans. He's waiting for his mom. The last thing he wants is to sit around for the boring discussions of what they should have done when Margot dropped her phone. Postmortems, his mother calls them. When Adam asked her what that meant, though he sort of knew, she made him look it up. What he found on the

Internet scared him, though he'd seen it a thousand times on TV. But somehow he hadn't known that it was real, that a stranger in surgical scrubs can cut you open after you are dead, just when you are probably thinking that nothing worse can happen to you.

Luckily no one leaving the theater recognizes him. They're jostling and pushing each other like people fleeing a burning house. Without the monkey suit he's invisible. No fool's going to come up to him and say, Aren't you that amazing child actor who played Mister Monkey? Can I have your autograph? Your agent's name? Would you be available to star in a TV pilot?

Adam's free to scan the crowd for that rude little piece of shit. Grandpa, are you interested in this? Everyone in the theater heard.

Quite a few kids have come with grandparents. And no one's signaling, I'm the little dickwad who ruined your show. But among the stragglers, there's one kid, maybe five or six, his grandfather is bending over to hear what he's saying, bending lower than the other grandpas. Is it gay of Adam to notice that the boy is pretty, with glossy black hair and pale skin? The kid could be a star. Adam never will, not unless he gets a face transplant and a massive infusion of growth hormones.

That's the kid. Adam's sure now, though he can't say why. He stares at them, and he must have *some* kind of power, because the grandfather catches him looking, and it's as if he's hit the old man with a laser. Pow. As they walk away, Grandpa turns back to see if Adam is following them. It would calm him down to know that Adam can't go anywhere because he has to wait for his mom.

A few people are hanging around the theater entrance, mostly tourists, stunned like vampires in the light. There's one youngish couple who look foreign and almost cool until the guy fires up a fruity E-cigarette and blows fake smoke in Adam's face.

Both of Adam's grandfathers died young, of smoking-related causes. Adam has promised that he'll never smoke. His mom made him swear on the life of his baby half-brother Arturo. Derek smokes, and Adam probably will too, but for now he's superstitious.

Adam wishes he had a grandpa like the one in the TV ad about grandparents keeping secrets. If Adam had a grandpa, could his loving grandfather keep the secret of what just happened onstage with Margot? Adam would only spoil everything by always thinking about how old his grandfather was and how soon he was going to die.

What's taking Mom so long? She always finds a reason to talk to Roger, though Roger never listens. It usually takes Mom a while to realize that Roger's blowing her off and then to recover from Roger's having blown her off. The second week of rehearsal, Giselle asked Roger to give Adam some notes. Roger perched on the edge of the stage, and Adam and Mom sat in the front row as Roger told Adam to play Mister Monkey like someone who hasn't done anything wrong, but whenever anyone accuses him of anything, he thinks he *might* have done something wrong. Did Adam know anyone like that? Adam did. *He* was like that. How did Roger know? The last thing he wants is Roger poking around in his head, reading his mind in that scary way his mother does, sometimes.

Should he have picked up Margot's phone? What will he say to her tomorrow afternoon when they will have to act as if *nothing* happened and do the Sunday matinee? He humped her leg! Are they not going to mention that?

*   *   *

ADAM IS ALWAYS shocked by how happy he is to see Mom, as if some part of him secretly feared that she'd died or disappeared and he would never see her again. But here she is, and now the second part kicks in: Mom always looks older than he remembers, weirder and heavier and less put together. Mom hugs him and kisses the top of his head, which she means to be sweet and loving and maternal but which only reminds him of how short he is.

The streets are crowded, and no one is paying attention to them, which is fortunate, because even before they reach the subway, Giselle has begun her own postmortem. Slice, slice, saw through the rib cage, take out a handful of guts, then start in on Adam's brain. Well, fine. She's serious about his acting. Too serious. She rattles on without noticing that Adam has dropped behind her so that people will think she's talking to herself. First he likes the pitying or contemptuous looks on their faces, then he doesn't.

As they near the subway, Adam's mom pulls him closer, raising her voice so that every stranger can hear how he lost focus for the last part of the show and how he needs to concentrate. All the time Mom's ripping into him, she's calling him *honey* and *sweetie*. Sweetie, this isn't day camp any more. Honey, if you're going to do this, do it right. Adam stops listening. He hears disconnected words. Monkey. Moon. Margot. Your cue.

Giselle doesn't quit talking till they reach the subway steps, which require *her* full concentration. Clinging to the railing, Mom slows everything down, annoying everyone behind her. Adam hates how they glare at the panting, asthmatic old hippie in her gypsy skirt and scarves, even as some dark secret part of him thinks it serves Mom right. Serves her right for *what*? Oh, poor Mom, poor Mom. Even Adam blames her for things that aren't her fault.

He and Mom get seats on the train, and now the people facing them can watch her ranting about the play. Adam is *really* acting now, impersonating a normally angry, resentful kid listening to his mom, when in reality he is a boy in hell. Everybody is acting. His dad is acting the part of a successful corporate lawyer, of Heidi's adoring husband and Arturo's doting dad. His mom is acting the part of his mom, but she's not doing so well. *She* could use some notes on a less maddening way—something less annoying than a poke in the shoulder—to rouse her dozing son when they reach their stop.

Trailing his mom through the fascist corporate wasteland otherwise known as Battery Park City, Adam hopes the elevator will be empty so they can ride in privacy up to the thirteenth floor. According to Mom, they got a deal on their apartment because people are superstitious, even in New York. The elevator door opens. No one's inside: the first answered prayer all day.

Giselle takes forever rummaging in the tasseled Tibetan feed sack she uses as a purse. Adam could find his key in a second, but he has to let her do it. Once he'd gently bumped her out of the way and unlocked the door, and she'd burst into tears.

"Bingo," says Giselle. She steps aside to let Adam enter first, half polite, half afraid he'll bolt if she turns her back. But where would he go? To Heidi and Dad in Park Slope? He could go to Derek's, but last time they hung out there, Derek played a DVD of *Requiem for a Dream* because he said it reminded him of Adam and his mom. That was completely unfair. Adam's mom is his acting coach, not some junkie blowing up like a Thanksgiving Day Parade balloon and trying to squeeze through a keyhole.

When the door closes behind Adam and his mom, it's like being thrown down a hole, or in solitary, the camera zooms in on the prison door getting larger and slamming shut, and the screen goes dark. Adam reminds himself, This is not some CIA black site! This is a nice two-bedroom apartment with a view of the harbor. During the divorce, his parents fought over the furniture: neither of them wanted it. His mother said she refused to live with a couch on which his dad had put his ass. Now Adam can't look at the couch without thinking about that.

When Adam pulls the drapes, his mother says, "Leave them open, honey. That view is why your father and I moved to this godforsaken hole. Lots of people would die for a view like that."

So why can't Adam look at it without thinking about how they're all going to die, and how he and Mom are going to die first because of their proximity to the water? Is there a name for Adam's problem? A few times he's tried to Google it, but he doesn't know what to search. One site said that some people are afraid of their own desire to jump out a window or off a bridge. But that's not what he's afraid of. Adam closes the curtains, and this time his mother doesn't protest. Natural selection: a human woman mates with a monkey boy, and they survive the apocalypse.

Giselle says, "What would you like for dinner? I can cook, or we can order out."

Neither is the right answer. If they call out for Chinese, Mom always gets General Tsao's chicken, which Adam doesn't like, and she eats the entire carton. She always makes him open the door for the delivery guy and figure out the tip.

She says that calculating 20 percent is the only math skill a person needs. The alternative is that Mom will cook a pound of pasta, and they'll compete to see who can eat the most, fastest. The more Adam eats, the less Mom gets.

"Let's have pasta," he says.

"*Cacio e pepe?*"

Adam nods.

"Excellent choice," his mom says. "Simple and delicious."

Giselle opens a bottle of white wine and gulps down a full glass, as if it were water.

Adam gives her wine the hateful look he usually reserves for her cupcakes. She pours another glass, fills a pot with water, and puts it on to boil.

"To Mister Monkey," she says. "Long may he run."

Adam likes watching her in the kitchen, stripped down to a black T-shirt and her witchy skirt, no scarves or shawls to catch fire. When he tries to imagines how Mister Monkey felt when he saw his monkey parents and his human step-mom get shot, he pictures his real mom going up in flames at the stove. Giselle's on her way to impaired, but she's not there yet. The cooking part of her brain is still intact, and the food is ready in no time. Grated cheese, cream, pepper, butter. Everything Adam likes.

After a while he hears Mom chanting something, or maybe singing lyrics, unintelligible until the nonsense sounds resolve into words.

> *Five little monkeys jumping on the bed*
> *One fell off and broke his head*
> *Mama called the doctor, the doctor said,*
> *No more monkeys jumping on the bed*
> *Four little monkeys . . .*

Mom says, "Want to hear something funny I just re-membered? I guess it's because we've been talking and learning so much about monkeys. Anyhow, when you were little, three, maybe four, you and me and Dad drove up to Boston to see Dad's cousin, and the whole way there you sang that rhyme about the monkeys. The whole way there! We couldn't stop you. Dad kept trying to dial it down, he'd say, 'Okay, Adam, one little monkey jumping on the bed, we're down to one!' But as soon as you got down to one, you'd push the number back up again, seven little monkeys, ten little monkeys . . ."

"What's the funny part?" says Adam. How could Mom imagine that such a sad story—her and Dad and him all happy and singing in the car—is humorous? Adam wants to weep. What happened to that cheerful kid? Where has he gone? How could he have been taken over by the mentally disturbed humanoid who lives inside him now, halfway be-tween a boy and an animal, halfway between a boy and a man, not human, uncivilized, molesting Margot onstage?

He wonders if Margot's out on a date, or with friends, or having dinner alone. Maybe she's ordered takeout. Is she thinking about him? He would give anything just to see the inside of her apartment. Is her kitchen like theirs? Does she have a scary view?

"I don't know," says Mom. "It just seemed funny for a second. Aren't I allowed to have even one nice memory?"

He and his mother take their seats at the counter, and for a few moments it's almost pleasant with the lights dimmed low, their faces damp with fragrant steam rising from the pasta.

Adam knows the right thing to say: the pasta is delicious. And he knows the wrong thing to say, which is what he says:

"Hey, what about that sucky little kid asking his grandpa if he was interested?" It's a test. A normal mother would say "What a brat!" and go back to eating her pasta.

But his mother fails that test. His mom says, "The kid was sitting right next to me. He was shouting in my ear." Then she puts down her fork, leans on the table, and lets her chin sink into her hands.

"I'm sorry," Adam says.

"Why should *you* be sorry?" his mom says thickly. "You did nothing wrong."

Oh, if she only knew! If she only knew that today, during the matinee, her sweet darling son had weird transgressive public sex with one of his costars. *Does* Mom know? Adam hopes not. It's alarming how often she knows things about him that he never told her. He stares at her, searching for a sign. But Mom has her eyes closed. At first he thinks it's because she's enjoying the pasta, until he realizes that she's crying. From behind the granny glasses tears slip down her cheeks.

"I'm sorry. I'm so so sorry." She weeps quietly for a while. She should be on medication. Derek's mom is, and it's helped. Adam has asked his dad to bring up the subject with Mom, and Dad said that he's the last person who could have that conversation with her.

The mood is spoiled. The pasta tastes like crap. Adam puts his dish in the sink.

"I think I'll have another little taste," says Mom. "And maybe a drop more wine."

Adam says, "Good night, Mom," and goes to his room, though it's still early.

He lies down and opens *On the Origin of Species*, an antique edition his mom found in a used-book shop. Its dark green cover sheds red velvet crumbs, revealing a rust-colored layer beneath. The title is stamped on the spine in gold.

Adam reads, "We shall best understand the probable cause of natural selection by taking the case of a country undergoing slight physical change, for instance, of climate. The proportional numbers of its inhabitants will almost immediately undergo a change, and some species will probably become extinct."

After a while, Adam hears the super-gloomy Miles Davis track that Mom plays to put herself to sleep. Probably she *is* asleep. What could be more depressing? He walks into the living room where he discovers that Mom has opened the drapes he made a point of closing. Does she want the whole world to see that nothing fun—correction: *nothing*—is happening in their apartment? Does she want the terrorist pilots deciding that theirs is the window they should crash into?

The round gigantic moon reminds him of the lights they use for interrogation and surgery—and torture—on TV. He raises his arms, Mister Monkey style. Mother, can you hear me? Not with that sad-ass trumpet blaring.

He no longer wants to go to the moon. The moon doesn't want him there. The moon wants to be left alone. Who can blame it? But no, what the moon *really* wants is to fuck with Earth, to churn up the tides and winds and water. Tsunami time!

Adam gazes at the sparkling skyline of scenic New Jersey, then out at the harbor. He watches the dark storm clouds thicken, split by zigzags of lightning like furry black broken hearts. Marionette strings of moonbeams yank at the waves until the current boils up, splashing over the sidewalk, lick-

ing the trees. Now only the points of the Statue of Liberty's
crown are visible, poking holes in the clouds through which
the rain sheets down. Fish ride the swollen river, which
dumps them on the rooftops, where they flop around, gasping and dying, until swarms of hungry seagulls swoop down,
and a red curtain of fish blood and guts slicks Adam's windows. It's messy, but he can see through it. He sees something
on the horizon, pitching and rocking on the waves.

It's an ocean liner. Though Adam knows better, he thinks,
Look! It's Noah's ark! Two of every species, culled and saved
to replace the drowned and repopulate the planet.

Sorry! He's read his Darwin. The earth's inhabitants will
undergo a change. Species will become extinct. Humans
will be the first to go. Then who is on the boat? Space aliens
with opaque almond eyes? Amphibious creatures with blue
skin and hair, fins and water wings? Adam—in some other,
superior, more efficiently adapted life-form?

The boat floats under his window, where the water has
risen so high that Adam can look inside the portholes. In the
elegant dining room, tables are set with silver, china, and
crystal goblets. Chandeliers glitter above the dance floor, but
no one is dancing or sitting in the deck chairs draped with
plaid blankets. It's as if the *Titanic*'s been struck again, this
time by a neutron bomb. So that's it. The end. It's over.

Grief wells up inside him. It is *so* unfair! He's still a kid.
He hasn't had his life yet. Let this happen to the selfish shithead grown-ups who caused the problems in the first place.

The only thing that comforts him is the memory of how
good it felt when Margot had her arms around him, and he
pressed his hips against her. He wonders if that feeling could
save him from the storm, if it could pluck him out of the end
of the world and lift him above the flood.

And if the world doesn't end tonight? He has to see Margot again.

Closing his eyes, he begins to pray. Please don't let the world end. Please don't let the planet die. Please don't let Margot hate me.

CHAPTER 3

THE GRANDFATHER

AFTER THE PLAY, a disheveled little man, needing a shave, wearing sweatpants and a saggy yellowed T-shirt, blocks their path and shakes first the grandfather's hand, then the child's. The grandfather recognizes the director, who'd appeared on-stage to take a bow, though the cast of *Mister Monkey* hadn't beckoned him to join them, as actors often do.

He thanks the grandfather and the child for coming to the play.

"Thank *you*," says the grandfather. "We enjoyed it immensely." The child is looking at him, as if he has caught him in a lie. Then the three of them stand there until a woman in a gypsy skirt, a fringed shawl, and a long gray braid approaches the director and sets them free.

"I was being polite," the grandfather explains, though he isn't sure if the child's expression was accusing or simply curious. The child is naturally polite, not counting sometimes, like today, when he forgets that someone might be listening. Grandpa, are you interested in this? Should he talk to the child about being quiet in a theater?

Outside, the audience has dispersed, except for a tourist couple studying a map and a short thin boy standing off to one side and glaring at the grandfather and the child in a way that makes the grandfather uneasy. Something about the jittery way he's bouncing on his feet reminds the grandfather of Mister Monkey, and though the grandfather knows it's probably just paranoia, he is suddenly afraid that the boy is the actor, and that he recognizes his grandson as the one who asked if he was interested.

The grandfather wants to explain to the boy who played the monkey, if that's who he is, that his grandchild, in all innocence, simply wanted to know. It would be harder to explain that the grandfather heard in the child's question the voice of his wife, calling his name in the night, because she'd woken from a nightmare and was in pain and needed to know that he was there. The child was waking from a dream of an orphan monkey in danger.

The grandfather is not going to say anything like that to the boy, who might not even be the person he thinks he is. He doesn't want to embarrass his grandson. But the kid's stare is so hostile that, after they walk away, the grandfather turns to see if they're being followed.

The grandfather hasn't been feeling well. Lately he's had some chest pain and a few dizzy spells. He's obviously not himself if he imagines that a gloomy boy is going to harm them.

"Did you like the play?" asks the grandfather. Sometimes he feels as if he and the child are on a first date and he's desperate to make conversation.

The child nods. "I'm hungry and thirsty." He's not demanding to be fed but merely stating a fact. Another kid might pout or whine. The child's mother used to. The grandfather must have been patient, or patient enough, because his daughter has turned out well. She's happily married, a loving mother, with work—she's a public defender—she respects and enjoys. Being with his grandson is more exciting than it was to be with his daughter when she was little, but even his most lighthearted moments with the little boy are marred by hopeless yearning. Because the force of the grandfather's love can never be returned, because the child is who he is, because the grandfather is who *he* is, and because it would go against the natural order for the child to be as obsessed with him as he is with the child.

"We're pretty far west," the grandfather says.

"Look, Grandpa. Over there." The child points across the street at a Korean deli. "Could I please have potato chips and a soda?"

A girl in a neon-chartreuse blouse, a black miniskirt, boots, and a bicycle helmet struts past them, pumping her arms. The child and the grandfather stop to watch a yellow scooter driven by an elderly cowboy in a Stetson hat, bare-chested but for a beaded vest. Is the child glad *that* man's not his grandpa? That's not how the child thinks.

In the store, they head for the refrigerated drinks section and the child gets a Coke, which his parents won't let him have. The grandfather is thirsty and would love some cold water, but when he's with the child on the street and the subway, he feels that he needs to have both hands free. He can wait to drink some water until they get to his daughter and son-in-law's apartment.

The child takes the grandfather's arm and guides him to the rack of chips, near the register. The child is not by nature affectionate, not physically warm. The grandfather sometimes thinks of the child as his unhappy love affair.

The intensity of the child's focus on the bags of chips grabs the grandfather's heart and squeezes it, playfully, but in a bullying way, not letting him breathe till it stops. Pangs of

love. He hopes. He should probably see his internist. Dr. Gro-
eder wasn't great with Jane, at the end, and a distance opened
between them.

The child looks up at the grandfather. Must he decide in a
hurry? The grandfather steps aside so he and the child won't
hold up the line. The grandfather is ashamed of his desire to
instruct the child, though he feels that is part of his job.

He no longer remembers why he chose that play. Maybe
because the tickets were cheap. He has taken the child to
the theater several times. So far their favorite show featured
a troupe of teenage acrobats, kids from a circus school in a
Rio favela, hip-hop trapeze artists and high-wire walkers
performing without a net. He and the child still talk about
it, another secret kept from the child's parents, who might
worry that their son would try a stunt like that on his own.
Maybe that's why he chose *Mister Monkey*. He'd read that the
title role was being played by a child gymnast: by the boy
outside the theater.

"What's wrong, Grandpa?" says the child.

"Nothing. Why do you ask?"

"You look a little . . . funny," says the child.

"I'm fine. Really."

Soon after he'd bought the tickets he'd told the child that
Mister Monkey was based on a book. The grandfather read
Mister Monkey aloud, two or three chapters at a time until
the child lost interest. The grandfather didn't like the book
either. It seemed obvious and preachy, full of improving lessons about race and class, honesty, justice, and some kind of
. . . spirituality, for want of a better word. It seemed almost as
if Mister Monkey were a stand-in for some sort of god.

Though the child is only in kindergarten, he already
knows how to read quite well. But he refuses to read in front

of other people. It's private, he says, a word that is sacrosanct in the child's home. Mommy and Daddy are having *private* time. Could *you* do *private* things? The grandfather loves his daughter and son-in-law and mostly approves of how they are raising the child. But they lie to their son, lies of language. *Private. Special. Grown-up.* That's a *grown-up* drink. Their childless friends are *child free*.

One thing the grandfather can offer the child is the promise that he will never lie to him. Unlike your parents, he almost said once. But if he'd been disloyal, the child would have thought less of him. He'd lied to the child in the theater. He'd said he was interested in the play. Not a lie of language. A lie of interpretation.

He *had* been interested, though not in the sense that the child most likely meant. How could anyone *not* have been interested in that cast and their manic desperation? The two teenagers and the kid in the monkey suit might have been having fun, and the pretty, redheaded woman who played the father's lying, treacherous girlfriend seemed to be enjoying herself. But the other actors and presumably the director never expected that they would wind up doing that play—in that theater. Whatever they'd hoped to achieve in their careers certainly wasn't that.

The grandfather had been particularly interested in the actress in the purple suit, a few years older than his daughter and an obvious mental wreck. Her wretchedness should have made him feel sorry for her instead of better about his daughter and himself. He must have been a good father: his daughter hasn't wound up like that!

The child stands on tiptoe to put the chips and soda on the counter.

"No BBQ?" says the cashier, a handsome African-

American guy, all Maori-tattooed biceps and sweetness, the kind of man whom kids look up to. "No cheddar and garlic? No jalapeño?"

"I don't like flavors," the child says. The grandfather feels a twinge in his chest, a bright star of pride and pain.

"Me neither," the grandfather says.

"Me neither," says the clerk.

The cashier is a test case. Maybe he has younger siblings, but at this point in his life, the grandfather's willing to bet, he has no interest in kids. Maybe he's even scared of them—anxious about the trap they represent. First comes love, then comes marriage, then comes the handsome deli clerk with a baby carriage. The grandfather can remember when having children seemed like punishment: the dire consequences of sex.

But even the cashier is impressed by the child. It's not just the adoring grandpa who notices that the boy is a beauty.

"What's your name, little man?" asks the clerk.

"Tony," says the child. The grandfather stares at him, shocked. The child's name is Edward. Early on, his parents made it clear that he was not to be called Ed or Eddie.

"Pleased to meet you, Tony," says the clerk. "I'm Eduardo."

Almost like *your* name! the grandfather almost says. Edward's a great name! See? But that would mean calling the child a liar, exposing him and ruining everything. Maybe forever.

"Hi, Eduardo." With his enormous dark eyes and long lashes, the child reminds the grandfather of his own father, who died when he was twelve; his father was thirty-six years younger than the grandfather is now. There is never a moment when the grandfather has to stop and calculate how long he has outlived his father; he always knows.

He has seen the world take notice of the child's delicacy and self-possession. He has been reprimanded by his daughter for telling the child that he is beautiful. The child's parents fear that he may attract the wrong kind of attention, or that he will take advantage of something unearned; that he will learn to use the gift of beauty for leverage or as a shortcut to getting what he wants. The grandfather has a different fear: that the child's beauty will incur some sort of bad luck. The grandfather thinks, I've become a superstitious old man.

Watching the clerk watch the child, the grandfather thinks, The child will grow up to be a lot of people's unhappy love affairs. It's not that the child is cold. When sadness engulfs the grandfather, the child comes and rests his head against the grandfather's shoulder. But only for a moment, and if the grandfather so much as ruffles his hair, the child drifts away.

Fortunately those onslaughts of sadness are growing less frequent. The year before the child was born was the worst in the grandfather's life. He'd lost his job at the museum, though everyone agreed that he was smart for taking the generous buyout that would have been foolish to refuse. No one predicted that Jane would die before she could help spend the buyout money.

"Grandpa," says the child. "Are you okay? You paid already. Let's go."

"Stay fresh, little man," the store clerk says.

"You too," says the child.

"You want me to open that soda for you?" says the clerk.

"My grandpa can do it," says the child.

"Are you good with that, Grandpa?" the cashier says.

"I'm good," the grandfather replies.

He kneels in front of the child and twists off the cap and

hands it to the child and manages to get back on his feet without tipping over. Again he wishes that he'd gotten a bottle of cold water. Well, fine, he can make it. If the train comes reasonably soon, it's forty minutes to his daughter's apartment. If necessary, he can ask for some of the child's Coke. The child has a generous nature. The grandfather wouldn't love him less if he were one of those children whose every other word is *mine*. Even if the grandfather drank his entire soda, the child would try to find it funny. Crazy Grandpa.

The child takes a long swig of Coke, swallows, and grabs a handful of chips.

"Chew slowly," the grandfather says. "You have all the way home to finish."

The child holds on to the chips, the grandfather takes the Coke, and with his free hand grabs the child's hand.

The street is much more crowded than it was when they entered the store, swarming with people, like zombies in a horror film. The soda and the chips are props, creating a little bubble of privacy and safety as the grandfather and the child find doorways, bus shelters, quiet spots in which to make hasty exchanges of savory and sweet.

At the top of the subway stairs the grandfather pauses, preparing himself to brave the tricky descent, the noise roaring up the stairwell, the subway riders so intent on their destination that they'd recklessly knock the grandfather down and just keep on plowing ahead.

In fact the other passengers range from uninterested to tolerant to excessively smiley, wanting the grandfather to see how touched they are by this vision of love across the generations: grandpa and grandchild holding hands, looking out for each other. Does the child know that strangers wish they had a grandpa like his?

The child looks at everyone they pass, registering and re-
cording. The grandfather and his son-in-law have spent several pleasant Sunday mornings at the playground watching
the child ride his scooter up to strangers and stare at them
until they noticed his presence, at which point he'd scoot
away. Adults and children alike were startled by the steadi-
ness of his attention and the suddenness of its withdrawal.

The grandfather pulls the child farther from the platform
edge and moves to a less crowded area, where a German
family—mother, father, a teenage girl, a boy of about ten—
are shouting with excitement and all looking in one direction. The father is filming, on his phone, a large black rat
scurrying back and forth on the subway tracks. The family is
thrilled by this authentic New York experience that they can
show their friends at home.

The child asks the grandfather what's going on, and the
grandfather, just about managing the chips and Coke, lifts
the child in his arms so he can see the rat. His grandson
sees the rat, then looks again at the family, and winks at the
grandfather. The grandfather imagines a future in which the
child will say, Grandpa, remember when we saw the family
filming the subway rat?

The child is interested in science, especially dinosaurs.
The grandfather has bought the child a set of tiny plastic
dinosaurs, which the child keeps, in the grandfather's apartment, in a wooden jewelry box that once belonged to Jane.
Last week, the child divided the dinosaurs into three groups:
herbivorous, carnivorous, and omnivorous. "How did you
learn those words?" the grandfather had marveled, and the
child had turned his face away so the grandfather couldn't
see him smile, despite himself, with pride.

When the train roars in, the grandfather flinches, but the

child doesn't. Years ago the grandfather witnessed an argument between his daughter and son-in-law about how early was too early to take the baby on the subway. He can't remember who took which position, or who won, but he recalls that both were briefly worried that the child was deaf or autistic because he didn't react (as he still doesn't) when the train arrived.

When the doors open, the grandfather gently pushes the child in front of him, and a young man gets up and gives them his seat. It's always the toughest black guys who are courteous that way; somebody brought them up right. The hipsters and the college girls will slither in and steal the seat right out from under you. The grandfather sits, and the child climbs onto his lap.

Across the aisle, a teenager is sleeping with his head on his backpack, his face so completely covered by his hoodie that he looks like a headless person. The grandchild pokes the grandfather, who has read him *The Legend of Sleepy Hollow.* Everyone else is deeply into some electronic device. It's just as well. Too often people look at him and the child and grin, as if they are a pair of newborn puppies. An elderly Indian man, his thin arms sticking out of his short-sleeved business shirt, stares at them as if the grandfather and grandson possess the explanation of something that has happened or a warning about something that hasn't.

The child reaches into his grandfather's pocket and takes out the pages that the grandfather vaguely remembers getting from the chubby girl, also Indian, who showed them to their seats. How proud and grown-up it had made the child feel that she gave them each a copy! The grandfather is suddenly eager to read about the cast. The actress in the purple suit—what brought her to *Mister Monkey?*

When the child says, "Can I keep mine?" the grandfather says yes. He'll hold it for the child, and give it to him when they get to his apartment. The child hands over the folded, stapled pages, and the grandfather reaches around too fast when he stuffs them in his pocket. He pulls a muscle, near his armpit. The pain makes him miss Jane and the ease with which she could comfort him, until she couldn't. Now he'll have no one to complain to in the middle of the night. He'll read the program later, then add it to his collection of zoo tickets and theater programs, sentimental souvenirs of his outings with his grandson.

The child says, "I want to bring it in to school. For show-and-tell."

He must have liked the play if he wants to tell the class! The grandfather feels joyous. Everything has been worth it. He likes the old-fashioned sound of *show-and-tell*. When his daughter was in school, they called it *sharing time*. He would give anything to be there when his grandson talks about the play.

The grandfather can't help himself. "What are you going to say?"

The child shrugs and pretends that the train is making too much noise for him to answer. When it surfaces to cross the bridge the child climbs up on the grandfather to look out the window over his shoulder.

They exit at the Seventh Avenue station. The grandfather is panting by the time they've climbed the stairs, and his breathing catches and sticks as he takes the child's hand and they walk down the leafy Brooklyn street.

The grandfather says, "*Did* you like the play?"

"Yes," the child says. "Did you?"

"Yes," says the grandfather. He *hasn't* lied to child. He

was mesmerized by the look on the face of the actress who'd dropped her phone. He could not have been more curious to know what she was going to do, or more startled by her solution. His heart goes out to the woman so obviously at the end of her rope. He understands what that feels like. He'll find out about her when he gets a chance to look at the program.

The child likes to push the elevator call button, and then the button for his floor. By the time they've reached the apartment door, someone has unlocked it. The child races down the hall to the kitchen, and the grandfather arrives in time to see the child fling himself at the back of his mother's knees. She turns from the stove on which she is sautéing onions and kneels and hugs the child, who buries his face in her neck. The grandfather suppresses a jealous pang. Of course the child loves his mother. He *wants* Edward to feel that love.

His daughter wipes her hands on her jeans. How it used to irk him, when she was a teen, that ragged edge of sloppiness, so unlike her mother. Now he treasures anything that reminds him of the girl she was then. The child watches his mother kiss his grandfather on the cheek.

"Could I possibly have a glass of water?"

"Of course, Dad. Sorry. I should have offered."

"No need to be sorry." He hadn't meant to sound annoyed.

His daughter takes a bottle of Perrier from the refrigerator, which—again, he can't help himself—irritates him. How many times has he tried to convince them that city water is safe to drink—and free? She leaves fingerprints all over the glass, but he gulps the water, greedily. How cold and delicious it is, and how well it knows how to open his parched, constricted throat.

"That's better," she says, as if he were the child's age.

He and his daughter and son-in-law couldn't have been more thoughtful or kinder to one another during Jane's final months. It was only afterward that awkwardness set in, as if he and his daughter are embarrassed by the shared secret knowledge that neither of them has recovered, though it has been seven years, and a child has come into the world. Maybe he is imagining this. *Projecting.* Jane's death should have brought them closer, but the opposite has occurred. Grief has sealed him off, and by now it's too late and too difficult to break through.

"Where's Mark?" asks the grandfather.

"Running," says his daughter.

"Running from what?"

"Hilarious, Dad. How was the play?" she asks the child.

"Good," the child says.

"Good?" she asks the grandfather.

"Interesting," the grandfather says, to his instant regret. Wrong word! The child gives him a searching look. Does the child think he is mocking him? The grandfather's smile is reassuring. He would never make fun of him or expose something he wants to hide. It's another secret they share, another memory for the child to carry into the future: the time my grandpa lied and said he was interested in the play and didn't tell Mom that I talked too loud and everybody heard.

"Heartbreaking, actually." He's glad his daughter doesn't ask what he means. She'll assume he meant that the play was sad. He doesn't want to say, in front of the child, how sorry he felt for the actors.

The child runs off to his room.

"Say thank you, Grandpa," his mother says.

"That's okay," the grandfather says. "He doesn't have to thank me."

"He *does* have to thank you," his daughter says, and turns back to the stove.

"Why so many onions?" the grandfather asks.

"Friends are coming for dinner."

"I should go," the grandfather says.

"We want you to stay. Mark told you about it. We assumed you were staying."

Did his son-in-law mention it? The grandfather can't remember. In any case, he's disappointed. He'd imagined a relaxed, intimate family dinner. What convinces him to stay is that his daughter says the guests are the parents of his grandson's friends; the kids are coming too. The grandfather can't resist the offer of information about the child's life in the larger world.

His daughter is making tomato sauce: pasta for the kids, eggplant Parmesan for the adults.

She says, "I can never remember which parents are vegetarians." She'd said *friends*, but now it's *parents*, which makes the grandfather think that maybe she does want him there as a buffer against strangers. She was always shy. She used to make him and Jane ask questions for her. Where is the bathroom? Can I play with your pail and shovel?

Now she says, "Dad, why not rest until the guests arrive? Stretch out on the sofa."

The grandfather doesn't feel like resting. He doesn't see enough of the child, doesn't want to waste a moment. He leaves the kitchen, intending to go to the child's room and read to him or play one of the picture card games with simple rules which the grandfather needs explained to him, every time.

On the way, he passes the couch. It's been a long afternoon. Why not lie down for a minute?

The grandfather dreams that he and the child are in the

subway station. This time the child has fallen asleep on the platform and refuses to move when the train pulls in. The grandfather tries to lift him, but the child is too heavy. How will they get home? In terror, the grandfather calls for his wife. He knows she is coming to help him.

The grandfather wakes to find himself surrounded by children staring down at him. This must be how Goldilocks felt looking up at the three bears. He reaches out to touch his grandson's face, but the child gives him a feral look and shoots off to his bedroom. The other children pause, as if sniffing the air, then turn and follow his grandson.

Their parents have gathered around the kitchen counter. The grandfather tries to remember if he has met any of them. His daughter is cooking, his son-in-law opening a bottle of wine. It's restful to stand back and watch them, but he can't, not for long. When he approaches, the parents' stares match their children's, precisely.

"I'm the grandpa," he says, and everyone smiles, as if he were a child saying something unexpectedly grown-up. Then they return to their conversation about the children's cooperative grade school, and its German director, Hugo. The grandfather has heard about Hugo from his daughter and son-in-law. Mark says that Hugo is pretentiously spiritual, overly crunchy, and Teutonic. His daughter says he's a bully.

The grandfather realizes that what his daughter has described as an informal gathering is in fact a meeting to plan a coup to overthrow Hugo. The parents take turns heaping abuse on Hugo, on his arrogant laziness, on his disregard for the children as individuals, on his humorlessness, his habit of sending kids home with another child's hat or mittens and then not only refusing to acknowledge his mistake but also insisting that it was an intentional lesson in *sharing*. And what about his completely inappropriate ideas about dance? Teaching hip-hop to the kids, who have shocked their parents by shouting and crouching, grabbing their crotches and stabbing the air with overhand hooks.

And don't forget those odious fund-raisers that Hugo made the parents organize and attend, teeth-rotting, hard *German* cookies repackaged in silver foil and sold for exorbitant prices, the recycled picture books—some scribbled in, one with teeth marks—they'd been strong-armed into buying. And who, in this day and age, would still imagine that a goldfish, gasping and dying in a plastic sandwich bag, was an appropriate prize for the child who won a ring toss? Surely not Hugo, so outspoken in his concern for animal rights?

Hugo's deficiencies hadn't seemed quite so problematic last year, when the kids were in pre-K, and their days mostly involved luxury babysitting and finger painting, but now that they've started kindergarten, which actually *matters*, when their education has in theory begun, the parents can no longer ignore the fact that Hugo is not a confidence-inspiring teacher.

They should have suspected him from the start, after the fuss he made about what to name the school, e-mailing the parents twice a day, soliciting suggestions, taking votes, doing surveys till the exhausted parents agreed with Hugo's idea: The Sunflower School: Growing Toward Learning.

"We should have called it the Xanax School," a mother says.

"The Hitler Jugend School," says one of the dads, and they all fall silent, looking at the grandfather. Do they think he is a Holocaust survivor? A World War II vet? He was born nine months after his father returned from the war.

Last week, there was a serious problem. Alex, the Brazilian boy, has a life-threatening peanut allergy, but Hugo consumed, at lunch, a carob and peanut bar, discovered only when the parent on cleanup duty found the wrapper in the trash. Even then Hugo refused to own up. He'd insisted that the candy was 100 percent organic, so the nuts weren't processed in the way that would endanger Alex.

The grandfather checks to see if any of the children are listening and is disturbed to see his grandson eavesdropping just outside the kitchen. His daughter and son-in-law underestimate how much the child takes in.

The grandfather says, "Just yesterday I was thinking that these allergic kids are the victims of one of those plagues that mysteriously appear and disappear throughout history. Like the bubonic plague. Like all those hysterical crippled Viennese girls coming to Freud for treatment."

The parents stare at him, then direct grimaces of sympathy, even pity, at his daughter and son-in-law. Look what they have to put up with! An old geezer with dementia! The grandfather sees his son-in-law wipe his hands on his pants, a nervous tic that his wife and son tease him about.

One of the fathers says, "Plague is still endemic in many regions of the Third World." The grandfather has no idea why he said that about peanuts. He has tried his theory out on Henri-Jean, the elevator operator in his building, when Henri-Jean complained that he'd gotten a letter saying he wasn't allowed to eat nuts within two hours of coming to work. Henri-Jean had said, "You are right, sir," but now the grandfather wonders how much Henri-Jean understood. For years he tried to make Henri-Jean stop calling him *sir*, but he's given up.

In any case, the violence directed at Hugo subsides. The parents agree they should step back, take a collective deep breath, and reconvene next weekend to decide what to do next.

Conversation falters. Mark refills everyone's glass. The party fractures, and as the grandfather drifts from group to group, the circles expand just enough to make room for him but without interrupting the conversation which, no matter where the grandfather goes, is about the children: their character, quirks, strengths and weaknesses; how they're adjusting to school, what they need from school, this school or any school, what the school isn't providing, where else they might apply, which school is a better school, more project oriented, more progressive, more likely to give their child what their child needs. The effort required to break into these heated discussions and tight circles reminds the grandfather of some girls he watched jumping rope in the schoolyard near his apartment; what dexterity and courage it took to join the rope-dancers without tripping or breaking rhythm.

The grandfather takes advantage of the brief lulls in these conversations to introduce other subjects, like a host offering hors d'oeuvres, tidbits of current events, morsels of a TV series he's been watching and imagines the parents might have too. But no, they haven't. It's too violent, or it's on the air before the kids' bedtime. Nor have they seen the films he mentions, nor read the new books he thinks they might know. They don't get out all that much, and at night, after putting the kids to bed, they're too tired to read or even watch TV. Their heads hit the pillow, lights out. They glare at him as if he is Satan tempting them into sin—the sin of talking or thinking about anything besides their kids.

They are obsessed with their children, just as the grandfather is obsessed with his grandson. But they have a right to be obsessed. They are young and vital and sending their precious darlings out into the world, children whose existence attests to their sexual viability. Whereas his obsession is pitiful, sweet, and sad: the tenderness between generations, one of which has recently entered this life while the other hovers near the exit.

"Well," says his daughter with panicky cheer. "Let's everybody eat!"

The group migrates toward the table, then stops, unsure of where to sit. Rescued from the stall, the women rush to help their hostess arrange the children on the floor around the coffee table and bring them bowls of spaghetti lightly laced with tomato sauce. Left behind, the men fall into the nearest chairs, and when the women return they distribute themselves around them. The chair beside the grandfather stays empty longer than the rest. He is relieved when the seat is taken by a pretty young woman he noticed before (though he has forgotten her name) because she is dressed like a rag doll, like Pippi Longstocking, whom his daughter used to love. Two jaunty red pigtails stick out of the sides of her head, and freckles have been painted on her nose and cheeks.

"I'm Edith," this saint of etiquette reminds him. She sticks out her hand, and the grandfather shakes it, a light mist of anxiety dampening his palm.

His daughter and son-in-law bring in two large baking dishes. Beneath a layer of cheese baked brown, the bubbling eggplant emits such delicious smells that the guests burst into applause.

Raggedy Ann pitches herself at him, enraptured before he has even spoken, a mannered gesture for which the grandfather is grateful. He is conscious of the tops of her breasts beneath the low neckline of her gingham doll's dress. The grandfather recalls a museum show of Japanese street-kid style. Edith isn't Japanese. She is *quoting* Japanese street-kid style, she would probably say. And he will have to try not to look at Edith's breasts.

The grandfather remembers a scene from the play: the victory celebration, when Mister Monkey jumped into his lawyer's arms. From his seat in the second row, the grandfather got the impression that the monkey was humping the lady lawyer, who wasn't happy about it, at all. Was that a regular part of the play? Did the director instruct them to do that? Was this another grown-up joke provided for the parents?

The grandfather found it so upsetting that there was nothing to do but pretend it wasn't happening. The actress dropped the monkey, and the moment ended. Grandpa, are you interested in this?

"Sally tells me you're a curator," Edith says.

"Retired," the grandfather says.

"I'm a painter," she says.

"Where do you show your work?" the grandfather asks, because he knows he is supposed to.

"Nowhere right now," says Edith. "I'm shopping around for a gallery, actually."

"I was curator of European painting."

"Awesome," Edith says. "I heavily reference the Old Masters in my process. In fact they're kind of my current subject."

"How so?" the grandfather says.

"I get large reproductions and cut them up into tiny squares. Then I piece them back together into images, like puzzles, like pixilated photos, and I glue them on a huge sheet, and then I paint a picture of the sheet. I always get something different from whatever I'd planned. So it's like a discovery—and a disappointment." She laughs and sits back and crosses her arms over her chest. Good-bye, Edith's breasts.

"Like life," says the grandfather.

"Like art mostly, I guess," says Edith. "Of course since Miles was born, I've hardly been able to work. Mostly I'm too exhausted. And that's okay with me. He won't be little forever."

"Is Max your only child?"

"Miles. His name is Miles. My husband and I are fighting about that. I mean, about having another kid. I think kids need siblings, don't you?"

The grandfather doesn't know what to say. Only children run in his family.

"What painters do you like?" he asks, to revive the stalled conversation. Otherwise Edith will turn to the young man beside her, and the grandfather will be left staring at the back of the head of the woman on his other side, who is talking to the man on her left.

Edith says, "Right now, I'm kind of into the Spanish painters. Velásquez. What a genius! Obviously, right? Murillo. Zurbarán. Oh, and Goya. At the moment he's my guy."

Obviously. Right. Any number of suitable banalities occur to the grandfather, but a swell of memory washes them away.

Instead he hears himself say, "Goya was my late wife's favorite painter. She was a very sophisticated woman with very subtle elegant taste, but her favorite painting remained the one she'd loved as a child, the Goya portrait of the little boy in the red suit with the bird cage." Is there a monkey in that painting? He can't recall.

He goes on, louder, willfully ignoring the fact that Edith no longer seems to know what to do with her bright faux-freckled face as he says, "We slept under that painting for almost fifty years. She died looking up at that painting, and when she died I ripped it down from the wall. To be honest, I never liked it. I took it out of the frame and tore it up into little pieces you could have for your art project, if you wish. They're probably around somewhere. I never throw anything out."

"A hoarder!" Edith's anxious face reminds him of the faces of the schoolchildren sitting on the museum floor in front of the Goya as he rambled on about his dead wife.

Edith says, "Oh, no thanks, that's okay. I like to do the tearing myself, that's part of my process too. I'm sorry about your wife."

There's nothing more to say. Mercifully it's one of those moments when the table talk expands to include the group, so that Edith and the grandfather can listen to the discussion about new restaurants that have opened in the area: the (for now!) affordable taqueria, the fried chicken place they adore but would probably skip if the kids didn't insist, the vegan café with the best green tea but so much attitude there was a drama when a child came in sucking a lollipop and the parents refused to get rid of the "corn syrup kebab," as the manager requested. When the parents finally took the lollipop away, the kid tore the place up. Led by the fathers, the dinner guests pump their elbows and cheer for the tiny hero of resistance. They are happy for the chance to make it clear that, while they may have food issues, they are not as far gone as the manager of the vegan café.

The grandfather says, "I've got a story." He decides to ignore the cautionary looks he's getting from his daughter. He can tell a story if he wants to. Long before any of them were born, he was telling stories at parties. And some were fancy benefit galas at which he was supposed to persuade his wealthy dinner partners to underwrite an upcoming museum show. So why is everyone acting as if the demented old fart can't say anything intelligent to a roomful of people who have forbidden themselves to think or speak about anything beside how to trick their children into eating quinoa?

The grandfather says, "I was in Portland, Oregon, visiting a museum donor we'd heard was interested in funding a show. This is a Portland story. I was having breakfast in a restaurant, farm to table, locally sourced. So the waiter goes up to the chef in the open kitchen, and I hear him say, 'Table Four. Nothing that moves, nothing that breathes, nothing with a face.'

"The cook says, 'Shit! Do dandelions have faces?'

"The waiter thinks for a minute. Then he says, 'I'll go check.' "

The grandfather has told this story before. He waits for the laughs. No one laughs. He recalls his daughter wondering how many of her guests were vegetarian. Probably they all are, and they probably think he's mocking them, which he probably is.

Why did he tell the story? Was it aggression, as they seem to believe? No, it wasn't, not really. At least he doesn't think so. He just wanted to say something funny.

There is a part of the story that the grandfather didn't tell.

By the time he went to Portland to beg for money from the donors, he'd known his career was over. And he knew why the museum had decided to offer him early retirement: the expensive Danish show.

Two years before, he'd gone to Copenhagen for a conference and fallen in love with the light in the nineteenth-century Danish paintings. In New York no one noticed the

Danish light, but they'd noticed (in a bad way) the image he chose for the invitation: an 1898 Borgensen of a lovely woman holding a monkey, its legs wrapped around her waist. He'd thought the painting beautiful, but according to the publicity department, no one else did. During the play, this afternoon, the painting kept appearing before his eyes. Was that why he chose that play? If so, he should go into therapy, the way his daughter kept suggesting after Jane died. He would rather spend the money on theater tickets, even if he picked the play to remind him of the mistake that torpedoed his career.

Anyway, he had reached "an age." He certainly didn't want to be one of those old guys who refuse to go quietly, who make fusses that people gossip about. Maybe he should have wanted to be one of those guys.

After Jane died, he'd volunteered as a docent in the museum where he'd been curator. His daughter said it was good for him to get out of the house, but maybe it would be wiser to choose another museum. He'd said no, he knew that one. He knew every painting in it.

Too well, as it turned out. After a few weeks he was let go. He'd upset the students and teachers when he told a grade-school group how much his wife had loved the Goya portrait of the little boy in the red suit, how he'd bought her a decent reproduction that hung over the bed in which she died. All he was supposed to do, the docent coordinator reminded him, was to ask the kids to point to the cat, the birdcage, the magpie. Not to ramble on about loss and death. Is there a monkey in the painting? It scares the grandfather that he can't remember.

In the hospital, his newborn grandson had been swad-dled in white, like an injured foot. How could a tiny human with two swollen eyelids and a blue sock on his head have so

changed his life? Most nights, the grandfather has only to
think of the child and he feels calm enough to fall asleep. Expecting a child to change everything was always too much
to ask. No wonder the child is cautious about how much of
himself he is willing to give.

The grandfather sees his daughter looking at him from
the opposite end of the table. He can tell that she can't quite
hear him, but her face has stiffened slightly.

Relax, the grandfather thinks. One consolation of age is
desensitization. You worry less about saying the wrong thing.
When you are young, you think you will die from shame,
but with time you learn that embarrassment won't kill you.
That is another reason why the young despise and fear the
elderly. They have no manners, no social sense. They will say
anything!

The parents want him to shut up. Well, they needn't worry.
He couldn't speak if he wanted to. He's paralyzed by a shy-
ness he hasn't felt since eighth grade, but this is worse than
eighth grade because then part of him hoped that his solitude
and humiliation wouldn't last forever. But now he knows that
it will, that at the end of the evening when the parents return
to their bright messy kitchens and their quarrels about whose
turn it is to put the kids to bed, and finally to their own warm
beds, with a warm body beside them, he will go home to
his neat apartment in which Jane's clothes have hung in the
closet for years, despite his daughter's efforts to persuade him
to give them away, despite his son-in-law's offer of help. No
wonder his daughter is wary of a man who shares his bureau
with the scarves and gloves of the dead.

These overburdened, overworked parents cannot know
how lucky they are: they are young and have someone to
help them. Even if they get divorced tomorrow! They are not

alone. The grandfather's grief feels sharp and new: beyond remediation.

The child helps. The thought of the child helps. The grandfather half rises out of his chair for a better view of the children's table. They are playing with their spaghetti, sucking it in and making mustaches of the dripping strands.

His grandson is the leader. The others look to him for direction. Again the grandfather feels that pain in his chest, the ache of loving the child with a hopeless love. When a little girl rubs spaghetti in her hair, his grandson shakes his head, and she stops. He is the king of the children, but he is also one of them, a child with an army of children who will do whatever he says. Perhaps he'll throw the first clump of spaghetti, just to see what will happen. Then the grandfather will have to watch how the parents handle the children's rebellion.

He wishes there were someone he could tell about *Mister Monkey*, about the actress in the torn purple skirt, playing out her own tragedy, separate from, parallel to, but much, *much* sadder than the play about the lawyer defending a monkey. And what does that woman receive in return? Getting humped by a boy in a monkey suit. The boy waiting outside the theater.

If only he could tell Jane. She would have understood how his sympathies went out to the actress. But who is he to feel sorry for *her*? A retired depressed old widower whose only tie to the world is through his grandson's intermittent love. And why would he have needed to tell Jane? His wife would have been in the audience along with him and the child she will never meet.

The grandfather closes his eyes. He hears his kindly son-in-law deflecting attention from inappropriate, fading

Grandpa with news of a cool new bar with a garden. It's just around the corner, not expensive, no attitude, a nice place to get a drink. This distracts the parents long enough for the grandfather to recover.

When he does, merciful Edith, forgiving angel of loving kindness, is waiting for him.

"How long have you been retired?" she asks, not actually listening. He could say "for a thousand years" and she wouldn't react.

He says, "Did you happen to see that Golden Age of Danish Painting show here in New York? Maybe seven years ago."

"I *wish* I had," says Edith.

"That was mine. It was wonderful. I felt as if I'd discovered a new country. I'd been in Copenhagen for a conference. I'd wandered through the museum, and the light that shone from those paintings . . . it was like the light of the first snowfall you see as a child. I remember feeling that peppery, almost painful stillness, like just after the snow stops falling."

Edith says, "Wow. What was the subject matter? The content?"

"Boats in a harbor. A coastal town, landscapes, a bonfire in winter. Women standing at their windows, or writing at their desks. Christ, it wasn't *the content*," he says, instantly sorry. He needs to lighten up. He's as bad as Hugo. Edith is being nice.

"It was the *light*," he says, almost pleading. "The show was beautiful. But almost no one came to see it."

"I hate when that happens," Edith says.

"When *what* happens?" says the grandfather, so loud that Edith jumps. "I even fucked up the invitations. I should have picked a pretty image. Something neutral. Flowers. A harbor.

But like an idiot, I went for the image that I thought would start people talking. And it did start them talking, it started them saying, I'm not taking a Saturday out of my busy life to take the kids to see a nineteenth-century Danish woman doing something unhealthy with a monkey."

"That sounds awesome, actually," says Edith. "Doing *what* with a monkey, exactly?"

"Holding it," the grandfather says. "Holding the monkey."

"And what was the monkey doing to her?"

"Nothing," says the grandfather. "Patting her on the head."

Edith says, "I don't get what the problem was. Who painted it? Anyone I would have heard of?"

The grandfather says, "Tell me all the painters you've heard of, and I'll stop you when you get there."

At first Edith can't figure out what he's said. Then her face reddens beneath the fake freckles. Poor Edith didn't deserve to be punished for being polite to an older person. What has she done to provoke the mean old bastard into making her feel bad about herself? He's sorry, but it's too late.

"Whatever," she says. "Excuse *me*."

The grandfather wants to apologize, but Edith has turned her back on him and is reaching for a lifeline of small talk from down the table.

Again the grandfather rests his head in his hands. Soon this will be over. All he has to do is wait. Maybe they will let him read his grandson to sleep.

These parents are giving their children everything they have. He can't fault them for having nothing left for themselves, or for each other, or for him. Especially him, with whom every interaction is a memento mori. In principle they like the idea of grandparents, of multigenerational families.

How marvelous for the children! They just don't like being reminded that being a grandparent means being *old*.

His grandson doesn't mind. The child knows who is old and who is young. The child is aware of everything happening in the room.

Something brushes against the grandfather's arm. The child has left his friends and has taken a moment to rest his head on his grandpa's shoulder. The moment will pass in a heartbeat, in a few irregular heartbeats. Bump bup. Pause. Bump. Long pause. Bip bip bip. His fluttering heart will toy with him until he's afraid, and only then, he hopes, will subside.

What stops it now is the child's hand in his jacket pocket. Edward takes out the programs from the play, keeps one and puts the other back in his grandfather's pocket. Holding his pamphlet above his head, flying it like a standard, Edward rears up, as if on a horse, and runs off to join his friends.

CHAPTER 4

EDWARD PUSHES THE elevator button, slams it with his palm, not because he wants to run away and leave Dad at his school, but because he wants the elevator to make Dad and Hugo stop fighting.

He tells himself that it hasn't been all that long, only a little while since Hugo asked Dad for the monthly tuition check, and his dad said, Could Hugo please wait a day, he was running late for a presentation, and Hugo said, No, thank—he said *zenk* you, he said no *zenk* you very much—he couldn't wait a day, the check was already a day late, and his dad said, A day late? A *day* late? Then Dad said he was sick and tired of feeling like Hugo's hand was scrabbling around in his pocket.

Edward hates the idea of Hugo's hand in his dad's pocket, the pocket in which Dad sometimes brings him a pack of sugar-free gum if he promises not to tell Mom. Hugo said *he* was sick and tired of parents pretending to care about their children's education, to want to be part of a cooperative school and everything it represents, except that they're too lazy and cheap to do anything to support it, and Dad, yelling now, said, "What school? The Sunflower Bullshit School."

The other kids, sitting on the rug, poked up their heads

like the prairie dogs Edward saw on Animal Planet at his
grandpa's house, where he is allowed to watch TV. Hugo said
something in German, obviously not nice, and Dad called
him a Nazi pig asshole. Hugo told his dad to please not use
language like that in front of the children, who, as his dad
may have noticed, had already started their school day;
Edward was *very* late. As usual.

Hugo's saying his name stripped off Edward's cloak of in-
visibility and left him standing there, not naked, but naked
was how it felt. Even his own dad seemed surprised to see
him. All the kids were watching now, but Edward didn't
care, the others would admire him even more for having a
dad brave enough to call Hugo a bad word.

His dad said, "What language? Nazi? Pig? Asshole?" He
said he was sorry about the Nazi part, but Hugo is an asshole.

THAT WAS WHEN Edward ran to the elevator, where now
he is pushing the button. The elevator door opens and shuts,
opens and shuts, without interceding, without rescuing
Edward, without even making enough noise to save him
from hearing every word.

Hugo says that Dad is the real asshole. His father is full
of shit (*zhit*) just like the other parents who don't give a *zhit*
about their kids as long as they get into Harvard or have fab-
ulous art careers and glorify *them*. Hugo's English is unusually easy to understand, even from across the loft.

Finally Dad and Hugo run out of insults, and they stand
there, red-faced, breathing hard. They seem to have grown
taller. Dad wipes his hands on the side of his pants, which
he does when he's nervous. Only then does Dad look around,
in a panic, as if Nazi pig Hugo could have made Edward
disappear.

"Dad? Over here? By the elevator?" It's lucky that Edward hadn't taken off his jacket or put his backpack and lunch box away in his cubby. So he doesn't have to retrieve his stuff with Hugo and the kids watching. Dad says he can push the elevator button if he wants.

The freight elevator rattles and moans down from a loft pretending to be a school, a school that was never really a school, no matter if Hugo calls it the Sunflower School, no matter how much kids' art Hugo tacks to one wall. On the other walls are Hugo's gigantic color photos of homeless people pushing shopping carts and looking even more un-happy than they do when Edward sees them on the street. When Edward passes the public school, he makes his par-ents stop so he can watch kids his age swinging like monkeys from the jungle gym in the school yard, and he longs for a real school, not a pretend school like this one.

Only now, he desperately loves his pretend school, only now that he sees it receding like something they are speed-ing past on a highway: smaller, larger, gone.

"Am I coming back tomorrow?"

"We'll see about that," says Dad.

In the elevator his father is still taking shallow panting breaths. Another upsetting question is: Will Mom be mad? His dad seems worried too until they get outside and he calls Mom. Edward can tell that Mom isn't mad even before his dad ends the call.

"Mom says whatever. It would have happened sooner or later."

First Edward and his dad are relieved, and then he can watch Dad thinking the same thing he's thinking: What will they do now?

Dad lifts him into the Volvo that Grandpa bought them,

which is double-parked, flashing its lights. Dad buckles him into his car seat and turns on the radio, which happens to be playing Edward's favorite song, a girl singing about someone lying on the cold hard ground.

At the office, Dad says he knows Edward won't mind hanging out with Sophie. Edward is embarrassed just to be in beautiful Sophie's presence. But Sophie, who is French, sweetly pretends not to notice how much Edward loves her. While his father is in the conference room giving his presentation, Sophie sneaks Edward a diet Coke and an energy bar and shows him how to make a chain from paper clips. She tells Edward to enjoy it because soon paper clips will be going the way of the rotary dial phone, cardboard matches, the typewriter, and the dinosaur.

The dinosaur? Edward loves dinosaurs! He knows everything about them! He thinks that dinosaurs are more interesting than people. He has a whole collection of dinosaurs, little plastic ones, at his grandpa's house. He keeps them in a box that used to belong to his Grandma Jane, whom he has learned never to mention in his grandfather's presence.

When he blew out the candles at his last birthday party, his wish was that he could see a real live dinosaur—one of the friendly ones, of course. The herbivorous ones. *Herbivorous* is a word he's recently learned. Sometimes he just says the word—*herbivorous, herbivorous*—because something about it tastes delicious, like food, tastes better than what the word means: leaves and grass.

Edward would like to continue this conversation about dinosaurs. He wants to impress Sophie with his knowledge, he wants to say *herbivorous*, and he thinks their talk could be steered to species extinction and from there to death, a topic he wants to know more about. Sophie might be more forth-coming about this mystery than his parents and grandfather.

When you die, does everything stop? How is that possible? And what happens then? Does a person disappear forever? The world is full of dead people. His Grandma Jane, whom he never met, is dead. Whenever he asks about her, his mother says, "She would have loved you." But that's all she'll say, and then she looks away or leaves the room. The last time Edward asked about his dead grandma, his grandpa's face froze so solid that Edward couldn't help thinking about how his grandfather was going to die too. His grandfather will die first. Then his parents, then him.

But before he can decide how to ask what he wants to know, the phone rings, and by the time Sophie hangs up, Edward can't think how to get back to the subject of dinosaurs, let alone death, so he keeps on stringing paper clips, which is boring. What is he supposed to do with the chain he's made?

If only he were back in the Sunflower School, where it's probably snack time. By now the kids will be drinking the cartons of milk that, according to Edward's mother, Hugo scams from the public-school education budget. As if the parents aren't paying enough for Hugo to *buy* the fucking milk! Will he be allowed to return to school after Dad yelled at Hugo?

That night his parents call the other parents, and by the next day *all* the kids have been taken out of the Sunflower School. There *is* no more Sunflower School, so now Hugo can take down the kids' paintings and put up more photos of homeless people.

Edward's mom tells him that Hugo had to go back to Germany. That's why he closed the school. Why does Mom think she has to lie to him when he can picture Hugo in his loft, waiting by the elevator for kids who won't show up, or sitting at his computer and searching for new kids to replace them?

He's heard his mom ask another mom, What the hell are they supposed to do now that fifteen former Sunflower School students are being flung on the nonexistent mercies of the Brooklyn public school system? What if he never finds another school and never learns to write and do math, or any of the things he needs in order to grow up? He'll be like those kids raised by wolves he saw with Grandpa on the History Channel.

That night, the night after he and his grandfather saw *Mister Monkey* and when the parents came for dinner, Grandpa was the oldest, so he should have taken charge. He should have made the parents calm down and be nice, instead of being so mean about Hugo. Grandpa should have stopped them before they went so far that Dad knew he could call Hugo bad names without getting into trouble.

Edward did hear his grandfather try to change the subject from Hugo eating a candy bar to peanut allergies in general. No one understood what he was saying. They just thought he was a goofy old man, and anyway it was too late. The parents had already said everything nasty they could think of to say about Hugo: the school, the name of the school, Hugo sending kids home with the wrong mittens and eating peanut candy. Edward can't remember Hugo eating the candy. But what if it had killed Alex? What if Alex died? If Alex died, then anyone could. He could.

Edward never liked Hugo, whose English is hard to understand and who gets impatient when the kids don't understand his English. He always seems uncomfortable around kids, which seems weird for someone who runs a school. And he makes everything so serious! Last year a kid began sing-

ing "Five little monkeys jumping on the bed," and the other
kids joined in until Hugo scolded them for laughing about
the fate of innocent animals who may have suffered concus-
sions or brain injuries as punishment for their rowdy unsu-
pervised games.

But this has been Edward's second year, and he's had time
to figure out how to make the other kids like him and do
whatever he says. Now, assuming his parents ever find a new
school for him, he'll have to start from scratch with all new
kids, who are probably already following another kid and
doing whatever *he* says.

Edward's real fear, his secret fear, is that he's brought this
on himself. That all of this is punishment for what he did
when they went to see *Mister Monkey*. When he'd asked his
grandfather if he was interested in the play, he'd meant to
whisper. He hadn't intended his voice to sound so loud. His
grandpa was too nice to make him feel embarrassed, but he
knows it was unforgiveable, and when they saw that mean-
looking kid outside the theater staring at them, he knew that
the boy knew that he was the one, the loud little brat who'd
spoiled the whole play.

His other grandfather, Dad's dad—whom they rarely see
because he's a judge and busier than the grandpa who retired
from the museum—knows someone on the board of education. And after a few days, when his mom and dad take turns
bringing him to work, which is fun at Dad's, hanging out
with Sophie, and not so much fun at Mom's, coloring in a
corner of her office while people come and sit at her desk
and talk about things he can't understand, one evening his
mother puts down the phone and claps her hands and says
that Edward has gotten a seat in the public-school kindergarten. The school with the jungle gym!

All the former Sunflower School students have been trying to get into PS 39, he's heard his mom tell another mom. Why do his parents never seem to notice that he's listening?

That Edward can go into Miss Sonya's kindergarten is a victory for his family. His parents are happy. He tries not to worry about the fact that public school started three weeks ago, which means that the kindergarten kids are already best friends. They might as well have known each other since they were born.

The school is very old and big and smells like sour milk and a refrigerator full of spoiled cheese sandwiches. In other words, a real school. He must have been crazy to want this. The principal, Miss Martinez, who also knows (or maybe has heard of) the friend of Grandpa the Judge, walks him and Dad to his new class.

Friendly Miss Martinez says he doesn't have to worry about finding his way around or getting lost because either his teacher or another kid will help him, and pretty soon he'll know his way around all by himself. He so loves the idea of knowing his way around a new place without grown-up help that he forgets to be nervous until they reach the classroom door.

The kids fall silent when they walk in. If he doesn't look at them, they won't see him, and by the time he opens his eyes, they will have disappeared. He forces himself to look at the teacher, who kneels in front of him so that their faces are on the same level.

"Edward," says Miss Martinez, "this is Miss Sonya. Miss Sonya, this is Edward."

Miss Sonya is almost as pretty as Sophie. She has yellow hair and is wearing a filmy pale blue dress, so much like the flower-petal dresses that fairies wear in cartoons that he half expects to see shivery wings fluttering over her shoulders. He knows those are girl cartoons. He shouldn't watch them, ever, and he certainly shouldn't be thinking about them now. Miss Sonya shakes his hand, solemnly and with just the right amount of pressure, unlike the painful squeeze that Hugo delivered to each child every morning, daring them with his wolf's eyes, his wolf's smile, to flinch.

Miss Sonya looks at him, then looks again, the way grown-ups often do. His grandfather told him that this is because he's such a beautiful child, but his parents overheard, and Mom suggested that Grandpa dial it down about the beauty. They don't need Edward knowing that. They don't want him to use it.

Edward knows that he's beautiful. It's a handicap, not a gift. He is pretty the way a girl is pretty, which is worse than being ugly, which at least gives you the option of scaring kids with your repertoire of ugly expressions.

Trying not to focus on any one kid, he takes in the patch-work of faces blanketing the room. None of them want him looking at them. He was the king of the Sunflower School. But he won't be here. It's way too late for that. He will be the lowliest slave in PS 39.

"Say, 'Welcome, Edward,' class," says Miss Sonya.

"Welcome, Edward," the class chants. Edward hates his name. He wishes his name was Tony, like the fat gangster he saw on TV when his parents thought he was asleep on the couch. Or at least Eduardo, like that guy in the store where his grandpa bought him a soda and chips. No one will be friends with him. That much is clear. The best he can do is not talk too often, not answer any questions, even when he knows the answers. At recess and lunch he will watch the others with a stiff little smile so Miss Sonya will think he's being included and won't pity him, which will just make him feel worse.

Miss Sonya will make the other kids include him, though they won't see why they should. In fact they're grateful to Edward for showing up just when they were figuring out that they were going to have to find one kid to despise and exclude. And now he can be the chosen one.

THAT SAME WEEK Miss Sonya asks Edward to bring in something for show-and-tell. It will only be the fifth show-and-tell this year. They don't have it every day. Their schedule is complicated, as Edward is just learning. The others already know what to do when, which makes him seem stupid. He was the smart one at the Sunflower School, where they did the same things every day. How could he not have appreciated how awesome that was?

The kids who haven't been chosen yet for show-and-tell resent the new kid for being picked first. Especially Terence, who is the boss, the way Edward was the boss of the Sunflower School. Terence is not about to surrender his power to a kid who started three weeks late and who looks like a girl.

At the Sunflower School, they'd sewn coin purses out of leather, braided together with shoelaces. But Edward knows that bringing in a handmade purse and telling the class about how his old school closed down because some Nazi fascist asshole had a fight with his dad is not the way to make the others see him as someone they want to befriend.

Edward is searching through his stuff when he remembers the program from *Mister Monkey*. He and his grandpa got it from the nice lady who showed them to their seats and whom he recognized later in a police uniform dragging Mister Monkey off to jail.

Part of him is afraid of ever mentioning *Mister Monkey* again, on the chance that his outburst in the theater *has* been the cause of everything that has gone wrong since then. And part of him thinks that if he talks about the play, maybe other kids will go see it, and somehow that will make up for his ruining the performance when he went with his grandpa. Maybe that will reverse the curse that made him leave the paradise where he was king and sent him to this smelly school where everyone hates him.

He's overheard enough to know that many kids in Miss Sonya's class go to plays and children's concerts, music lessons and gymnastics. They think that these activities are cool. Well, he's gone to a play. He is not an alien from Planet Sunflower School. Regardless of the weird feelings left over from *Mister Monkey*, he will tell the class about his afternoon at the theater.

SHOW-AND-TELL COMES right before lunch. The children clean up the tables at which they sit in groups of four. The first kids to clear their tables are the first ones allowed to come sit in the story circle. At Edward's table are three scowling boys who hardly speak. Because of their lack of teamwork, they are always last to join the circle, and today the circle is closed by the time Edward arrives; no one's moving to make room. Luckily, Miss Sonya motions for him to step over the circle—unluckily, into the center.

Terence's group is always first: three boys and a beautiful girl named Chloe who is Terence's girlfriend even though they are only in kindergarten. But today Edward doesn't care because he has a magic object, a helper: the pamphlet from *Mister Monkey*. Maybe it wasn't the greatest play, but he is pretty sure that he can tell the story and get the class interested—way more *interested* (the word still makes him cringe) than he and his grandpa were.

Miss Sonya says, "Listen, class. . . . Edward and his grandfather went to see a play. Edward, why don't you tell us about it?"

Edward stands in the middle of the rug and tries to look at the other kids, but they've merged into a blur of shifty eyes and smirking faces. Doesn't Miss Sonya see?

"It was a musical. From a book my grandpa read me. The book was about a brother and sister whose mom is dead. Killed in Africa by hunters who shoot elephants for ivory."

"Sad." Miss Sonya looks worried. She hopes Edward's story doesn't get any more tragic or violent. This is only her second year out of Teach for America. She is being closely monitored by the principal, Guadalupe Martinez, who is kind and supportive but who doesn't want any trouble. There's a budget crisis. Teachers are being fired, and Miss Sonya's only ace in the hole is that she is being paid less than the teachers whom they are letting go.

She asks, "Does everyone know where Africa is? Does everyone know what ivory is?"

Yes, say the children, including the ones who don't.

The children were with him at *dead mother*. They know the story is sad. They like sad stories. They like stories about death. They want to hear less about Africa and ivory and more about the murdered mom.

"The kids hardly remember her," Edward says, and then before the class can recover from the shock of this unimaginable thing, this obvious lie, he says, "They live with their dad and their housekeeper and a pet monkey their mom adopted. They call him Mister Monkey."

"A pet monkey? Awesome," Chloe says.

"It's a very famous book," says Miss Sonya. "Has anyone heard of it? Has anyone's mom or dad read it to them?"

Her voice trails off, and the children shake their heads no. In the Sunflower School at least some of the parents would have read the book to the kids, or the kids would have lied about it and pretended they had.

Encouraged, Edward goes on. "But the dad has a mean girlfriend who's kind of like a witch, and she hates Mister Monkey and wants to get rid of him. So she tells everybody he stole her wallet, but he didn't. And the cops arrest him!"

Miss Sonya wonders how many of the kids' fathers have mean girlfriends. She's certainly had her share of mean boyfriends. But this is not the time to reflect on her disappointing love life. This is lonely beautiful Edward's moment to shine so that the others will see his light.

The child thinks of Hugo with his hand in Dad's pocket. Stealing, like Mister Monkey. Except that the monkey didn't do it. Hugo wasn't stealing, either. He was just asking for what was his.

"Are you all right, Edward? The other children can't wait to hear how your story turns out."

It is not his story, but he feels as if it is. He almost feels as if he's making it up, as if the puzzle pieces of the story are putting themselves together in his mind as he sails into the part about Mister Monkey going to jail and the nanny persuading the lady lawyer with the funny hair to help him. The kids will know about lawyers and courts. Surely they've seen crime shows on TV, even the kids who aren't allowed to watch TV. His grandpa lets him play with his dinosaurs and watch TV at the same time. He sleeps over at his grandpa's whenever his parents want some *private time*. Grandpa says he can stay up all night, but Edward always falls asleep, and his grandpa turns off the TV.

"There's a trial. And the lawyer proves that the monkey is innocent and the girlfriend lied. Because she didn't have any fingernails."

"How did *that* prove that Mister Monkey was innocent?" Miss Sonya sounds worried. What if the children tell their parents they heard a story about an evil girlfriend without any fingernails and a larcenous monkey? This wouldn't be a problem if they'd read the book to their kids.

"I don't know." Edward can feel his audience losing interest, just as he lost interest around this point in the play. The monkey was free. Who cared if the kids' dad and the lady in the purple suit fell in love? And if the monkey jumps into the lady's arms and wriggles against her? That stuff was for girls. What about the dead human mom? And the dead monkey parents? Doesn't anyone think about *them*? What does *dead* mean, exactly? Maybe if he mentions the dead mom and the dead monkey parents again, Miss Sonya will enlighten them about what it means to be dead.

He's not going to tell them how the lady dropped her phone and then kicked it, though it's possible that this would make the kids perk up. The kids are looking around, bouncing up on their knees and sitting down again, picking their noses, flicking boogers at each other.

"That's it. And everybody lived happily ever after," he says.

"That's a beautiful story, Edward. Class, didn't you think that was a beautiful story?"

"Yes, Miss Sonya."

The story has not made them want to be friends with him or like him any better than they did before. And this was the only chance he will ever have. He's afraid he is going to cry. Nothing will ever be worse than this. Wrong! His grandpa will die, his mother and father will die. That will be worse than this.

"Edward, don't look so unhappy," says Miss Sonya. "Please, class, let's give Edward a big thank-you round of applause."

The children clap limply. Miss Sonya says, "Does anyone have any questions for Edward?"

Edward turns to ice, pure ice. No one told him that there would be questions. What will they ask him? Grandpa, are you interested in this? At first he'd been interested, and then he wasn't, just like them. He should have ended the story with the monkey in jail.

"Miss Sonya, can I say something?" Terence asks.

"Of course, Terence." Miss Sonya doesn't hear the threat in Terence's voice. But Edward does, and he waits, as if for an attack. Terence is handsome the way boys are supposed to be handsome. Blond hair, blue eyes, a face beneath which you can already see the hard sharp pitiless bones.

Terence says, "This isn't really a question . . ."

Edward is relieved, then annoyed because he can tell that this is not going to have anything to do with him or *Mister Monkey*. His moment in the spotlight is over before it's begun. In a voice that's louder and more certain than Edward's babyish whisper, Terence says, "My dad told me that human beings used to be monkeys. My dad says that before we were cavemen we were monkeys living in trees."

"My dad said that too," says a girl whose name, Edward thinks, is Jade. Yesterday at lunch, Jade—if that *is* her name—told Edward that her grandma cleans houses and works every Tuesday as a radiology technician. And Edward could tell that Terence was mad at Jade for talking to him.

Edward says, "No! Humans are descended from dinosaurs! The whole planet used to be one big jungle. The
cavemen lived in trees. The dinosaurs were as big as subway
trains, and they could kill and eat people. Dinosaurs ruled
the world. The biggest was the brontosaurus, but the stego-
saurus was the meanest. Some of them were herbivorous and
some of them . . . ate meat."

"Herbivorous!" says Miss Sonya. "What a wonderful word!
Go on, Edward."

Edward tries hard not to smile. Oh, how he adores Miss
Sonya! He forces himself to go on:

"Then something happened. An asteroid, maybe. The
cavemen lived, and the dinosaurs died. My grandpa said the
same thing, about how we used to be monkeys. But that isn't
true. One day a dinosaur mom had a baby that looked a little
like a human baby, and then that baby had a baby that looked
a little bit more like a human baby, and so on, for millions and
millions of years until the dinosaurs turned into humans."

He adds this last for good measure, though he's not quite
sure it's true. He's not sure if any of what he's said is true.
But now that he's said it, he'll swear to it. He'll swear to it
on his life.

"That kid's wrong." Terence has forgotten Edward's name.
"He's lying."

"His name is Edward," prompts Miss Sonya. "And that's
a little harsh. I know you don't mean to be harsh, Terence.
Maybe you should apologize. Edward isn't lying."

Edward's chest aches with gratitude. His teacher is taking
his side.

Chloe says loyally, "Terence is right. About the monkeys.
My dad told me the same thing."

The class looks at Miss Sonya. Everyone knows this is serious, and that she is the judge who must decide the life-or-death question of whether Edward or Terence is right.

Chloe says, "Miss Sonya? What do you think?"

Miss Sonya is silent for so long that the class wonders if she's heard. The clock on the wall gets louder to fill the unbearable hush. Tick tock tick tock tick tock. Even the clock sounds nervous. A siren wails outside. Maybe school will end before Miss Sonya has to decide. Everyone knows that's not possible. It isn't even lunchtime.

Miss Sonya says, "Different people believe different things about how human beings developed. Many people believe that God created the world in seven days, that he made Adam and Eve on the sixth day and then rested. Many people believe that humans started as creatures so small you'd need a microscope to see them. And many people believe that these creatures lived in the water, and then the water dried up, or the water didn't dry up and we crawled out of the water and started breathing air, and our flippers turned into lungs and wings and feet. The lizard turned into the chicken, which is why you can still see the lizard in the eye of the chicken and in the tilt of its beak. Then came the wild animals with fur, and a tail for balance. Some of these creatures are extinct now. Like the dodo. Do you know what a dodo is, class?"

The children laugh. *Dodo* is a funny word. They have no idea what it means.

"Yes," they reply, in unison. They want to see where this is going. Ultimately Miss Sonya will have to decide between Edward and Terence. Edward has a bad feeling about this: she hasn't mentioned dinosaurs, though they too are extinct.

Miss Sonya says, "Little by little these creatures got more

like humans. They stood up on their legs and walked and
had families and started schools and became teachers and
kindergarteners at PS 39."

Terence holds up his hand. Edward wishes that his grandfather had never taken him to the play. It's all Grandpa's
fault. It was a stupid story, a stupid play. No one would love
a pet monkey like a sister or brother. No one would accuse a
monkey of stealing her wallet. No one would try a monkey in
court. Even the actors thought it was stupid. The kid who'd
played the monkey was waiting for them outside the theater. The monkey-boy knew that Edward was the one who'd
talked out loud. Edward was scared, and then he got more
scared when he realized that his grandfather was scared too.

Miss Sonya is saying, "And then there's natural selection.
Some day you children will learn all about Charles Darwin
and his voyage on the *Beagle*. The survival of the fittest,"
she says, and then she shuts her eyes and puts her hands over
her face. Her fingernails are pearly pink, but the polish has
chipped, leaving ragged empty spaces.

Terence says, "But which one is *true*, Miss Sonya? The dinosaurs or the monkeys?"

Another silence. Edward hears a chanting voice deep
inside his head: No more monkeys jumping on the bed!

"I would have to go with . . . the monkeys." Miss Sonya
says *monkeys* so softly that the children can barely hear.

The dinosaurs have betrayed him. Edward never wants to
see another dinosaur again. He doesn't want to think about
dinosaurs. The next time he goes to his grandpa's house, he'll
throw all his dinosaurs in the garbage.

"Thank you, Edward," Miss Sonya says, "for inspiring
such an interesting discussion. Class, let's have another big
round of applause for Edward."

Clap clap. Terence has won. Miss Sonya has betrayed Edward. He will never get over this humiliation. Clap clap. Losing makes his chest hurt. Clap clap. This is how he will feel the first time the kids call him Mister Monkey, the first time he is caught in the rain, the first time he gets lost on the subway, the first time he fails to get something he desperately wants, the first time he loses something he cherishes. This is how he will feel after his first unhappy love affair and all the others that follow.

CHAPTER 5

MISS SONYA HAS A DREAM

MISS SONYA DREAMS that a very large and threatening chimpanzee is sitting cross-legged on her living room floor. He's cradling a cardboard box in his lap and pulling out sheets of paper, tearing them up and flinging the scraps in the air. His giggle is terrifying, his sharp incisors glisten with spit.

In the dream Miss Sonya knows that the pages are her poems, not the poems she wrote in college but the poems she wanted to write and would have written had she not been accepted by Teach for America, and then, thanks to her mother's friend who works for the board of education, been hired to teach kindergarten at PS 39, one of the best public schools in Brooklyn, a job for which Sonya feels grateful, even in her dream.

She awakes in a Xanax haze. Apparently it's morning, a bright sunny morning in . . . she has no idea where she is. All right, she's in her room. In her bed. She no longer wonders if she's becoming dependent on sleeping pills. She *is* dependent on sleeping pills. If only she could remember how a normal person falls asleep. She needs to close her eyes and watch the thoughts cascading like a deck of cards shuffled and thrown on the . . . What she really needs is to tell someone that she has a problem.

Last week she asked the children to describe their bedtime routines, mostly to find out if their parents read to them or not. Her attention had wandered as they'd prattled on about their electric toothbrushes and stuffed toys and pajamas, and then the room went still, and it was her turn. She'd said, "Every night I take a sleeping pill at eleven o'clock."

If just one kid tells just one parent, and if that one parent tells the school, her teaching career will be over. And it won't help to explain that her harmless miniconfession was a cry for help. Now Sonya knows why she had that dream. Yesterday, in class, beautiful Edward, the new boy, told the class about *Mister Monkey the Musical.* Sonya knew the plot. She'd read the book as a child. It was one of those books she'd never liked as much as her teachers did, though she'd never admitted it, because it felt like a personal failure

Sonya knew what Edward was trying to say, even when he mangled the plot. She could have interrupted and helped him. But sometimes interceding is worse for the kids; it would have been a mistake with Edward. She will bribe and cajole and manipulate the others, even confident heartless Terence, until they are nice to Edward and want to be his friend.

Edward told his story about the monkey in the play, and then Terence started in about evolution. Sonya looks out her window at the gnarled, half-dead hickory tree reaching up from her neighbor's yard and she thinks, Cavemen in the trees. Herbivorous. Please dear merciful God don't let some parent complain because evolution is *definitely* not on the kindergarten curriculum.

Her principal, Guadalupe, makes all the teachers feel as if she is on their side. But Guadalupe has her own back to watch, her own career to consider.

Miss Sonya closes her eyes, and at the edge of sleep—only

now, too late!—a banner flutters, no, a poster on the wall of some long-forgotten classroom, an image of a monkey growing taller and standing on two legs and looking progressively more human, trudging along in an increasingly gloomy procession from the carefree joyous primate swinging from trees to the man who walks upright but whose heart is sadder and whose shoulders are more stooped than the chimp's, a human stumbling into a future in which the species will mutate again . . . into what? A humanoid fish with gills capable of surviving on the toxic sludge at the bottom of the ocean that has covered the earth. But before that can occur, the line from monkey to *Homo sapiens* takes a sharp turn and slouches faster, faster, then begins to run—and rushes straight at Sonya, brandishing a club, like the ape in *2001: A Space Odyssey*. Or is she remembering that wrong?

What's done is done. Don't worry about what happened yesterday, or about what might happen today, and besides, as they used to say in Teach for America, every mistake is a teachable moment. A lesson. In this case, a lesson about prompt intervention, about ending the instructive, interesting, though extremely unwise discussion of whether humans descended from the monkeys or the dinosaurs. Instead of redirecting the class, Sonya dived into a pit of self-indulgence and regaled her captive audience with her own evolution fantasy, which might not even be true. Who knows what Darwin actually said? Not Sonya, who could be in real trouble. Last night she frantically Googled Darwin, her racing heartbeat slowing only when she read a speech in which a famous biologist said that everyone has his own way of interpreting Darwin. Well! That was a relief!

Rolling out of the bed and into the shower and getting dressed and checking the weather on her phone makes her feel competent and in control. Competent? Not even remotely. Here's the proof: she's walked the five blocks to the DeKalb Avenue station and gotten on the first of the three trains she has to take to school when she checks her phone and sees that she's gotten a text message from someone named Greg, with the address of the restaurant where's she's supposed to meet him . . . tonight. For a date! A competent person doesn't forget such things. Memory loss is the number one side effect of prescription sleep-aid abuse.

Sonya and Greg "met" (she can't even *think* the word without quotation marks) on Truelove.com. His photo showed a guy (blond and so handsome she couldn't believe he was contacting *her*) in jeans and a black T-shirt sitting on the steps of a brownstone. No naked-to-the-waist bodybuilder weirdness, no baseball cap hiding God knows what.

He listed his profession as "environmental lawyer" and his personal motto as "Saving the planet, one case at a time." Sonya imagined listening, enthralled, as he told her how he'd fought for the life of an adorable tree toad with giant goggly eyes or a brilliantly colored jungle bird threatened by Big Oil or some luxury ecotourist resort.

After a few encouraging e-mails, Miss Sonya and Greg had their first and so far only phone conversation. Given that Greg's profile said that he was born in Georgia (the other Georgia!) and that he has been in this country only five years, Sonya was surprised that he didn't have more of an accent. She was charmed by the few English phrases he got slightly wrong.

"Sonya," he'd said. "Is that a Russian name?"

Did he want it to be? Do Georgians hate Russians? As he waited for her answer, she searched for Georgia on Wikipedia (why hadn't she done this earlier?) but got the state, not the country. Anyhow she might as well tell the truth, which would emerge soon enough.

"No," she said. "I'm not Russian. My mother likes Russian novels."

"Good," said Greg. "Excuse me, but I didn't come all this way to date Russian girls."

"I'm not Russian," repeated Sonya.

It took her a while to understand where he was saying they should meet.

"An-sos. In Bensonhurst. Everyone knows An-sos. Where you can't get a table unless you're not just *any* Mafioso but like a crime-family head or district attorney or supermodel or Marty Scorsese."

"Oh," she said. "Enzo's!"

"An-sos," he said. "I love it. It makes me homesick. It's just like where the gangsters and the bigwig politicians hung out back in Tbilisi. Same food, same upholstery, same everything. Only difference, maybe: more wine and pasta, less vodka and kebabs."

Already this was more interesting than what she mostly hears from guys, who talk about their former girlfriends and their social media presence and their promising careers. And this may be her only chance to have dinner at Enzo's.

Now Sonya checks her reflection in the black subway windows, then glances away and back again, as if in the interim a fairy godmother might have tapped her with a magic wand and given her something nice to wear, taken her out of her mousy teacher disguise, polished her nails, and dressed her in the first-date equivalent of Cinderella's ball gown.

It will be another long subway ride from school to Bensonhurst, and seeing as how it will be five o'clock before she finishes straightening up the classroom and doing her paperwork, and dinner is at six (Greg apologized for it being so early, but it was the best Enzo could do), she won't have time to go home and change. She'll have to buy a cheap lipstick and a tube of mascara on the way. But that won't alter the fact that she's dressed to tell Guadalupe Martinez that she's sorry she lost control of the class and will never let anything like that happen again, instead of like a woman who plans to seduce a thirty-two-year-old, six-foot-two, blond, athletic, foreign-born environmental lawyer.

Sonya knows the route to school so well she can navigate on autopilot, freeing her mind to scurry back and forth between worry about her job and anxiety about the date. Perhaps the monkey in her dream was tearing up her paycheck. Or the note that will be in her mailbox if Guadalupe wants to see her. Maybe it was Greg ripping up the paper on which he's scribbled her number, though he would be more likely to delete it from his phone.

Sonya has so clearly pictured her mailbox with the note in it that when she gets to school and finds the note in her mailbox, it seems less like a real event than a déjà vu. *Please see me at your earliest convenience. G. Martinez.*

The note is all that Sonya can think about as she seats the children at their tables. She'd planned to do a counting game, with kids coming up to the blackboard and filling in missing numbers. They'd called it Hangman when she was their age, but of course she can't call it that now. Instead she gives them crayons and pages to color. She grabs a sheaf of paper from the coloring cubby and has handed half of them out before she notices that they're line drawings of Curious George, probably donated by George's publisher.

The children are coloring monkeys! A monkey riding a tricycle! A monkey eating a banana! Monkeys are the last thing she wants the children thinking about today. Terence flashes her a triumphant smile, as if she is using Curious George to communicate with him, to validate what he told the class yesterday: humans used to be Curious George.

Edward won't look at her. His eyes are almost closed. How beautiful his lashes are, two glossy black crescent brooms.

At recess, Sonya goes to the front office and asks Guadalupe's secretary, Miss Gladys, if Guadalupe has a minute. Gladys's concerned expression tells Sonya that her goose is cooked.

Miss Gladys says, "Let me check."

GUADALUPE RISES FROM her seat, leans across her desk, and presses both of Sonya's hands between her warm palms. She does this with parents, faculty, kids; everyone seems to like it. Her smile is kindly and genuine. There is no secret that she is trying to pry loose, nothing she wants to ferret out, or to extract from Sonya.

She says, "I got three very upset phone calls this morning from three very unhappy kindergarten parents with students in your class. Can we assume that you know what this is about?"

Sonya nods, though why should she assume anything? Maybe the parents were saying what a great teacher she is. Except for those two words: *unhappy* and *upset*.

"Darwin with the kindergarten kids? Seriously, Sonya?"

"I'm sorry. I knew it was a mistake. I guess I lost control. I want them to learn so much that sometimes I lose sight of what's appropriate for them to know."

Guadalupe says, "Look, I'm a practicing Catholic. Darwin is probably right, but I feel more comfortable going with the teachings of the church on this. Anyhow, my faith isn't the point. Sonya, do you watch the news?"

Sonya nods. Can Guadalupe tell that she's lying? Maybe napping during the early evening—when the news is on— and then ordering out for Chinese food may be part of the reason she can't sleep. Is it legal to fire someone for having a sleep disorder? Sleep deprivation is a torture technique! Sonya loves her job, she loves her students, she loves their bright sweet open faces, their dusty milky smell. Her heart is heavy with love for them, especially now that she may be about to lose them. Isn't that always true with love? Or maybe that's just immature love. Maybe you can grow past needing the sharp goad of loss.

Most of Sonya's friends are in love with men who don't love them. Sonya has mostly stopped seeing her friends. Is that a sign of depression? She tells herself it's exhaustion. Let them do what she does every day at school. Let them see how much energy they have left for clubs and art openings and the tedious plays and poetry readings they pretend to find enthralling. Maybe she should videotape those events and watch them to help her fall asleep.

"Well, then, Sonya, if you pay attention to the news perhaps you saw the story about the fifth-grade teacher who got fired when he assigned a demented math problem about the slave trade. If a slave ship with the capacity for five hundred slaves drops off half its human cargo . . . What was that man *thinking*? Couldn't he have said, bags of candy? They fired the principal too. Or maybe you heard about the English teacher who took the whole school administration down with her by mentioning some famous essay about how Huckleberry Finn and Jim were gay lovers? Or the history teacher who lost his job for assigning seniors to write about 9/11 conspiracy theories?"

Sonya vaguely remembers hearing about something like

that, so nodding isn't, strictly speaking, lying. She thinks, I wanted to be a poet!

"Need I go on, Sonya? With even more depressing examples of hardworking teachers and administrators axed for having imparted actual knowledge or expressed a reasonable opinion? Dedicated teachers punished more severely than pervs who diddle kids and get away with it for decades? Need I, Sonya?"

Sonya shakes her head no. Judge, the prosecutor is badgering the witness. Guadalupe waits for Sonya to regain her composure and ask, "What now?"

"Let's wait it out." Guadalupe takes off her glasses and rubs one perfectly groomed eyebrow. "My gut says that this will blow over. The abusive phone conversations with me may be all that the parents want. But you've got to promise me that nothing like this will ever happen again." She crosses her wrists to demonstrate that her hands will be tied.

Sonya nods again.

"Let me give you some advice," Guadalupe says. "You know that reality show, *The Dog Whisperer*? The guy who teaches Hollywood starlets how to train their pups?"

Sonya watched it once: a super-skinny starlet's pug kept vomiting on her Jimmy Choos. The Dog Whisperer accompanied his client to the vet (she'd been too anxious to go alone) to make sure that there was nothing physically wrong with Perrito: the problem was all in his mind, which had been permitted to become undoglike, competitive with costly high-heeled sandals. It seemed to Sonya that Perrito might have learned about vomiting from his owner, but this theory was never mentioned, and in the last sequence, the starlet and her pug were happy. Two by two, her shoes gleamed, backlit, in her closet.

"I love that show," lies Sonya.

"You don't have to love it," says Guadalupe. "Just watch it a few times. Do what the man says, only with children instead of dogs. You are the leader of the pack. Calm assertive authority. Trust me, it works. And be ready to fall on your sword if the parents get crazy."

"I will," Sonya promises. "I'm sorry." Later she will sort out how she feels about apologizing for having told the truth.

"Take care now." Guadalupe gives her the thumbs-up sign, and Sonya does the same. Like two monkeys.

Somehow she gets through the afternoon. The kids will think of words beginning with *A* all day if they get the shriveled apple (another *A* word) she's offering as a prize and if they can keep the others from winning. She sees Edward holding back, knowing more words than his classmates and pretending not to know any. It makes her want to stop the game and take a nap.

Terence wins the apple. His victory word is *armadillo*. She can't tell Terence that he can't have the apple because Edward knows more words but won't say so. How can she even be sure?

Calm assertive authority. She is the leader of the pack. Today the pack gets an extra-long rest period. She can say that the kids were tired from working so hard on the letter *A*. Why can't she just have a bad day like everyone else without thinking that she is failing the children?

Just when she is beginning to fear that the bell will never ring again, the bell rings. One day less of her twenty-sixth year, one precious day of her students' only childhoods, never to be repeated.

It's her responsibility to walk the kids to the door and make sure they get picked up. She'll look for Edward's mom or dad. She wants to tell them something. But what can she say without betraying his trust? Anyway, he is almost always collected by a beautiful French girl named Sophie, whom Edward's parents have put on the after-school pickup list.

Edward has told Sonya that Sophie works for his dad. Stylish girls like Sophie, who seem to care nothing for style, make Sonya feel like a homely undateable kindergarten teacher, which naturally reminds her of her upcoming date with Greg.

Edward runs to Sophie and flings his arms around her long beautiful legs, which today are sheathed in leggings printed to look like tattoos.

"*Dites 'merci, Mademoiselle Sonya,' Eduard,*" Sophie says.

"*Merci, Mademoiselle Sonya,*" says Edward.

How does one say *You're welcome* in French?

"*De nada,*" says Sonya.

Greg probably speaks French. He probably speaks many languages. He should be dating Sophie! Sonya wants to cancel her date but won't, partly because she has never Internet-dated before and doesn't know the etiquette. *Etiquette* is her mother's word.

Anyway, there's something wrong with Sonya's phone. It refuses to send messages, though at least she still gets texts. She doesn't have time to get it fixed or enough money to upgrade to a new one.

She completes the attendance sheet and the lesson plans and files them and punches out. Feeling the need to hurry ratchets up her anxiety level as she rushes to the station. She doesn't like unfamiliar subway lines, though she never minded them when she lived with Warren. But if she were still with Warren, she wouldn't be dating Greg, though that never stopped Warren from dating girls *he* met on the Internet, as Sonya eventually discovered.

The trains arrive rapidly, not too empty, not too crowded, not too hot, not too air-conditioned. She never once thinks she might be lost. She emerges from the station directly across from the restaurant. And she's right on time. Like magic, Sonya thinks, briefly saddened to realize that this is what magic means now: not being late, not getting lost on the subway. Whatever happened to the fairy godmothers, to all those bunnies yanked out of hats?

Enzo's is more or less what Sonya expected, and yet she is unprepared for the energy generated by diners who love the feeling of being special and chosen, of being *among* the special and the chosen. She feels nearly faint with gratitude for the kitschy beauty of Christmas lights in September, for the glittering holiday cheer too warming and familial to be confined to one short season, and for the doughy but vigorous handshake she receives from the charming gnome who turns out to be Enzo.

"Buona serra, Signora!" He ushers Sonya to a table from behind which a tall young man rises to greet her. Even as she is deciding that Greg is twice as good-looking as his TrueLove .com photo, she intuits, from the slight but perceptible dip in the temperature of his smile, that Greg is deciding that she is only half as pretty as hers. Well, of course! She forgot to buy lipstick and mascara. Should she throw herself on his mercy and tell him that she went to work expecting to get fired? Who would go on a second date with a woman who introduced herself with such an embarrassing over-share?

As she puts out her hand, he's already wrapped one arm around her shoulders, and they exchange what must surely be the most awkward handshake-hug in first-date history.

"Please. Sit down," says Greg. Sonya can't bring herself to stare directly into the radiant sun of his perfect face. So perfect it's almost boring, she thinks, as she lowers her gaze and feels a shaming urge to fondle the weave of his expensive black jacket. Everything about him is perfect except for his tie, which is purple with a weird iridescent red sheen. Why would Mr. Perfect choose a tie that color? And why is Sonya analyzing everything Greg is wearing, when she can only hope that he is not lavishing the same critical attention on her please-don't-fire-me skirt and granny-gray cardigan sweater?

She says, "Thanks for texting me the address . . . That was very thoughtful . . . I mean, I could have looked it up, I *did* look it up but . . ."

Greg puts his thumbs against his chest and splays his fingers.

"That's me," he says. "Mr. Thoughtful."

Just then, the Angel Enzo reappears. "A nice red for Romeo and Juliet?" Greg looks at Sonya, who nods, though red wine gives her a headache and so exacerbates her insomnia that no (safe) amount of Xanax will stop her from waking at three in the morning, certain that she is going to lose her job and die alone and be eaten by the cats she will have acquired by then.

Enzo says, "Mario will be back with the wine in a minute."

"Catch you later, An-so," Greg says. Then to Sonya, "An-so's a friend of my dad's."

Sonya's father, whom she adored, has been dead for fifteen years. Bringing up her personal tragedy now would just make her seem sad. A sad case. Even thinking about her dad is a bad idea. She can feel the memories tugging down the corners of her mouth.

"How was your day?" Greg asks, which seems like a good sign. Of what? Politeness? Interest? She'll settle for politeness.

She says, "Good. Good enough. If the kids are good, I'm good."

Greg says, "I get it. It was good. You said *good* four times."

"Did I?" says Sonya. That's four lies, and they've only just met. How tactless of him to notice.

"But who's counting?" he says. "A good day is a good thing." Why would Greg care if a bunch of five-year-olds were well behaved and happy? He's probably looking for a supermodel who wants to party and have lots of edgy sex before he dumps her and finds a wife whom his family will approve of. But it was Greg who got in touch with Sonya. He knew what she does for a living and what she looks like.

Her friends, the friends she's too busy and borderline depressed to see, posted her profile and treated her to a manicure to celebrate her toe-dip into the dark, churning waters of computer dating. That manicure has peeled, so that now her nails look like ten tiny pink row houses, weather-beaten, in desperate need of a paint job. On the dating site, under hobbies, her friends made her write, "Work. I work all the time." No point pretending, they said. She'd be better off looking for a work-obsessed maniac like herself.

At first Sonya refused, then agreed to let them do it. It had begun to occur to her that she could stay single forever. An elderly kindergarten teacher and her feline friends.

A tall waiter with an unusually long, cylindrical head appears with a bottle and glares at them with hate, pure hate. He pours a taste for Greg, who pinches the air, approvingly. The waiter fills their glasses and leaves.

"Waiter Frankenstein," Greg says. "That dude never waited on me when I was here before."

There's a silence. How many girls has he taken here?

"With my dad," Greg adds.

He drinks most of his glass in one gulp, sluiced down by his pistoning Adam's apple. Sonya takes several swallows to keep up, and Greg refills her glass. All right, let's see how this goes. Sonya's not a prude, and Greg doesn't seem like a potential date-rapist. Though girls always say that, after.

"What does your father do?" she asks.

"He's in business." Greg hooks his fingers around *business*. "If I knew what kind of business he was in, he'd have to kill me." He laughs, and so does Sonya. Okay, she can date an oligarch's son. It's not Greg's fault, what his father does. Greg's an environmental lawyer.

"I actually don't know . . . ," says Greg, and some as yet unseen (by Sonya) emotion disturbs the glassy calm of his features. Is he afraid of his powerful father? Sonya will never know him well enough to know. She doesn't want to know him that well, and yet the thought that Greg's deepest emotions will forever remain unknown to her makes her sad.

"How was *your* day?" she says.

"Lousy," he says. "Worse than lousy."

Actually, so was hers! But he's allowed to tell the truth, and she isn't. Such are the rules of dating. "What happened?" she asks, her voice honeyed with womanly sympathy.

"It's starting to look like we're going to lose a big case."

"Bastards," Sonya says. "They can always outgun us. Outspend us. What's it about?"

"The Carolina speckled mouse," says Greg. "Size of your fucking pinky. Endangered species. The usual bullshit. So three thousand North Carolina men and women who would have gotten jobs are going to stay unemployed and unable to feed or clothe their kids because some morons in Washington strong-arm the fucking lumber companies into protecting a fucking rodent who could just move the next county over. Excuse my language."

It takes Sonya a while to understand: they mean different

morons and bastards! She'd assumed that "environmental lawyer" meant Greg fights *for* endangered species, not for the right to wipe them out. Is Greg representing the lumber company? No matter how she turns the page, that is the only way she can read it. She pictures swarms of teensy mice screeching with terror as they dodge the giant tree trunks crashing down around them. Then she thinks of Edward telling the class about Mister Monkey. Wasn't there a lawyer in that? How can she not remember? She read the book as a kid. She remembered the story yesterday. Trying to make sense of it feels like trying to glue together the shards of a dream. A dream about a monkey. Did someone put something in her drink? Wine on an empty stomach is enough to start the room slowly revolving, scattering colored Christmas lights.

She finishes off her wine and lifts her glass. She is going to drink it, and then she is going to think about whether this new information about Greg's job changes her situation. Or not.

Greg stands and twitches his head and one shoulder toward what must be the men's room. He seems embarrassed, like a kid, which Sonya finds endearing.

"Please," she says. "Go ahead." Is she giving him permission?

His departure takes her anxiety with it and turns the roar of voices into the sound of a beneficent machine humming softly behind a thick velvet curtain. But she's not too woozy to know that she can never go out with Greg again. Never. Not that he's going to ask her. The distance between them is too great: the size of a mouse as big as her pinky. Though maybe she's being too negative, too knee-jerk liberal. Is it always right to choose the life of the mouse over the welfare of human beings? There's another side to this story that, at the moment, she can't recall. Greg's an interesting guy. And doesn't love conquer all? You hear about those couples, Katharine Hepburn and Spencer Tracy, different politics, different ideas about this and that, they fall in love, and it works. Maybe Sonya could change Greg. He'll do a complete one-eighty and work on the side of the angels, saving the miniature mice.

Just when Sonya has begun to notice that Greg has been gone for a *very* long time, she sees Enzo guiding a couple to the table beside hers. Enzo's hand rests on the arm of a dark-skinned middle-aged man, Latin or maybe Sicilian, with black 1950s nerd glasses. He is wearing a pale straw fedora and a beautifully tailored caramel-colored jacket, unbuttoned to reveal a crisp white shirt, no tie.

With him is a much younger woman, tall, angular, and proper, wearing high heels and a simple lemon-colored dress, a rich woman's dress. She's the kind of woman who looks as if she's been drawn in a single continuous line, without the artist's hand leaving the page. Beside her Sonya feels like a figure sketched in a moving car.

Enzo squeezes the man's arm and hands them on to the waiter, who knows the man in the fedora and is *way* friendlier to them than he's been to Sonya and Greg. The waiter starts to pull out the woman's chair, but the man rushes to do it himself, tenderly cupping the woman's shoulder in his palm as she slides into her seat. Are they married? The woman is Sonya's age.

Sonya tries not to make eye contact, but it's already too late. The older gentleman says, "Good evening."

"Good evening," says Sonya, turning her head from the

man to the woman without looking at either. She hopes that, when Greg returns, he won't notice the woman's beauty, which will only make him more aware of what Sonya lacks.

By why should Sonya care, especially when she isn't sure that she even likes eco-criminal Greg? Did he lie in their e-mails? Or intentionally mislead her? She'd automatically assumed—foolishly, she sees now—that a good-looking guy who seemed decent enough had the same politics she does. How *does* one weigh the welfare of families against the life of a mouse? It's not as if humans are in danger of becoming extinct. Not unless you take the long view. Dinosaurs, Sonya thinks. Edward has stolen into her thoughts again. No more monkeys jumping on the bed!

The older man looks over at her. He looks *worried* about her, which is nice but not very flattering, and Sonya gives him a wan smile meant to signal that she's fine. Really, she's fine.

The waiter reappears with their wine, and the older gentleman makes a show of giving the waiter an envelope, from which he produces two tickets.

"Enjoy the show, Mario."

"Thanks, Mr. Ortiz," the waiter says.

"Ray," the man corrects him.

Sonya can't stop thinking about her students, school, Guadalupe, evolution. She's so obsessed and distracted by the events of her day that when the couple beside her clink glasses in a toast, Sonya distinctly hears them say, or *thinks* she hears them say, "To Mister Monkey."

That is not even possible! Of course they can't have said that! And she certainly can't ask them. Excuse me, I didn't mean to eavesdrop, but did you just say, "To Mister Monkey"? They'd think she'd gone insane. But if they didn't say that, what *did* they say? Sonya shouldn't drink. She *is* going insane. She takes another sip.

More time passes—how much Sonya couldn't say—until Greg finally returns. The man at the next table says "Good evening," and the young woman smiles at Greg. After all, it's Enzo's. They are the chosen ones, the special ones. Family. They're practically related.

Greg beams at the young woman. Of all the tables in the room, why did Enzo have to sit them here? Sonya doesn't want Greg, yet she's sick with anguish at having lost him to this woman who could have him if she wanted, which she doesn't.

When the waiter appears, the man repeats, quite loudly, "Enjoy the show, Mario." He doesn't seem to remember that he already said this, and that the waiter already thanked him.

"I will," the waiter says. "Thank you."

Greg leans across the table toward Sonya and whispers, "What show?"

"Theater, I think," says Sonya. Why does she think that? Edward was talking about a play. That's how all the trouble started with her students—

Greg asks, "So what do the kids call you?" Excessive drinking often makes her think that people can read her mind.

"Miss Sonya."

"Miss Sonya," says Greg. "That's sweet."

"That's me," says Sonya. "Miss Sweet." She splays her fingers over her chest, like Greg did before, except that, in her case, her breasts get in the way.

Enzo hunkers down beside Greg. He looks at Sonya, but he is talking to Greg as he recites the choices. Clams casino, clams oreganata, baked clams, fried clams . . .

Sonya wants every kind of clam they have! At lunch she'd

lost her appetite because her job might be at risk and because no one would sit with Edward. Now Edward is home, eating dinner with his mom and dad, or with beautiful Sophie. He's not thinking about Miss Sonya.

Enzo smiles as he lists more food than two accomplished eating-competition contestants could possibly consume. His hands open prayerfully to encircle each temptation in a glutton's paradise of fried eggplant, eggplant Parmesan, lasagna, penne alla vodka, veal, swordfish, greens in garlic and oil. Greg will order some of it, or all of it, or any of it. Sonya's glad she doesn't like him. Liking him might make her self-conscious, which would make it harder for her to enjoy her food. What would she be having at home? A bucket of General Tsao's chicken, followed by a goopy dessert of guilt. If music be the food of love, if food be the music of love . . .

Now the wine is affecting her in a good way. She's not ready to leave this shimmering moment when everything seems promising, vaguely intriguing, and marginally funny. Greg chooses the dishes she would have picked. It's as if he possesses some sort of menu ESP. Maybe the guy's more sensitive, caring—more telepathic—than he appears. If he's not going to be a boyfriend, then maybe they could be friends. Is it pretentious and pious to let a teensy rodent stand in the way of a genuine human connection? Does it matter that it's not one little mouse but an entire mouse species? Is it even a species?

Species, she thinks. Darwin. Evolution. Edward. My job.

"What's the matter?" says Greg.

"I don't know." Sonya forces a smile of gratitude for his having registered her anxiety.

"Okay, then." Greg holds up the empty wine bottle until the waiter is forced to see him, and to bring another bottle and uncork it, sneering. A fleeting tic pulls his Frankenstein features sideways. Is it a wink at Sonya, or has he flinched when the cork popped? Wasn't Enzo's where *The Godfather* was filmed? The scene in which Michael Corleone finds the gun hidden for him behind the toilet tank. Sonya can't ask the waiter. He might think she was anti-Italian. They aren't all Mafioisi. Well, of course! Sonya knows that.

Greg and Sonya toast once more. "To clams à la An-so," Greg says.

"To clams alla Enzo," says Sonya. She studied Italian in college and spent a semester in Florence. What's the Italian word for *clam*? Herbivore, she thinks.

Greg says, "Don't worry. I'm not driving. I'm Uber-ing it all the way."

This should reassure Sonya. This is not a guy who pounds down two bottles of wine, then takes his Beemer out for a spin on the BQE. She's watched too many episodes of *Law & Order* in which the sleazy restaurant-owner covers up for his friend's son, the spoiled rich date-rapist, reckless driver, and serial killer. She watches too much television. No wonder she can't sleep.

"What other cases are you working on?"

It's not what Greg wants to talk about. "What can I tell you? Not one, not one fucking case where I like what way it's going."

Is his English deteriorating? He's drunk even more wine than she has.

So maybe he doesn't mean what she thinks he means when he says, "Sick kid. Chemical plant. The company has already gotten an A, a fucking A-plus for cleanup. Impeccable. Trust me. And the so-called science, the kids' lawyers' science, it isn't all that good. I wouldn't take the case otherwise. I like to sleep at night. Right?"

"Right," mumbles Sonya. Are the signs of her insomnia visible on her face?

"It's a kid. The parents. Christ." Greg shrugs. "There is just no evidence that it's the company's fault." He *does* mean what she thinks he means. There is nothing else he could mean.

"People always assume the company's to blame. But it isn't. Not always. And the factory employs five hundred people. Who's supposed to feed *their* kids? Like I said in my profile: saving the planet for human beings, one case at a time."

Sonya thinks, This is sickening. This guy is the godfather's consigliere, only worse. He's the evil lawyer representing the wicked corporation. Sonya will get through this. She'll enjoy the food and spend an evening with a guy who will defend a company responsible for the sufferings of a child. She is not morally compelled to stand and denounce him as an agent of the devil and stalk out of Enzo's, ruining everyone's meal. She will do what she has to. She'll be a whore for the food and find some graceful way to end the date. Greg won't object. He wouldn't mind if it ended right now.

The waiter brings the baked clams in shells the size of a baby's fist, little boats with their delectable cargo of bivalves, bread crumbs, parsley, garlic, and oil: the exact recipe of the long-ago cook who made the baked clams that Sonya's parents bought in boxes from the neighborhood Italian place and served at the parties at which everyone seemed so happy. This is comfort food. Really. Not comfort in the sense of, Oh, you have a sore throat, here's some chicken soup. Or, Oh, you've had a bad day. Order a carton of General Tsao's chicken and eat it all by yourself. It's the kind of comfort that takes you back to your last known place of comfort. Clams oreganata. Oilier, more garlicky and delicious than a madeleine! The baked clams do that for Sonya, and Greg has brought her here.

But it's tricky to chew and swallow with Greg watching. She can tell that he doesn't like the way she eats. Too much appetite, maybe. Too much pleasure. And it hurts her feelings. Even if she doesn't care about his opinion. Even if she cares a little. He's drinking and not eating. There's no olive oil on *his* lips. His napkin stays in his lap.

"You go, girl!" says Greg. "One thing I hate about American girls is how they never eat. Are they going to live on kale salad for the rest of their lives? Nothing but beer and lemons in the refrigerator. Maybe a rotten avocado. Are their children supposed to survive on Smartwater and low-cal gluten-free rice thins?"

Is he saying Sonya's a fat pig? She sinks back against her chair, away from the food.

She says, "Can I ask you something?"

"Anything," says Greg. "My life is open book. Almost open. We just met. Be gentle with me. Okay?"

"Obviously," says Sonya. The word *gentle* is an obstacle, a roadblock that she will have to get past. Because the way he says *gentle* has sex in it; it's not just her imagination. The last thing she wants is to be melted by a two-syllable word. *Herbivorous*, now *that's* a word.

"You're going to think it's a strange question."

"Try me," says Greg.

"Okay. What do you think about evolution? Charles Darwin. Whatever."

Greg raises his eyebrows and opens his eyes as wide as they'll go. It's not especially attractive, but it is a sign of interest. "Why are you asking me this?"

"I don't know. Something happened in school."

"Fucking Darwin! Are you fucking with me? Messing with my head? Was this on my profile? Did you Google the inside of my brain? I am obsessed with Darwin, since I was a boy in Tbilisi. Did I say that on the phone?"

"I don't think so," says Sonya. "I had no idea. I just asked because—this is crazy."

"Crazy," Greg agrees. "Could be a coincidence."

"Could be," Sonia says. Is it coincidental? What *is* a coincidence, anyway? Or is Greg just pretending to be interested in Darwin because he thinks it will make her want to have sex with him? Does he want to have sex with *her*? How does anyone know that another person wants that? It's been so long since she's had sex with anyone she can't remember how it begins. Does *she* want to have sex with *him*? She doesn't know that, either.

Even as Sonya is trying to process this coincidence, if that's what it is, together with all its possible implications, she is again acutely aware of the couple beside her. Their food has arrived. They are having a wonderful time, passing their plates back and forth, tasting each other's dishes, laughing. As wrapped up as they are in each other, they can tell that she and Greg are on a first date, and they can't help being curious about how things will turn out.

"So why *do* you ask?" Greg looks at Sonya as if he can't decide whether she has witchy powers or not, and if it's sexy or alarming. "About Darwin."

"I told you. Something happened in school. Some of my students got into an argument about evolution."

"You got kindergarteners fighting about Darwin? That's quite a class, Miss Sonya. Well, you've come to the right person. I just read two new books about it."

Even if it's true, even if Greg is obsessed with Darwin,

she's sorry she mentioned it, because now she is going to have to listen to a right-wing rant that will justify the extinction of helpless mice and defend the rights of a company to kill a child unlucky enough to live where they dump their toxic crap. Natural selection. Survival of the fittest. A new mutation will give birth to a new race that will thrive on PVCs. Everyone has his own way of interpreting Darwin.

Greg says, "The voyage of the *Beagle*. You know this story, right?"

"Don't insult me," says Sonya.

"Sorry," says Greg. "The ship's captain, FitzRoy, he's twenty-three, brave and crazy, later he kills himself. Bipolar, sudden rages, but a serious Christian. So while Darwin is stuffing and sending thousands of dead animals and birds and insects and plants to England, he and FitzRoy are sharing a cabin and having long philosophical conversations. More wine?"

"Please," says Sonya.

"FitzRoy hires Darwin, he sort of likes him, though in his opinion the guy thinks too much and is all the time seasick. They share a cabin, eat together for five years, Darwin is starting to think that the history of the natural world might not be so exactly like the Bible says. So right after Darwin finds dinosaur skeletons, the big humongous fuckers, he asks FitzRoy, all innocence, maybe not *all* innocence, he asks the dude how a creature so big could have fit on Noah's ark. Fitz-Roy says all the creatures didn't make it onto the ark, some of them drowned in the flood, and Darwin says the dinosaurs didn't drown. Two highly educated men, a scientist and a cartographer, and they're arguing about whether a brontosaurus couple can fit on Noah's ark! And you want to tell me nothing has changed? Some things have changed. Believe me."

Sonya says, "I believe you." How does Greg know all that? She's already forgotten what she just told him she believed. "So why *did* the dinosaurs disappear?"

Into the tar pits, she thinks. But maybe she's only thinking that because molten lava seems to have pooled in her chest, where it's burbling, sticky and noxious.

Greg says, "I've been trying to figure that one out since I was your students' age."

Your students! Her students! Greg not only remembers, he knows and cares what Sonya does. Part of her is delighted, while another part—the sensible part, or maybe the paranoid part—wishes he hadn't mentioned the children. She sees her students lined up: Edward, Terence, Chloe, Jade, their beautiful eyes welling with tears. Tears for her. Miss Sonya isn't coming back. Miss Sonya has been fired. She shouldn't have said that humans are descended from Mister Monkey. This is your new teacher, Miss Sonya's Replacement. Say hello to Miss Sonya's Replacement, class.

The waiter removes her bowl of empty clam shells and slams down a plate of pasta with cheese and pepper, butter and oil. Is it wrong to feel happy because she is being served good food at the invitation of someone on the wrong side of every argument?

Her stomach heaves with nausea. Or something. How much Xanax is still thumping sluggishly through her bloodstream? She puts her hand over her glass. Too late. *That* train has left the station.

"And what about the monkeys?" she says. "I mean the monkey component."

"The monkey component?" says Greg.

The heat inside her thickens. It's nausea, all right. How embarrassing. She takes a bite of pasta, an *extremely* bad idea.

The sauce is thick and white, grainy and cloyingly sweet. She needs some air, maybe water, some room in which to breathe.

She grabs her purse and excuses herself, nearly tripping over the black leather backpack which the young woman beside them has left under her table, practically in the aisle. Bitch! Someone could get killed!

"Sorry!" The woman in the yellow dress kicks her backpack under her chair, with an extra kick for being naughty. "It goes on walks when it wants to."

"Bad boy," says the man in the fedora.

From beneath the fuzzy blanket of sickness, Sonya forces a smile. If she opens her mouth she'll vomit. She keeps her gaze level and, looking neither right nor left, glides across the room with both arms extended, as if the floor were slicked with ice. Her path is blocked by two men, one playing the accordion and the other singing "Come Back to Sorrento." It's a horrible dream, worse than her nightmare about the monkey on her floor. At least the monkey wasn't singing Neapolitan ballads.

She needs to navigate past the musicians, but she's too tired, too sick. She pushes past them, grabbing the accordionist's arm for balance, so he hits a wrong note and hisses, "You stupid piece of shit!"

Bracing herself against the corridor walls, Sonya makes her way to the dimly lit bathroom with its white subway tiles and vintage black and white octagons. *Was* this where Al Pacino got the gun hidden behind the toilet tank? The fact that she remembers *The Godfather* seems like a good sign, suggesting that she is not going to pass out.

The nausea subsides a bit, but she still feels dizzy. What she really wants, what would actually help, is to go back to the dining room, grab some bread from the basket on her

table, and bring it back here to eat in the cool quiet bathroom. She splashes her face with cold water.

It's pure luck that the bathroom is empty. By the time
someone walks in, Sonya will be safe, hidden inside a stall.
She touches more surfaces than she would if she weren't
drunk.

Sonya opens the door to the farthest stall from the door,
enters, locks it, and sits down, fully dressed, on the toilet.
She's beyond her usual fear of being locked in a public re-
stroom.

She rests her wet face in her wet hands. Trying to dry
them with toilet paper would only make things worse. It's
been a terrible day! She should have patience with herself.
Hours on the subway, school, the meeting with Guadalupe,
and now this first date from hell with a wealthy psycho who
by some grotesque coincidence is obsessed with Darwin—
the genius who may get her fired.

She just needs to recover a little before Greg starts to
wonder where she is. Before he sends someone to check on
her, or pays and leaves, neither being desirable options.

She has no idea how long she has been sitting on the toilet
when she hears: buzz buzz moan. What *is* that? Her phone.
Someone's sending her a text. Probably Greg is checking on
her. She finds her purse, which has fallen on the floor, even
though she has read about fecal culture samples taken in
public bathrooms. The clarity and disgust with which she
remembers this gives her hope that she can recover enough to
go back and finish her first and last dinner with Greg.

She remembers everything now. Enzo's. Greg. Their table.
The happy couple beside them. Clams. White pasta. Red
wine. Texting is what a decent human being does when he
realizes that his date has been gone for an alarmingly long

time. Probably she is perfectly fine and will thank him for caring. On the slim chance that she isn't all right, he can gallantly intercede.

The message *is* from Greg. The letters spell out *Nathan, dude.*

Nathan? Only slowly does Sonya realize that the message is meant for someone named Nathan and not for her, that Greg is drunkenly texting the wrong person. And he's hit SEND. He gets credit for being able to write. She can hardly read.

She has a dark premonition about what might happen next. She wants to stop the letters before they appear on the screen. She wants not to look. She wants to put away the phone without seeing what Greg has written.

Another message box appears below the first.

Dude, on the scale of one to ten, she's a 4.

Sonya is so instantly sober that she can do the math and think. There is a slight chance, an infinitesimally slight chance, that Greg doesn't mean her. There is a bigger chance, a much bigger chance, that he does. There is a slight chance he wasn't texting his friend and sent her the message by mistake. There is a bigger chance that he was.

In a few moments she will have to return to her table and say something, or not say something, about the fact that Greg texted his friend to say that she's a four. Commodified her precious self, her only self, rated her body and soul. But if she's being honest . . . is it the fact of the rating or the number that upsets her? Would she be so insulted if he'd said she was a ten?

In a few minutes she'll return to the dining room, and soon after that she'll go home. At home she'll take a Xanax, and slide into sleep. She'll have nightmares, awaken, and, she hopes, fall back asleep. In the morning she'll teach her class, if she still has a class to teach.

But for now she sits in the stall and watches her thoughts swing from vine to vine, backward through the day, all the way to last night's dream. Again she sees the monkey sitting on her floor, tearing up paper and giggling. But now she recognizes Mister Monkey, who isn't laughing but praying for mercy with a secret rite involving paper snowflakes gusting up to the deaf ears of the monkey god in his distant monkey heaven.

RAY ASKS THE driver where he's from, and when the driver says Chad, Ray knows that it's in Africa, but not *where* in Africa, so the conversation lags until the driver asks Ray if he wants to let the evening in. It takes Ray a while to understand what he means. It's a goddamn poem. By all means let in the evening, though technically it's late afternoon, broiling for late September.

The driver pushes a button, the windows roll down. Has someone told him that *evening* is English for the carbon monoxide, grit, and whatever airborne toxins blast into the car as they stop at the red light at Park and 125th? English for the bone-shaking rattle from the train trestle, the smell of stewing garbage, the half-delicious, half-crematorial smoke from the halal food truck, and a plume of rage from the mother pushing a stroller halfway into the intersection: her semaphoric *fuck you* to the traffic? What blows in through the open window is like a concerto in which each musician is playing whatever note he wants, all of them playing at once. The Sun Ra Arkestra. Whatever happened to them? There is no one Ray can ask, except maybe his second wife. Kathy. He could call her in Chicago, but he's left his phone at home.

So what? He hates the fucking phone. He just hopes he won't need it, hopes there's no problem finding Lauren, whom he's picking up on the corner of 55th and Sixth. There's never been trouble before. Sweet Lauren is always where she says she will be, not a minute before or after she says she'll be there. People made and kept dates for centuries before cell phones existed. An old man's thought, Ray knows.

Ray concentrates on loving the city outside. It's his city, and he is riding in a car-service luxury sedan, being driven to pick up his beautiful girlfriend Lauren at her office in midtown and from there out to Brooklyn to have dinner at Enzo's. The future looks bright. At least the immediate future. Another old man's distinction.

"Thank you," he tells the driver. And thank you, Mister Monkey. For the millionth, the hundred-millionth time, he thanks an imaginary chimpanzee. Sure, Ray wrote the book. But it always felt as if that little primate son of a bitch wanted to be born, as if thieving tough Mister Monkey muscled his way into the world.

"Highway or street?" says the driver. "Both ways, heavy traffic."

"You're in charge," Ray says. The Klonopin and the half Percocet are starting to work. As usual Ray feels it first in his jaw, which he has to clamp shut because he so wants to open his mouth and say, "I'm so fucking *happy.*"

"Street," the driver says. "I'll take Park."

"Absolutely," says Ray. "You're my man."

On Park and 115th they pass the projects: brick walls the color of watery piss, the lawns more garbage strewn than they were when Ray grew up there. The whole city is luxury glass-and-steel doorman condos; this is the only place that's deteriorated. When Ray was a kid, the guy who lived downstairs

was murdered by the Cape Man, and when they staged the
Broadway musical, the director, the producer, Paul fucking
Simon himself, they took Ray out to lunch, picked his brain
about Cape Man and sent him front-row seats. The music
was okay. To be honest, it pissed Ray off, how much better
Cape Man was than *Mister Monkey the Musical*, which he
has always despised.

Whenever *Mister Monkey* is produced, which, given how
bad it is, still happens surprisingly often, the contract speci-
fies that Ray gets two tickets. He gives the tickets to Mario,
his favorite waiter at Enzo's, where Ray spends the royalty
checks for the play.

Blowing the (minuscule) theatrical royalties on dinner at
Enzo's is a family tradition that all of Ray's wives and girlfriends have liked. Not the checks from his publisher and
licensing firms, the Mister Monkey puppets, the speaking
engagements and wise investments from the years when
Mister Monkey was still being optioned for the movies, and
the option money was still good. Sometimes he senses that
a nosy stranger is wondering how Ray manages to live so
large on the back of a twenty-five-year-old monkey. The
answer is: investments. But it's none of anyone's business.
Ray has never minded buying and selling houses, moving
from one apartment to a fancier apartment, and his luck has
been good. So far.

"Knock on wood," Ray says aloud to himself, in the absence of wood to knock on. His money is money from God
working through the mysterious agency of a children's book
that has stayed in print, that has been translated into dozens
of languages, and which is still being read in classrooms all
over the world. Those checks pay the mortgage and the IRS,
the grocery and cable bills.

The money that buys dinner at Enzo's is distilled from the trickle of proceeds from *Mister Monkey the Musical*. As Ray tells his girlfriends and wives, the checks are reparations, payback for all the things he hates about the play.

For example, Carmen, the slutty, dopey, heart-of-gold Latina maid. In Ray's book she's brilliant, like Ray's sister Carmen, who cleaned houses to pay for college and is now a sociology professor at Fordham. When they were kids she always took Ray's side, the way Carmen takes Mister Monkey's. Another crime against his book is that bullshit song and dance in which Portia and Mr. Jimson fall in love on their cell phones. That's not in his novel, either.

Sometimes the royalties pay for an appetizer, sometimes for an Amarone from the top of the list plus the veal chop for two and the grappa. It doesn't matter. Ray makes up the difference, and every so often, for old times' sake, Enzo tells the waiter (always Mario) that Ray's dinner is on the house.

"Look at that," the driver says.

Two cops have three kids spread-eagled against a massive concrete column beneath a trestle. Jagged spikes of oily rust drip down the concrete.

"The cops up here do what they want," says the driver.

"They always do," says Ray.

"Same everywhere," says the driver. The light changes, and he hits the gas, flinging Ray back against the seat. The neighborhood still sucks, and Ray is lying every time he tells kids that they can get out of it, they can better themselves, like he did. Half lying. They can escape if they get a one-in-a-million lucky break and meet a succession of lovely, helpful women who are decent and nice even after you dump them. Ray feels his mood track toward the dark until the delicious meal before him dances through his mind like a cartoon

character, joining its cartoon hands with those two kindly
fairies, Painkiller and Muscle Relaxant.

Ray has been coming to Enzo's ever since *Mister Monkey*
became a bestseller and Ray's then-agent, Con (one of those
joke-descriptive names), took him there to celebrate. Ray was
still a kid then, a deer-in-the-headlights boy afraid even to
ask how Con knew Enzo.

It just so happened that Enzo's son Ricky was a big *Mister
Monkey* fan. The kid wasn't much of a reader, but he'd read
Mister Monkey four times. Enzo had shaken Ray's hand with
the dignified macho of a man thanking another man for doing
his son a favor. The second time Ray went there, this time with
his editor-girlfriend Emer, Ray brought a signed copy. *To My
Man Ricky, Keep reading!* That holy relic had briefly made
Ricky the star of his class at St. Ignatius Academy.

Enzo has a famously good memory. All these years later,
Ray can still get a table. So that's become the tradition. The
day the check comes in the mail, Ray drops everything and
calls the wife or girlfriend. Now it's text. He texted Lauren.
Enzo's? Pick u up at 6? Boom.

Even this far uptown, the traffic is so heavy that they sit
alongside the projects, waiting for two lights to change. The
projects were ahead of their time, fully prepared for the crack
cocaine years, by which point Ray was out of there, trading
up through Manhattan and Brooklyn before landing back in
Harlem, in a high-floor loft with a downtown view of Cen-
tral Park, a doorman condo that he was savvy enough to buy
years before Harlem got crazy.

Sometimes he tells the drivers, I grew up here! And the
drivers say, No kidding. They could give two shits. Less than
two shits. Ray doesn't care what they think. Right now he
doesn't feel like talking.

He's had an interesting day. This morning he went to a public school up in the Bronx to read aloud from *Mister Monkey*. So what if they're still using prehistoric fossil Raymond Ortiz as living proof that a kid could come from the streets and get famous? He is still a poster child: the upwardly mobile Puerto Rican. He didn't make it all that high, which may be part of the reason he's invited to these schools. J. Lo isn't stuffing her insured-by-Lloyd's-of-London ass into those tiny chairs, reading to first-graders. Ray has succeeded just enough to write a book that the teachers read to the kids, year after year, and feel they have to assure Ray: their students still really like it!

Ray always enjoys these visits. He likes seeing the kids' faces, each child so unique, all of them already so *themselves*: the adults they'll turn into, the old people they'll become, boiled down into a cute little concentrate, like a bouillon cube, or like those tiny Japanese sponges his daughters loved; dropped in the water, they swelled into flowers and pink brontosauruses. He'd loved those magic sponges, just like he loves the heroic (and hot!) teachers who this morning herded three depressingly overcrowded classes into the cramped library and sat the kids on the floor. They made them sit on their crossed legs (crisscross, applesauce!) and then the teachers prayed, silently but so intensely that Ray could practically hear them: please make the kids be good.

The kids *were* good, good as gold, but if Ray can't remember one moment that made today any different from any other *Mister Monkey* reading in any other classroom, it's not because the kids were good or bad, but because *Mister Monkey* is always the same, as are the questions. Ray is always playing the world's oldest ex-street-kid ex-gang-member turned successful children's writer.

Did you like reading when you were a kid?

He tells them how his high school English teacher gave him *Down These Mean Streets* by Piri Thomas. That was when he first understood that books were written by people and didn't just pop up like mushrooms out of the library shelves. He said what he always says: "You kids need to wait till you get older to read *Down These Mean Streets*. That book's got some grown-up parts. I know your teachers will be mad at me because my saying that is gonna make you kids want to read it *right now*."

The children laughed uncertainly. The prettiest of the teachers gently reminded him, "Mr. Ortiz, this is a reading *readiness* group."

Before Lauren, Ray would have checked out the teacher to see if she was someone he wanted to fuck. But not now, which is a good thing, because Ray is getting a little long in the tooth for casual hookups and first dates. Sometimes he wonders what men his age did before Viagra.

"Meanwhile," the pretty teacher said, "I'm sure our students are eager to know what made you write *Mister Monkey*."

Ray said what he always says. "I went to the zoo and saw a monkey. The Bronx Zoo, actually. It's not all that far from here. It cheered me up and made me want to go home and write a book. Have you kids been to the zoo? Your teachers should take you on a school trip."

The children had loved him even more. He was trying to set them free!

Ray sees no need to mention the fact that every so often he goes to the zoo and stands in front of the monkey cage and cries. He is still surprised when (not every time, but sometimes, with a mysterious sense of relief) he finds himself in tears. He doesn't want to know what he's feeling. It seems wiser not to know. It feels good to cry, alone (in a crowd) and in a relatively controlled situation.

Ray does remember one incident unlike any he's experienced in a classroom situation before. A few months ago, a little boy raised his hand and asked, "How much money do you make from your writing?"

Ray was so taken aback that he'd mumbled something about paying for food and the phone bill, but the kid wasn't having any of it.

"No," he said, "I mean how much?" Other kids took it up: How much? How much? How much? Until Ray had to tell them that it was none of their business. What they'd wanted to hear was: a lot. Otherwise why were they wasting their time, listening to him?

The driver swerves right and brakes.

"Come on," says Ray. "What the hell, man?"

"Sorry," says the driver. "These limo guys go slow as they want."

"They're getting paid by the hour," says Ray. "What do they care?"

"Exactly," says the driver.

No one ever has any idea what a tiny fraction of the true story Ray tells. The monkey he'd seen at the zoo, all those years ago, had made him feel the opposite of cheered up. He'd gone there with Astrid, his teacher in the writing class for Vietnam vets at Bronx Community College. Every day for months he'd been typing the words *My Bronx*, and then nothing else, certainly nothing he wanted to show Astrid or the class. So he was feeling a little . . . *discouraged*, when Astrid asked if he wanted to go to the zoo.

It wasn't a date, just a friendly teacher-student outing— until he had a meltdown outside the monkey house. Sobbing like a little bitch. It's embarrassing to remember, even now. Back in those days, he cried a lot. He'd start talking about the war, about Vietnam, and the next thing he knew: waterworks. Maybe he had a teensy-tiny touch of PTSD. You didn't hear much about that then. It wasn't a real diagnosis, or anyway, not in his corner of the Bronx. No one ever knew what to do when he started to blubber. Some girls seemed to like it, some didn't, not that Ray cared whether they liked it or not. Mostly people would ignore it, looking slightly past him, waiting patiently the way they did around someone with a debilitating stutter. He doesn't cry much anymore, except at the zoo, but then again, he hardly ever talks about the war.

Astrid brought him back to her apartment and tucked him into her soft, sweet-smelling bed; she'd slept on the couch and nursed him back to (relative) mental health on a diet of daytime TV, Valium, and miso soup. She'd joined him in bed a short time before he was well enough to leave it.

They both agreed that, given the change in their situation, he should drop her writing class. By then he'd moved out of his mom's apartment in Washington Heights and was living with Astrid in the East Village. What was it about the monkey house that had made him fall apart? He'd told Astrid he didn't know. Technically, a lie. He still has some memories of the war he'd just as soon keep to himself. In fact he's never told anyone, nor does he intend to.

It was Astrid who suggested that he write about a monkey. Get to the root of the problem! She'd given him a personal monkey reading list. He'd wondered why so many of these books were horror stories—"The Murders in the Rue Morgue," "The Monkey's Paw"—or books for children: Pippi Longstocking, Curious George. Did no one think that adults could be interested in monkeys unless there was an element of terror? His favorite was *A High Wind in Jamaica*, about a group of children kidnapped by pirates who have a monkey whose tail has fallen off from cancer and who steals food from a pig. Ray had loved the novel, but he couldn't see how reading about children on a pirate ship would help him write his own book.

He wrote *Mister Monkey* in three weeks, on Astrid's typewriter, while she was teaching. He'd meant it as a book for grown-ups, and he and Astrid broke up not long after she read it and liked it and then asked if he thought it might not work better as a story for kids.

"Excuse me?" the driver says.

Ray seems to have said "Hostile bitch!" out loud. Thirty years later, certain feelings stay painful and fresh, though Astrid was right, and Ray owes his life to her. Astrid was such a saint that even after Ray left her, she sent Ray's manuscript to a friend who worked for an editor, an Irish redhead named Emer who persuaded him to change his book in every way Astrid suggested and also in some ways that Astrid wouldn't have dared to suggest.

Mister Monkey's adoptive family morphed from poor and Puerto Rican to rich and white. Did Ray want his book to sell—or was he okay with a niche market? He wanted his book to sell. Without knowing that it was something to want, he wanted a table at Enzo's. It was Emer who persuaded Ray to describe Mister Monkey as "super-cute"—an expression he would never have used—on the book's first page.

"Sorry," Ray tells the driver. "Talking to myself."

A ribbon of green lights unfurls before them as they cross the border from welfare Park Avenue to billionaire Park Avenue and cruise past the stately apartment blocks.

The midtown traffic jam is like death, Ray thinks. You

want to believe it won't happen to you, but inevitably it does. As the cab idles on 57th, Ray meditates on the strangeness of coming full circle. All these years later he's living with Lauren, who works at the same company that published *Mister Monkey*, where he met Emer, whom he made the mistake of marrying. A quarter century. Jesus Christ.

He'd walked out of Emer's office when she told him to relocate Mister Monkey's birthplace from Vietnam to some unspecified African jungle. East Ooga-Booga. Ray had been to Vietnam. The whole point was Vietnam. Did Emer know that animals—whole monkey families—were victims of so-called collateral damage? He'd stalked out of Emer's office and stood on a midtown street corner—the same corner on which he's about to pick up Lauren, as a matter of fact—and wept like an infant whose mommy has taken his pacifier away.

When he cooled off and came back, half an hour later, Emer said that Ray needed to understand: people want to forget. Human Psychology 101. Didn't *he* know that war was the kiss of death for juvenile fiction? What mattered was the story. The story you invent. Emer quoted Bertolt Brecht: no one can make his own suffering sound convincing. If your stomach hurts and you say so, people will just be disgusted.

Ray went to the library and looked up Bertolt Brecht. That was when he knew that he had fallen in love with Emer. And when he figured out that it was probably a good idea to stop talking about the war.

Emer had been wrong about a lot of things, but not, as it turned out, about *Mister Monkey* and its sales potential. After all the arguments, Ray had rolled over for every one of her editorial suggestions. Mister Monkey's parents were no longer killed by soldiers but by poachers. Mister Monkey wasn't adopted by a military family but by the grieving husband and children of a primate biologist. Ray said that Emer's version was boring, and Emer said that people liked their kids to be bored. Kids preferred to be scared, but the parents were the ones who bought the books.

Not long after they broke up, she quit publishing, and she went into film. Emer is now a studio executive in Hollywood. Every year she sends massive, expensive Christmas cards with photos of herself and her partner, Jill, and the twins. Tinsel and colored lights in the palm trees.

Ray and Lauren have talked about Emer only because it's such a coincidence: his being involved with two women who worked at the same publishing house, decades apart. Though really it isn't so strange. Ray and Lauren met at the publisher's party celebrating *Mister Monkey's* twentieth birthday. A short person inside a monkey suit had draped a medal embossed with Mister Monkey's face over Ray's bowed head.

His current editor, Grace, gave a speech about what an honor it had been to work with Ray Ortiz, though during all the time she's been Ray's editor, they'd only "worked" together once. That was right after 9/11. Grace called to ask if they could take out one sentence from the beginning of *Mister Monkey.* It was: "What if the buildings fell down?"

Sure, Ray told Grace. Cut it. He'd understood. Let the first paragraph read: "Mister Monkey was scared of the tall buildings. He couldn't get used to the noise of the traffic . . ."

What did an orphan monkey's arrival in the Big Apple have to do with 9/11? But like everyone else, Ray had been so sad. Way too sad to argue about a sentence. At this point they could put that sentence back in, and it would be fine with the kids, who are always watching apocalyptic disaster films about tall buildings exploding or crumbling.

Even as Grace was giving her speech, Lauren caught Ray's eye from across the room. Those few seconds had telegraphed a promise: she would come over and find him after the bullshit was over. So Mister Monkey had played Cupid just as he did for Portia and Mr. Jimson.

Lauren is in marketing, in Ray's opinion a more modern and youthful occupation than being an editor or a writer. They'd left the *Mister Monkey* celebration early and gone to a Japanese businessmen's hotel bar that Ray knew about, a quiet place in midtown.

The reissue of *Mister Monkey* featured a vintage author photo of Ray as a handsome, moody street kid in the army fatigues he'd put away forever to take Astrid's writing class. Where did those cheekbones go, and will they really never return? Luckily for him, Lauren has an imagination. She can look at this Ray and see that one, though to be honest, Ray has no idea what she sees when she looks at him.

From halfway down the block, Ray spots Lauren standing on the corner. Perfectly calm, perfectly on time, perfectly poised, perfectly his. Slung over her shoulder is a stylish leather backpack. In her crisp yellow dress, she looks like a rich high school girl rocking two grand's worth of imported Italian calfskin. Lauren comes from money. Her dad, who is not much older than Ray, made a fortune buying cocoa butter from Third World countries and selling it back to them as toxic beauty products with American labels.

On their first real date, Lauren told Ray that her dream was to make amends: reparations for the damage her father has done. And Ray had said that was funny, not humorous funny but coincidental funny, because he'd written *Mister Monkey* to make amends for some things that had happened in Vietnam. He'd come to think of the book—and the money it made—as reparations for the damage that the war had done to *him*.

If Lauren wondered what he'd meant, she'd known better than to ask. She'd waited politely while he went off to the men's room and returned, his eyes red from weeping.

Anyhow they'd had that in common, the idea of reparations, which seemed deeper and heavier than what connects most couples. And now they're going to Enzo's to enjoy some delicious payback for the humiliations of *Mister Monkey the Musical.*

"That's my girlfriend over there," Ray tells the driver. "The young lady in yellow." Is Ray imagining that the driver's shoulders straighten when he sees who is going to be riding out to Brooklyn with them? Lauren slides in, kisses Ray, snuggles against his shoulder.

"Tough day?" says Ray.

Lauren says, "Not bad. And you?"

"The school kids were amazing," Ray says. "I could have stayed there forever."

"You're a generous guy, Ray," says Lauren. Just the sound of her throaty voice gives Ray a semi-hard-on. Not bad for sixty-two, though his erection subsides when he thinks of the very different compliments she could pay a hot young guy. Like the driver. Generous Ray. Big deal.

"What's wrong?" Lauren says.

Ray flexes his palms to include the car, Lauren, the East River, the sky.

"What could be wrong?" he says.

As they cross the Brooklyn Bridge, the daylight bouncing off the skyscraper windows flashes a friendly shout-out. We remember you, Raymond, say all those tiny orange suns. We knew you when you were a boy. He and Lauren have left Manhattan and died and gone to heaven.

Lauren says, "It's so beautiful. This is so much fun."

That's exactly how Ray wants her to feel and just what he wants her to say. That it is beautiful and fun to be out with a guy twice her age who has been married three times and doesn't want to get married again. Or have kids. Ray already has three girls and a boy. His middle daughter is two years older than Lauren. Not one of them earns enough to live on. His youngest daughter is battling depression. Hereditary, from his side, Ray sometimes fears. They all depend on Ray.

Ray's kids get along with Lauren. The kindest of his children, Miranda, works in a bookstore in Fort Greene and texts him whenever someone buys a copy of *Mister Monkey*. She likes telling her customers that she's the writer's daughter. For Father's Day, she gave Ray a volume of Shakespeare's sonnets. Ray only needed to read a few lines to realize that thoughtful Miranda had given him literature's most moving description of what it is like to love a younger person. Though what was his daughter *really* doing? Because in Ray's opinion, and for Miranda's information, the person Shakespeare loved seemed to have treated him much worse than Lauren treats Ray.

Ray would like to know who made the rule that people are only allowed to fall in love with people their own age. It's just a pity that Lauren wants to get married. She is too cool to say so, but Ray heard it in her voice when she asked, oh so casually, "Would you ever think about getting married again? Ever think about having kids?"

"That would depend," lied Ray. What was he supposed to say? Absolutely not? That was over a year ago, and Lauren hasn't brought up the subject since. Ray hopes she has gotten past it, accepted it, made up her mind to let all that go and enjoy the beauty and pleasure of a car, the Brooklyn Bridge, the promise of dinner at Enzo's.

As they turn onto the expressway, Lauren says, "I put in an order for *Mister Monkey* coloring-book pages. We'll give them out free to the schools. Curious George has them. Why not us? It's good for the schools and for the book."

As they pull up to Enzo's, the driver gives Ray his card. They should call him five minutes before they want to leave.

"Shit. I forgot my phone," Ray says.

"I've got mine." Lauren takes the driver's card from Ray, and it seems to Ray that she and the driver exchange a look that lasts a beat too long and that conveys the knowing forbearance of the young in the presence of the elderly dementia patient. Ray's just being paranoid. He should have remembered his phone.

"*Bon appétit*," says the driver.

As always Enzo appears after a very short wait.

He says, "Raymond, how are you? You still writing books?"

"You still serving pasta?" says Ray.

"And the lovely Lauren," says Enzo. "Good evening, *Signorina*."

What a memory, thinks Ray, who over the past months has come this close to calling Lauren *Emer* or *Vicky*, the names of his first and third wives.

Even at six-thirty, the place is mostly full, and Enzo shows them to a table a little too close to the one beside it.

"You should have called earlier," Enzo says. "My apologies, Raymond. I can only do what I can do. It's busy."

"We appreciate that," says Ray.

Ray phoned Enzo this afternoon. They are lucky to get

this. And Enzo and Mario will make them feel like honored guests: the most important people in the restaurant. Enzo leaves, and Mario takes his place. Ray and Mario shake hands.

"*Buona serra*," Mario says.

"*Buenas noches*," says Ray.

As always, Mario starts to pull out Lauren's chair, and as always Ray laughs and beats him to it. He wants an excuse to touch Lauren's shoulder. For decades, this dance has stayed the same, though the ballerinas have changed. Gentleman Ray lets Lauren face the room and takes the seat facing the wall.

At the next table is a young woman, pretty enough, but nowhere near as striking as Lauren. And (Ray can't help noting) she's frumpily dressed. She is alone, but the crumpled napkin across the table suggests that someone was there.

The young woman scans the restaurant, as if she is worried that her date might never return from the men's room. A schoolteacher, Ray thinks. More schoolteacher-like than the three sexy teachers he met in the Bronx this morning.

Ray says, "Good evening," mostly to take her mind off her missing date. Ray hopes he's not young and handsome, sitting where Lauren can see him. Lauren isn't that type of girl. But a woman can't help comparing.

"Mario," Ray says to the waiter. "What can I do for you?" He and Mario laugh again. Not real laughs, more like friendly snorts.

Mario must be pushing fifty by now. Ray has known him for years. He is tall, and his looming presence spares him the throat-clearing and "Hi, my name is" chatter that other waiters rely on to announce themselves. Mario has only to stand there and Ray reaches for the wine list.

Mario says, "Should I choose?"

"I trust you," says Ray.

Mario puts one hand over his heart. Ray hands him an envelope containing two tickets to *Mister Monkey*. For Sunday afternoon, when the restaurant is closed. Mario treats Ray well, and, tickets or no tickets, Ray leaves him a 20 percent tip, even when Enzo comps him. Ray isn't one of those cheapskate celebrities who try to pay their bill with free stuff.

"Enjoy the show, Mario," says Ray.

"Thanks, Mr. Ortiz."

"Ray."

Mario reappears and pours the wine: a wizard casting a spell of silence.

"To *Mister Monkey*," says Ray.

"To *Mister Monkey*," says Lauren.

The young woman at the next table is staring at them, slack-jawed with shock. What could they have done to provoke such amazement? Has she recognized Ray? It happens. Rarely. But it happens. Someone saw him at a bookstore reading, a teacher remembers that he came to her school. Somebody IDs Ray as the author of their favorite children's book.

After two umbrella cocktails at the Japanese businessman's bar, Lauren had asked why he hadn't published anything since *Mister Monkey*.

Ray said what he saves for certain girls. "Have you seen *The Shining*?"

"I love that movie," Lauren said. "It's the scariest movie ever!"

"All work and no play makes Ray a dull boy."

"Are you warning me that you're an ax murderer?" Lauren said.

"I'm warning you that I'm a writer," said Ray.

Lauren took the bait, as they all do, though, like all of the women who have fallen in love with Ray, Lauren is too smart to think that she could give Ray what he needs to start writing again. A woman who imagined she was going to be his muse wouldn't have made it past the first night.

The girl beside them has stopped staring and gone back to scanning the room for her date.

The candlelight flatters Lauren, but so does every light. Crossing the Brooklyn Bridge, she'd said *beautiful*. She'd said *fun*. Ray needs to enjoy the moment and not worry about the future.

Lauren says, "Don't you ever want to go see your play? Aren't you even curious?"

"It's not my play," says Ray. "It makes me sick to think that anyone would associate me with that mindless piece of crap. If I didn't know that Mario will go see anything, in any theater, anywhere—"

"I understand," Lauren says. "But if you ever wanted to go, I'd go with you. It could be fun."

"I just gave Mario the tickets. You saw me." Ray shrugs.

"Maybe next time," says Lauren. "Or I could take my nephew."

Ray loves her assuming there's a next time, but he hates her mentioning the nephew. Lauren is going to want to have a child, and that is when she will leave him.

"Next time for sure," says Ray.

Two months ago Lauren moved into his condo, and they've been happy. In the mornings, Ray makes coffee, Lauren takes the subway to work, and Ray goes to his study, where he spends a few hours staring at the screen on which he types the words *My Bronx*, just as he used to all those years ago, when he got out of the service and the Veterans Administration sent him to college, where he took Astrid's writing class because it seemed like four easy credits requiring no work. He was less qualified than the other students, the ambitious future writers, but he was Puerto Rican, a former Marine, and handsome, and when he appeared in the classroom that first day and caught Astrid's eye, what passed between them was an early draft of the look he'd exchanged at the *Mister Monkey* party with Lauren.

When at last the guy at the next table returns, Ray has to fight the impulse to put his hands over Lauren's eyes. To show he's not worried or competitive, he says good evening to the movie-star handsome young man, and Lauren smiles a little too brightly and says hi. Ray refuses to go there, to do that self-loathing *Othello* shit.

Blessed Mario reappears.

"Enjoy the show," Ray tells Mario, too loud. He's aware that he's already said that, but now apparently he needs to make a point of his generosity. Apparently he needs to sound like a fucking idiot. Generous Ray. Certainly Lauren must notice. Mario's already thanked him.

"I will," Mario says. "Thank you. So what will it be? The usual?"

"Bring it on," says Ray.

Part of the tradition is that Ray lets Mario decide. The trust between them is such that it never crosses Ray's mind that Mario might bring them a menu item that isn't selling, or anything but the freshest and most delicious dishes.

Tonight it's a platter of clams oreganata and a dozen oysters.

Ray loves to watch Lauren going after the last drop of oyster liquor, the last crusty morsel of oily, salty, garlicky bread crumbs. Only a fool would worry about the future when someone is doing that with a clam shell! Was it Astrid or Emer who took him to see *Tom Jones*, with its erotic dinner scene? Has Lauren seen it? Ray can't risk asking. Most likely she wasn't born when the film came out.

Lauren signals with a slight sideways nod: check out the couple beside them. Ray tries to look without being too obvious. The woman seems unhappy; the guy telegraphs annoyance to anyone interested in picking up his signal. Meaning *everyone*, or so he thinks. Who *wouldn't* be fascinated by every nuance of his shifting mood? Meanwhile he and the woman have run out of conversation; it's a first date gone wrong. Ray can tell that Lauren is thinking the same thing, and he feels guilty for being glad that the young couple's misery is making him and Lauren appreciate their own happiness even more.

The couple start talking again, just when Ray and Lauren are devoting their undivided attention to the scallop and razor clam risotto that Mario has delivered.

"Delicious," says Lauren, licking her fingers.

The young man has gotten louder, and now the words *fucking Darwin* pierce the companionable fog of wine and food into which Lauren and Ray have slipped.

"Oh, please no," whispers Lauren.

Once more Ray knows what she's thinking. It thrills him to realize that he and Lauren have been together long enough to free-associate to the same thing. The word *Darwin* reminds them of one of the many reasons why Ray so hates *Mister Monkey the Musical.*

Maybe Ray had expected too much—expected *anything*—when Gavin Leaming, who'd had several Broadway hits, approached him about doing *Mister Monkey* as a musical. How could Ray have predicted that, six months into the process, Gavin would become a strict Creationist who believed that Charles Darwin was the spawn of Satan. Having accepted

Jesus into his heart as his personal savior, Gavin told Ray that he thought of *Mister Monkey* as a Christian redemption story. The mercilessly cheerful songs, the hysterically upbeat lyrics have always reminded Ray of *Godspell* and Christian rock music. Ray had said as much at one rehearsal, but by then Gavin wasn't listening to godless Ray, who saw it twice, maybe three times before he'd had enough. Even the kids in the audience had seemed mystified, or perhaps just stupefied with boredom.

Ray hates the play. Those ludicrous songs and dances. "Monkey Tango." That bullshit cell phone song. Gavin thought cell phones were cute. Ray thinks that if you want to talk about the workings of Satan, you should start with cell phones. It shocks him that people will still pay to see such a pointless piece of shit when they can read a book or stay home and watch the world end on their HD home theaters.

What is the young couple talking about so excitedly? *Fucking Darwin* is all that Ray and Lauren hear, because the music has started up. An accordion and a tenor are serenading the customers. "Come Back to Sorrento" and "Funiculì, Funiculà" are the hazards of dining at Enzo's. Fortunately, Enzo knows who likes the music and who doesn't. Ray has never had to suffer through an embarrassing musical interlude. Except once when he and Emer were having one of their screaming fights. The musicians are Enzo's second-line bouncers; when a table gets too loud, he sends over music, the food of love, on the house.

The young woman beside them vaults out of her seat. As she squeezes past Ray and Lauren, her ass practically in their faces, she trips over Lauren's backpack, tucked under the table. She actually *kicks Lauren's backpack*.

A spike of adrenaline zaps Ray. She can't treat his girlfriend's stuff like that. But Lauren, saint of decency and for-giveness, model of civilized behavior, smiles at the woman and says, "Sorry!" With one foot Lauren slides her backpack farther under her seat. "It goes on walks when it wants to."

Just knowing Lauren, just having the privilege of watching her, makes Ray a better person.

"Bad boy," he says to the backpack, and Lauren's social smile brightens into a genuine one as she turns back to him.

The young woman's date, who has seen this all go down, shrugs and rolls his eyes. Don't blame me. She's not even my girlfriend. Neither Ray—nor, Ray is glad to see, Lauren—acknowledge him. Of course the poor girl got drunk to console herself for being out with a jerk like that!

The jerk takes out his phone to keep him company while she's gone, and as he taps away at his device, Lauren says, "Fuck Curious George, anyhow."

"Excuse me?" says Ray.

"Have you read it lately?" Lauren says. "It's an apology for imperialism. The man with the yellow hat kidnaps Curious George, and it's supposed to be fine. The monkey's taken out of his home, and of course he keeps getting into trouble. He's blamed for whatever goes wrong."

"So is Mister Monkey," says Ray.

"That's different," Lauren says. "Mister Monkey is inno-cent. And when he's unjustly accused, everyone goes to a cer-tain amount of trouble to help him. I love Mister Monkey, I do. I haven't been faking it all this time just because I want your body."

Is it possible to die of happiness? Take me now, Ray prays.

"We should all boycott Curious George," Lauren is saying. "Just like no one reads *Little Black Sambo* anymore. It's racist imperialist propaganda."

A lot of what Lauren says could be taken in two ways. Ray could see it as evidence of her passionate youthful idealism and adore her even more. Or he could conclude that only a very young person would say such a thing, which would then remind him that he is no longer young. He decides to take the first option, the more loving, less depressing view of her hatred for Curious George. This allows him to bask in affection for Lauren and in the anticipation of the delicious main courses—did they want the swordfish or the veal, or the swordfish *and* the veal?—that Mario has promised.

Ray *feels* the young woman return, coming up behind him. Something prickles on his skin: a barometric change. He swivels around and watches her lurch toward the table, both shoulders raised as the implacable goddess of female vengeance and fury emerges from beneath the mask of the kindly grade-school teacher.

She stands behind her date until the young man notices that Lauren's startled gaze is focused on something just over his shoulder, and he turns.

The woman says, "You asshole! You stupid son of a bitch. You think this is a fucking wine tasting? Swish swish, spit, I give the cabernet a four. Or some celebrity game show? I give that talented break-dancing ghetto youth a four. Or some hotel Web site? I give the Nashville Airport Ramada Inn a four. Or Amazon? I give *War and Peace* a four. Though on the travel sites and Amazon that's four out of five, which is better than four out of ten, which is what this asshole gave me."

The words *this asshole* make Ray realize that she has shifted her focus from her date to him and Lauren. They are the witnesses and the jury at his trial. Ray can tell that this isn't what this woman usually does, or says. He and Lauren and the guy are watching a once-in-a-lifetime performance, Ray hopes.

"Sonya, please," says the young man.

Sonya covers her face and sways slightly. The young man shakes his head, as if to dislodge an insect buzzing in his ear. Performing, Ray thinks. For them and for himself.

Sonya lets her hands drop and asks Lauren, "Do you know what this asshole did? While I was in the bathroom he texted his frat-boy friend and told him that I was a four out of ten, except that he's so fucking stupid he texted *me*."

"I didn't," the young man says. "Jesus Christ. I would *never* do that."

Ray wants to say, Hey, a four is not so bad. Not to defend his male brother but to make the woman feel less awful. A person could marry a four, it could be a happy marriage. But why would he lie to this poor girl about the guy she's out with? And what does he know about happy marriages? Her rage and grief seem reasonable. Maybe she wants to get married. Maybe she has begun to suspect that she could have one bad date after another until she gives up and moves back in with her mom and dad.

"Don't say *Jesus*," she says. "You did it, and you know it. You called me a four."

Again she turns to Ray and Lauren. "I'm a teacher. I teach kindergarten."

Ray knew it! He wants to say that just today he was reading his book to a grade-school class, she's probably heard of *Mister Monkey*, she probably read it as a child. Seeing as how she's a teacher, she's probably used it in class. But he says nothing. Women prefer you to listen. And he doesn't want Lauren thinking that he's just another guy trying to make this all about *him*.

The teacher, Sonya, says, "Every day I've got the minds of twenty-five little people in these two hands, and it's my job to help turn them into the smartest, most productive, happiest little human beings they can be. And every day there's a crisis. Right now I could lose my job because one of my students mentioned evolution."

That explains why her date said *fucking Darwin*.

She says, "Doesn't that entitle me to go to the bathroom and take a piss without getting a text that says I'm a four?"

"Totally," says Lauren.

Ray's nodding like a bobble-head doll. He can't seem to make himself stop.

"Absolutely," he says. Where is Enzo? Where the hell is Mario?

The woman turns and heads for the door, where Enzo, gallant knight, puts his arm around her shoulders and gently guides her out into the street where he will call her a cab. The young man watches her go, then takes a show-offy breath, exhales, turns to Ray and Lauren.

"What that bitch doesn't realize," he says, "is that it all means nothing. I could rate her a four, a ten, a fifty billion. And it would still mean nothing."

He is very drunk. Ray feels torn between the desire to protect himself and Lauren from whatever the guy's about to say—and the desire to hear it. For the first time Ray picks up the faint traces of an accent, but instead of disordering the guy's syntax, the alcohol's making him more fluent.

He says, "It's all going to end. We've passed the point of no return. The glaciers are melting, the polar ice caps are shrinking, the sea is rising, first the basements go under, then the lobbies, then the people on the sixtieth floor watch their downstairs neighbors float away. The future is fucking dark. Dark. So whether the bitch is a four, or a ten, or a twelve, whether I work to save the mouse or to exterminate every last fucking rodent . . . Global warming? Hilarious. Global dying. I don't mean to ruin your evening, but there's nothing we can do to stop what is *going* to happen."

Ray and Lauren are silent. Ray has no idea what to say.

Lauren says, "She called you an asshole, and you *are* an asshole. Not just an ordinary asshole but a gloomy nihilistic asshole. I refuse to believe that it's over, that nothing can be done."

The young man leers at Lauren. "*Nihilistic.* Big word meaning what?" He asks Ray, "You speak English well enough to understand your girlfriend here?"

Lauren says nothing. She crosses her legs and turns as far away from him as she can. She's done with him. He'd have to reach over and grab her to make her pay attention.

The guy's not going to grab anyone. He totters to his feet and heads for the door, where Enzo is watching everything. Enzo thumps him on the shoulder. Ray can lip-read Enzo mouthing *your dad.*

Mario brings a platter of swordfish, a smaller plate of veal, a dish of greens in olive oil with garlic and salt. He neatly divides the greens, not an easy task, between Ray and Lauren.

"What was *that* about?" Why is Ray asking Mario, who made a point of absenting himself?

"I don't know," says Mario.

"Bad date," says Ray.

"That's what I figured," Mario says.

"So are you going to use the tickets?" Ray wants to die of shame.

Mario says, "I enjoy seeing the different ways that different actors do the play."

When Mario leaves, Lauren says, "It's a beautiful book, really, Ray. Look at what it still means to Enzo and Mario and probably those kids you read to, today. It's nothing like Curious George. It has heart, Ray, real heart."

"Thank you," Ray says. "That means a lot."

"You're a real person, Ray, not some . . . artificial construct. Not some phony monologue about a man who has a soul. It's been hard for me to find that with guys my age. I feel that if I hang out with you, I could learn to be a real person."

"You *are* a real person," says Ray. This is a conversation that young people have. But he can pretend to be young.

"I'm trying," Lauren says. "Tell me you're listening, okay?"

"I'm hanging on every word," says Ray.

They seem to have finished the wine. Ray raises the bottle just enough to catch Mario's eye.

"I'm listening. I swear," says Ray.

Ray eats his swordfish, tastes Lauren's veal, and then uses his tongue and even discreetly his napkin to make sure he doesn't have greens in his teeth. That he can't grimace and ask Lauren to look at his teeth proves they are still in love, though maybe that's the sign of an immature love. Maybe real love is being able to ask, Do I have greens in my teeth? Is it too late to find that with Lauren? Does he want to? Shouldn't he be looking for someone willing to take care of him in his . . . Wait. Lauren seems to be saying something about a *boyfriend*.

"I had this boyfriend," Lauren is saying. "Briefly. Once we were having sex in his room beside an open window and he said, 'Feel it. The breeze is a sex toy.' "

The story makes Ray miserable. Why can't Lauren see that? Is she trying to ruin his evening? What's left of the Xanax and codeine can't stand up to this.

She says, "Have you ever heard anything more pretentious? More of a buzzkill? We're in the middle of doing whatever, not that it was all that great. Believe me. And he says *that*?"

More than anything, Ray wants to believe that it was not all that great.

"And he can't resist the temptation to come up with *some perfect line*. I know this guy, he probably used this same line with fifty other women. Did I mention that he was a writer? I swore off writers after that."

"But you made an exception for me," Ray says.

"A big exception," says Lauren.

What Ray feels is like a drug, or like after sex, or like the first few moments when a painkiller kicks in. He feels as if he's levitating slightly above this red-sauce paradise in which people all around him are doing things—serving food, pouring wine—designed to make other people happy. He wants to give Lauren something. He wants to do something for her.

After a silence Ray hears himself say, "In Vietnam, there were all these stories, these . . . I don't know what to call them. Urban legends . . . about monkeys."

This is what he is giving Lauren? Something he's never told anyone. A gift, all right, but not a gift that any sane person would want. Stories he's never told anyone because they come with their own illustrations, pictures he doesn't want anyone else seeing when they close their eyes. Is *that* his love-gift to Lauren: a case of contact PTSD?

He wants to tell this story without crying. After all these years, hasn't he earned the right not to cry if he doesn't want to?

"Everywhere I went, that's all anyone talked about. Monkeys. Was it a coincidence? I was too fucked-up to tell. I kept hearing about how somebody went to a restaurant or dinner party and was served monkey brains in a monkey skull. Everyone told it as if no one had ever heard it before. Once in Saigon the signal guy in my office said he'd had his wallet stolen by a monkey. He chased the monkey and caught it and tried to grab his wallet back, and the other monkeys came and formed a scary circle around him, and this guy kept saying he didn't care, the monkeys could go fuck themselves, it was his wallet. He could tell that the older monkeys were telling the little chimp to give it back. Which he did."

"Mister Monkey," says Lauren.

"Sort of," says Ray. "I guess."

No tears. He touches his cheek to make sure.

There's still one story he's not telling. The family of dead monkeys beside the path through the jungle. The dad and mom and two baby monkeys hung from the trees, in nooses, executed, like humans. What sick fuck would do that? American? South Vietnamese? The enemy sending a message?

All the guys saw it and stopped and looked. No one spoke, not even the motormouths, no one said *Jesus Christ* or *What the fuck?* No one knew what it *was*. That night, back in the camp, they talked about it. One guy said maybe it had nothing to do with the war. Maybe it was some lone psycho. There were sick fucks everywhere. And all of them, the Americans and the Vietnamese translators, took turns telling stories about the sick fuck in their town or neighborhood or village. It was probably the closest the guys ever felt to each other on that tour.

Maybe once a year the dead monkey family visits Ray's dreams. And he wakes up thinking that the success and lon-

gevity of *Mister Monkey* is reparations, after all—payback
for the murdered monkeys. And restitution to *him*, Ray, for
having had to see them when he was just a kid. A boy.

So far so good with the not crying. Almost home, Ray
thinks.

Lauren looks down, as if she can't remember what to do
with the dead green plants on her plate. Finally she says,
"Today at the office when I was supposed to be working, I
streamed a documentary on my computer. About this national park in the Congo where all these amazingly brave scientists and rangers are trying to protect the gorillas from the
soulless bastard mercenaries hired by oil companies which
want all the animals dead and the game preserves privatized
so they can drill. God, Ray, it was so heartbreaking . . . this
poor gorilla was murdered . . ."

"I hate that shit," says Ray.

"I thought of you, Ray, I thought of you telling me about
the clause in the contract of the play saying that no one can
mention evolution. How could anyone *not* think about it, and
how could I look at this film and not think how shocking it
was, killing creatures just one step down the evolutionary
ladder. Not that I know that much about evolution, Ray. I
hardly remember the science I took at college. I knew I was
seeing murders. But why should that surprise me, with so
much *actual* killing of *human* men and women and children
going on all over the world, every single day? Why am I telling you this, Ray? You were in the war.

"I thought about *Mister Monkey*, Ray. I thought of you. I
thought, How ahead of your time you were! Writing about
Africa and poachers and wildlife, all these things that needed
to be said, things that *still* need to be said. You were hiding

it in the story. And hardly anyone was saying it before you, Ray. Maybe Rachel Carson. You're a hero, Ray, really. *Mister Monkey* is not just some regular kids' book."

Maybe Lauren's reading too much into it, but whatever. She's young. If there are two or more ways to take what Lauren has just said, Ray decides to take it the good way. What the hell. Ray's happy. He'll worry tomorrow.

His eyes are wet. Let Lauren think that they are tears of happiness, tears of gratitude for her love for him, for their love for one another. Let Lauren think that they are tears of modesty, tears of sadness and resignation about the tragedies he saw on the horizon even as he sat down to write *Mister Monkey.*

Don't cry. Don't cry. Don't do it. He needs to think of something that will work like a charm. A charm to ward off tears. Something so hot and distracting that it will dry up his tears like a blowtorch.

He leans across the table and takes Lauren's hand. She tenses slightly, startled by the force of his grip. Then her smooth fingers curl around his.

"Okay," he says. "Here's a crazy idea. Why don't we get married?"

MARIO HAS A funny feeling about this church, which he has never noticed, surprisingly, because the church is beneath the High Line, where so many small theaters are these days, and where Mario often finds himself, on matinee afternoons. Could the narrow, slightly sinister, soot-blackened church have appeared out of nowhere? Mario's impulse to go to confession has also come out of nowhere, or so he thinks until he enters the church and realizes that he has been preparing his contrition ever since the night Ray Ortiz gave him tickets to *Mister Monkey*.

The Little Church of St. Francis. Mario's favorite saint. He loves the idea of Saint Francis as a ragged, smelly hermit kneeling to receive the laser-like stigmata of light wounding his hands and feet. Imagine not caring if birds shit on your robe! Passing the church, Mario pictured St. Francis hovering above the sidewalk, one outstretched arm covered with a line of black starlings unafraid of the toothy wolf nuzzling at the saint's hip. With his free arm, St. Francis had beckoned Mario into the church.

A vision of St. Francis. Who is Mario kidding? He went into the church because it was something his parents would have wanted.

Mario is on his way to see *Mister Monkey.* He hopes he can get in and out of the church on time. He's glad there's no line for confession. There rarely is, except in the Polish and Mexican churches, whose parishioners must have more colorful sins to confess. Or maybe: the fewer sins people commit, the more they want to talk about it. Forgive me, Father, for doing nothing wrong.

In the hierarchy of sins, Mario's sins are microscopic. Forgive me, Father, for I've had bad thoughts. I have felt hate for a fellow human.

The church is empty except for an old woman in black, kneeling at the altar. A sign announcing that the sacrament of confession will be available from noon to three is chalked on a blackboard. The parish must be saving on signage. The decor looks more Quaker than Catholic. Maybe a cash-strapped congregation has had to sell off its fake-Neapolitan paintings and brocade altar cloths. Ghostly white rectangles mark their absence from the walls. Jesus writhes on a polychrome crucifix above the altar. The baptismal font is a black ceramic birdbath.

The one large oil painting is so encrusted with gunk, so cracked and badly lit that Mario has to shade his eyes to make out St. Francis rapt in prayer, a dusty wand of light finding his palms like those searchlights that used to signal a film premiere or (in this once-rough neighborhood) the opening of a new disco. Though St. Francis is kneeling, he appears to be levitating.

Mario enters the confessional, and like one of those escalators that start when your foot hits the step, the priest begins. "In the name of Father, the Son, and the Holy Spirit, Amen." Why do the Latin American priests speak so quietly and have such high voices? Is it racist to notice?

"Amen," Mario says. "Bless me, Father, for I have sinned. I have sinned against charity. I have wished others harm. I have wanted them to suffer, and I have enjoyed watching them twist . . ."

"Suffer . . . how, my son? Twist how?" Mario hears in the priest's voice: Jesus Christ, God help me. On this otherwise nice Sunday afternoon he's not in the mood to hear a serial killer describe eviscerating cats, though absolving a cannibal pedophile might be the peak of his career. Forgive me, Father, for I have committed the sin of not making myself clear unless it's about the wine list or what a customer wants for dinner.

"Who makes them suffer, my son?"

"They do it to themselves. I watch these rich guys eat and drink like swine and ruin their lives, and I think: serves them right."

Mario can feel the priest's relief misting through the lattice. Venial? He can do venial on autopilot.

"How long has it been since your last confession?"

"One week," Mario says. Forgive me, Father, for I am lying. More like three weeks or four. Okay, a year. Could a year have passed since . . . ? Another year gone. Given how rarely—he's read on the Internet—American Catholics go to confession, once a year should get him a gold star. So why lie? Because he is confessing through the priest to his mother and father, for whom confession was a regular obligation, not an impulse decision, for whom a year between confessions would guarantee him an eternity in hell. But if his parents are angels, can't they look down and take pity on him? Doesn't being in heaven mean they can see into his heart without having to worry about him being so lonely that he has no one except this stranger, this priest, to complain to about an especially awful night at the restaurant?

Mario's father has been dead eight years, his mother five. He misses them, if not every day then often, his sorrow intensified by the fact that he is still living in his childhood room in his childhood house. Reminders of them are everywhere; pangs of grief lurk on the stairs. A snapshot of the three of them on vacation untangles itself from a gnarled extension cord and ambushes him from a kitchen drawer. He is forty-six, a number as unreal to him as the thousands of years the Old Testament patriarchs lived. He is too old to believe that his life is about to start.

Ever since his mother died, Mario has gone to different churches. He doesn't want Father O'Blah-Blah who's known him since he was a tyke, or father Blah-Blahbalino, who presided over his baptism, or the family priest, the incomprehensible mumbler, Father Machalski. Father Mitch is also dead and probably in heaven with Mario's parents, though one never knows about priests. Mario doesn't want a trusted spiritual adviser he meets for coffee and monitors to make sure he's not flirting with the altar boys, a guy with problems of his own, though no one's supposed to know that. Mario doesn't want a community. He has enough community at Enzo's: the other waiters, the wine stewards and busboys. Enzo still asking, now and then, How come Mario isn't married? Mario wants an intimate but impersonal sacrament, like sex with a stranger, though he's always been repelled by the idea of sex with strangers.

He wants someone objective, a professional who knows the score. This many Hail Marys for that much sin. Not that Mario's going to say the Hail Marys. He just wants to know how many. Talking for free to someone with a direct line to God is a bargain. People pay therapists fortunes to pretend to listen and doze off and say a few words at the end. Confession has helped Mario get through the hard parts of his life, or *around* the hard parts, the grievances and irritations, and oh yes, the occasional black spells of desolation and despair.

"I'm a waiter at Enzo's . . ." Mario always wonders whether or not to name-drop the restaurant. Maybe it helps the more celebrity-conscious priests visualize his temptations: most of Mario's sins have begun at Enzo's. As a young man Mario slept with the few waitresses—all beautiful—whom Enzo allowed into his male domain. Mario never mentioned marriage or even love. Wasn't pleasure and friendship enough? The women never thought so, though at first they pretended to share his point of view. The awkwardness never lasted long; Enzo fires his waitresses when they turn thirty, which is surely actionable, though no one—warned perhaps by the framed photos of Enzo with an ecumenical range of Mafia dons—has ever taken action.

Mario used to date customers too. Girls slipped him phone numbers right in front of their dates. Where did they learn to do that? Now they probably text, like that dumb bastard who texted his date that she was a four out of ten. If someone's getting phone numbers now, it's the younger waiters. There hasn't been a woman in Mario's life for . . . counting is bad luck. Anything could still happen, but he's stopped making the effort. How would he meet women? Having been table-side for the sorry spectacle of so many computer dates gone south, he'd rather avoid that route.

Father, are you listening? Have you fallen asleep?

"Go on, my son."

"So this week a customer comes in, one of those spoiled rich kids who can sometimes, not always but sometimes, Father, make me hate my job. He says, 'Bro? Can I ask you a favor?' This yuppie scum-sucker calls me *Bro*, and I have to call him *Sir*? There are times when the *unfairness* of it all makes me want to howl like a dog, Father. Though I'm not a communist. I know that certain inequalities are part of God's plan.

"Anyhow *Bro* is on a first date, and here's the favor. If the girl's a keeper, he'll do a thumbs-up when he hands me the wine menu, and I'm supposed to bring him something high on the list. But if she's a dog, because, he tells me, many women look *nothing* like the pictures they post, either because they've been Photoshopped or because it's not even her picture. More than one girl has admitted to him that she posted her hot friend's photo. In which case we go to Plan B. I bring the guy something drinkable but cheap. Check, please. Call it a night.

"So the girl arrives. She's pretty, beautiful skin, everything about her is sweet sweet sweet, but she's got pinky eyes like she's been crying. She looks like a kindergarten teacher instead of the lingerie model the guy obviously has in mind. He knows, and she knows, and Enzo and I know, and everyone in the restaurant knows she's not what he thinks he deserves. So I bring them a bottle that's rated ten out of ten by the staff for the red most likely to give you a crippling sinus headache. Is that a sin? Dickhead Red, we call it."

"Go on, my son."

"I felt hatred, Father, pure hatred. I *tried* to feel sorry for the guy, to find compassion somewhere in my heart. And then I thought, Not only do I have to bring this steroidal piglet cheap wine to swish around his mouth, not only do I have to bring him and his date delicious food they won't enjoy, because they're not going to enjoy anything, certainly not each other, but I have to conspire with him to break this poor girl's heart. Maybe the girl would love the food—

but only if she was too stupid to see that the guy just *hates* watching her eat. And I'm supposed to feel sorry for *him*? Could you have done that, Father? Then everything flips, and it just seems sad, these two young people not knowing how soon they'll be middle-aged, then old, then dead. And they're wasting one evening, one *minute* of their youth, making each other unhappy.

"Long story short, she goes to the ladies'. He takes out his phone, because he can't stand being alone with himself for five seconds. I see this all the time, especially with the money guys, their phones might as well be Gorilla Glued to their hands. There's a no-cell-phone rule at Enzo's. But texting's allowed. My man is so loaded he's putting the phone up to his face and stabbing at the numbers.

"When the girl comes back she's yelling her head off. The idiot thinks he's texting a buddy. He texts his friend that she's a four out of ten—and he sends it to *her.* Are you following this, Father? I assume you e-mail and text. And she rips this guy a new . . .

"So here's what I'm confessing. I *loved* watching the guy get reamed. No pity in my heart at all. I felt like a kid at Christmas. I signal Enzo: let her be. Let her get it out of her system. Let her tell the whole restaurant what this genius did. She comes up with some fairly raunchy curses for a kindergarten teacher before she runs out of breath and turns and weaves toward the door.

"Enzo puts his arm around her and walks her out. He tells all the crying girls his true life story. How he met one wrong girl after another, and he finally found the right one, and now they have nine grandchildren, they've been married forty-five years, and they're still as madly in love. Well, strictly speaking, it's not his *totally* true life story. Enzo married the first girl he had sex with, and he's had girlfriends, action on the side, all his life, even now in his eighties. Enzo tells them that God will see into the hearts of the girls who have been insulted and ignored and injured. God will have mercy on them and send them love, marriage, children. Then he puts her in a cab. He pays the cab fare up front. Big tip for the driver.

"Of course I was sorry for the girl. Poor thing didn't deserve it. But she had her moment. Whatever she'd gone through with that guy, or earlier that day, or, for all I know, her entire life so far . . . by the time she leaves Enzo's, Father, she's made everybody pay. She leaves the guy sitting there with his mouth open and his thumb up his you-know-what. No one will talk to him, no one will look at him. He says something to the couple at the next table, and then he starts ranting and raving. Spit's flying out of his mouth. I keep expecting Enzo to send over the musicians."

Has Mario said too much? What he's confessed to is *nothing*. A failure of compassion. Are other people ever afraid that their sins are boring? Would it be more fun for the priest if he *were* a cannibal killer?

"At last the guy leaves. Enzo has to bullshit him goodbye. His dad's high up in the Russian mob. And pretty soon the guy's just a crappy memory and a ten percent tip. Am I wrong to hate him, Father?"

The priest doesn't answer for so long that it puts Mario on edge. Then he says, "My son, it sounds as if you have already forgiven yourself."

What kind of priest says that? Who cares if Mario forgives *himself*? Isn't this supposed to be about God forgiving *him*?

"Is there something else you wish to confess, my son?"

"Envy," Mario says. "The sickening, gnawing, stomach-churning, humiliating kind of—"

"Envy of whom, my son?"

"That's another story. Or maybe it's part of the same story. The couple at the next table. This guy, Ray Ortiz, he's been coming to Enzo's for years. He's a writer. Kids' books. Every so often somebody puts on a musical based on his book, and he gives me tickets. It's a thing we have. He makes me thank him for the tickets, twice, three times. I don't mind stroking the guy's ego. He's not our biggest celebrity, not by a long shot, but he gets respect, he's a writer. A creative guy. Enzo's told me a thousand times, always in front of Ray, how Ray's book turned Enzo's son Ricky into a reader. Ray's book did the trick. Ricky's a thief and a shithead, so maybe the book didn't do him all that much good. But I'm obviously not going to say *that*. And at the end of the day I get tickets."

"To a children's play, my son?"

Was there a suspicious edge to the way the priest said *children*? Does the priest think he's a pervert? Would denying that he's a pervert prove that he is one?

"I love theater. I'm a fan. I go whenever I can. Broadway. Off-Broadway. Off-off-off Broadway. Festivals. I don't care. Sometimes customers give me tickets, sometimes I buy them, sometimes—"

"Envy?" prompts the priest. He doesn't want to talk about theater, though maybe he would, if he were better at his job, smarter at ferreting out the secret sins and lapses of faith that an ordinary person might not notice. Is it heresy that the theater gives Mario that mysterious . . . *something* that devout Catholics find in the Church? Mario would like to see this priest get through one shift as a waiter at Enzo's.

"Ray's always with beautiful women who are also smart and friendly and nice. He's been married I don't know how many times. The women stay the same age, and Ray gets older. Though that's not for me to judge, Father. I say more power to him. Ray's a gentleman. Polite, a generous tipper, a good guy all around. And young Master of the Universe at the next table is a total piece of shit. So which guy would you choose for your daughter, if you had a daughter, Father? I don't mean—"

"Please, continue, my son."

"I start to pull out his girlfriend's chair, but Ray gets there first. It's another thing we have, our little joke, like a secret handshake. But this time I see his hand resting on the girl's shoulder. He can't help touching her. *Tenderly* would be the word. That kind of love can be tough to see, though probably not for you, Father, if it seems likely to lead to a litter of Catholic babies. But it can be hard for a single guy. I can handle it, otherwise I couldn't work at Enzo's. Guys are always proposing, couples celebrating engagements, anniversaries, Valentine's Day, whatever. Hug hug. Kiss kiss. For the moment.

"Ray's telling his girlfriend something, and she's hanging on every word. She *adores* him. I bring them their escarole. Delicious. They're staring at each other: serious, confused, happy beyond anything that could possibly involve sautéed greens. Maybe she's pregnant, maybe he's proposed. I've seen it all, Father.

"No dessert, thanks. Ray and his girl order espressos. They're not planning on sleeping much.

"Finally Ray says, 'Mario, bring us a bottle of good champagne. No, make that a great champagne.' Because guess what? They're engaged!

"Congratulations! I have to smile and pop the champagne while my head is exploding from envy. Or maybe it's despair. I remember from Catholic school: despair of the distance from God is worse than murder or whatever. I may have gotten that wrong. When I saw them together I knew that happiness was a zero-sum commodity. More for them, none for me. I knew there was no hope for me, no chance for the friendship and love of a decent woman. I will never have what they have. And why? Because I'm not smart enough, not good enough, not handsome enough, not rich enough, not lucky enough—"

"As long as we are still alive, there is hope, my son. Infinite hope."

"Maybe. But not for me. To be honest, Father, I wanted the guy dead. No, not dead. I wanted him never to have existed, never to have paraded his love in front of me like something that everyone has *so much of* that we can all afford to be generous and *happy* for everyone else. Is that a sin, Father?"

"Don't be so hard on yourself, my son."

Don't be so hard on yourself? Seriously? What about the part where the sinner is told to scourge his skin raw, to let leeches feed on his flesh, to cross the burning sands on his knees to the holy shrine? Mario must have wandered into some progressive Catholic Worker–type shit. Go forth and feed the homeless. Ladle Thanksgiving turkey gravy over the instant mashed potatoes of the poor and despised, a job for which his lifetime career in the food services industry has left him extremely well qualified.

"Try to keep a loving heart and avoid sin, my son. Do your best to correct your faults and ask God for mercy. Go in peace, but before you leave, pause for a moment of prayer in the House of God."

"Will do," says Mario. So does that wrap things up? He doesn't feel any better or worse than he did when he walked in. Did the priest just catch him checking his watch? God sees.

"Good-bye, Father, thanks again." Mario stands, stumbling slightly. His knees aren't what they used to be. That's going to make his job harder. What bad knees will mean at Enzo's is what Mario is thinking about as he leaves the confessional booth.

The woman at the altar has gone. The priest told him to stay a while, and just in case he's watching, Mario's too self-conscious to leave. He sits in the last pew. What now? He bows his head, and with his eyes closed he sees what he was blind to, before. The church isn't just poor. It's dying. Everywhere around this slice of prime real estate, condos are going up. They're building high-rises in alleys. This square footage is worth a fortune. The diocese is not going to keep this place open, especially when an upscale church of St. Francis is thriving, a few blocks away. And what will happen to the priest? He'll be sent further down the food chain. A doomed priest in a doomed church has given the sacrament of confession to a man whose sins aren't serious enough to be damned for. He looks at the crucifix over the altar, and it seems to him that the tilt of Christ's head says, You think I died for *you*?

Cheer up. The day isn't over. He's looking forward to seeing *Mister Monkey*. Who cares if it's a children's musical about a chimpanzee? He likes seeing what different casts do with an idiotic play. Once he saw a production in which they did the whole first half in silent pantomime, and the kids in the audience were positively *shrieking* with boredom.

Not counting the Bronx Civic Opera *La Bohème*, which Mario and his eighth-grade pals mocked, warbling filthy made-up arias in their cracking voices, the first play Mario ever saw was *Uncle Vanya*. A Broadway producer gave Enzo tickets, and Enzo gave them to Mario only because Mario was the first waiter he passed en route to the kitchen. Such are the workings of God.

Lucia, Mario's fiancée, had left him not long before. She'd said he wasn't the person she'd thought he was, but in fact he *was* that person and was never going to be anyone *but* that person. She was the one who'd pretended to be someone else, someone who wanted a life of simple contentment with Mario. By then Mario had moved back to his parents' house for what he'd thought would be a few weeks. He'd been grateful for the chance to spend an evening out. Who cared what the tickets were for? A movie. The theater. A circus.

The Chekhov play was performed in a loft for an audience so small that everyone knew Mario didn't belong and probably suspected him of stealing the Broadway producer's tickets. Or so he thought until he became so absorbed in the drama that he was no longer himself but an invisible guest at Uncle Vanya's home, a visitor who knew these people better than he had ever known anyone. No one had ever talked to him so openly about their deepest feelings. No one, not even Lucia. Certainly not her. He had never imagined that anyone else suffered the loneliness that came over him, like an illness, in a busy dining room surrounded by customers depending on him not to find an empty chair and put his head in his hands.

Watching the play, Mario understood that you could never make someone fall in love with you, or stay in love with you. The actors were talking directly to him, telling him that he would never get Lucia back, that she would never love him no matter how many times she agreed to talk it over. When Nanny tried to comfort Sonya, tears welled up in Mario's eyes. Silent, looking neither right nor left, Mario wept silently through the final scenes. Why had he enjoyed feeling so miserable? A normal person—by which he means a normal male person—would never have gone anywhere near a theater again.

He's often wanted to say something after a play, to wait near the stage door and tell an actor or director how much he'd admired the show. But he's never known how to begin. Just the thought of it makes his heart race. It scares him to imagine talking to creative people, though he waits on plenty of them at Enzo's. An exhausted actor might not want to hear Average Joe Waiter's blubby admiration. People are likelier to be nice to you when you are bringing them food.

Sometimes late at night, eating a bowl of cereal by the refrigerator light, Mario thinks about a play he has just seen, or seen long ago. Though he has never given anyone advice except about what to order for dinner, he has lots of advice for the characters. He wants to warn the crippled girl to forget the gentleman caller. He wants to tell King Lear not to be so reckless. Sometimes Enzo reminds Mario of Lear. Enzo's son Ricky has grown up into a heartless shark who plans to rob his siblings blind. What will happen to Mario then? He is lucky to work at a place that values experience. Everywhere else in the city, the waiters are half his age and all look like fashion models.

By now Enzo's regulars know that Mario likes the theater. Cheapskates offer him tickets instead of a tip, but decent guys like Ray leave both. Movie stars ask him what he's seen lately, though they never listen unless he mentions a famous name, and then they say, I worked with that person. Mario reads theater reviews, but he goes his own way. It makes him happy to walk into a theater and see a spooky Richard Foreman set. He still remembers the *Twelfth Night* in which Viola and Sebastian dressed and looked identical, and Mario understood that Shakespeare was talking about finding the lost other half of your self. He often finds himself humming a Brecht song about a guy kissing a girl under a tree; a white cloud passes by, and years later the guy can't remember the girl but only the cloud. Mario likes the idea of forgetting the girl and remembering the cloud, though he sometimes worries that theater is the cloud, that he understands and loves people in plays so much more than people in life.

Of course he prefers it when great actors say beautiful lines, or when a brilliant director spins the straw of a crappy script into gold. But he'll settle for less, much less: actors, an audience, a stage or something like one. A children's play, if it's free. That he's seen *Mister Monkey* so many times lets him overlook the imbecilic plot and find out if the director has done *anything* interesting with the unpromising hand he's been dealt.

Mister Monkey! What time is it? How long has Mario been sitting in the back of the church? No one can fault him for daydreaming. A waiter can't afford that luxury on the job. Six days a week, all his adult life, he's had to pay attention. He deserves a few minutes of reverie in the House of God.

He checks his watch. Thank you, Jesus. He still has half an hour. He stands and sits down again. Something's thrumming in the air, a seismic rumble like a mild earthquake, the furnace kicking in, or a car radio blaring hip-hop so loud you can hear the bass line from half a block away. It feels like some dark scary premonition of . . . Could he be having a stroke?

But it's neither a stroke nor an omen. A pigeon has flown into the church, and the frantic beating of its wings feels like blood whirring in Mario's head. The bird makes several passes through the air, then bashes into the ceiling, drops slightly, stunned, then recovers and resumes its anxious swooping flight. Mario's superstitious: a bird in the house means death. Where is St. Francis when you need him to catch the feathered fucker?

Calmer, the pigeon perches on a rafter, growling softly, its bottle-fly-green iridescent breast rising and falling. Mario hurries out of the church. A bird in the house means death. It was an omen, after all. A prophecy of doom, but not—this time—for him. Before long, condos will rise from this hallowed ground.

THE ENTRANCE TO the theater admits Mario to a gloomy corridor smelling of dust and roach spray. He surrenders his ticket to a skinny, grizzled guy in a dirty sweatshirt. A young Indian woman in a blue policeman's uniform hands Mario a sheaf of stapled pages, more like a press release than a program, and shows him to his seat among rows of uncomfortable chairs.

Though Ray always gives Mario two tickets, he never invites anyone to go with him. The last time he brought a date—years ago—was a mistake. What had he been thinking to take Sally Ann, a pretty waitress at Enzo's, to a revival of *Frankie and Johnny in the Clair de Lune*? They cringed all through the sex scene, and their discomfort increased when it turned out that Frankie and Johnny worked at the same restaurant. Mario and Sally Ann couldn't look at each other as Johnny desperately attempted to make Frankie fall in love with him, and the whole play had seemed to them to be about how Mario was never going to do that. He wasn't even going to try. They never went out again, and Mario has never again risked an evening at the theater being spoiled for reasons unconnected to the play.

Another advantage of having two tickets is that he can choose which seat to take. Today that choice is made by the time he reaches his row. On the far side of his two seats sits a heavy middle-aged woman wearing layers of hippie fringe and her long hair plaited into a bristling gray braid. Mario is ashamed of the intensity of his reluctance to sit beside her.

He leaves an empty seat between them, settles in, and skims the program. Almost all the actors have been on *Law & Order*. The woman playing Portia toured with the road company of *Wicked*. A few cast members are currently studying at NYU. This is the first professional appearance of Adam Leigh, who will be playing Mister Monkey and who wants to give a special thanks and shout-out to his mom. Everyone wants to thank someone or give a shout-out to someone else.

Mister Monkey is traditionally played by a child. One production cast a small woman as the monkey. Mario read about it, but the show closed before he could see it.

THE LIGHTS COME up on the entire cast paired off in couples, arms outstretched for "Monkey Tango." Mario has seen the play often enough so that he usually knows who everybody is, but today he's confused. Which actress is Portia, and which is Janice? One of the women is wearing a chic black dress and a black bag, swinging from her shoulder. That must be Portia. The lawyer. The other is wearing a rainbow Harpo Marx wig and a tight shiny purple suit. She's got to be Janice. But as the dance continues and various pantomimes—miniduets foreshadowing the rest of play—take place, Mario realizes that the actress in the wig is playing Portia and the redhead in the little black dress in Janice. How strange.

Everyone flings themselves into a square dance, then 1970s disco, hey hey monkey time, a few booty shakes of salsa, then they extend their arms and arch their backs for a rigid-with-shame mock-tango. Mario can't stop staring at the woman in the rainbow wig, at the sad-clown suffering so visible on her happy happy face. Her eyelids snap open and shut like a doll's. How can she open her mouth so wide without unhinging her jaw?

> *Monkey Tango.*
> *Orangutang-o.*
> *You rang? Oh tango.*
> *King-King Kong-o. Mighty Joe Young-o.*
> *Monkey tango. Into the jungle. With me.*

The kid playing Mister Monkey isn't dancing with anyone but lacing his way among the dancers, creeping across the stage like a sadistic psycho in a home-invasion thriller. The rest of the cast seems afraid of him, especially the actress in purple, who visibly recoils whenever he comes near her. Has she found a new take on Portia: a monkey-phobic woman who refuses to let fear keep her from doing the right thing and defending an innocent chimpanzee?

Or not so innocent, maybe. The kid plays the chimp like a rooster, a cock of the walk, elbowing actors out of his way. A family is under the thumb of a primate juvenile delinquent. Something is very wrong. Interesting, *really* interesting as a choice for *Mister Monkey*. But also disturbing. Mario looks around. Are the parents worried about their kids picking up bad behavior from a monkey? The parents don't want to think too deeply about what the monkey's doing. They paid good money for tickets. The play is *supposed* to be fun.

The house lights go down, and a pale yellow circle—the full moon—rises against the worn curtain. There's no orchestra, just a tape. It's *Mister Monkey* karaoke. Even so, it's familiar. Mister Monkey is about to tell the moon, in song, the tragic backstory of what happened to his parents, killed in Africa by the poachers who also murdered his adoptive stepmom, the sainted Mrs. Jimson. He's about to sing about playing toss-the-coconut with his monkey mom and dad. Can his parents hear him? Where are they now? Before his own parents died, Mario used to think that this song was stupid, but now he finds it hateful, because it brings tears to his eyes.

Mario has never before seen an aggressive Mister Monkey stride out of the wings and hunker downstage front and pummel the audience with a hip-hop rant about how Mister Monkey came to live with the Jimsons. His shoulders are hunched, he's making those overhand lunges, pointing at the ground and (could this be true?) his crotch. And yet he doesn't look like a rapper. He can't quite carry it off. He looks like a child in a monkey suit, trying to rap. Of course Mister Monkey is angry at the criminals who destroyed his idyllic jungle existence.

It's riveting but scary, and Mario's surprisingly moved, because the subject, underneath everything, is the death of parents. Does the child playing the monkey worry, as Mario used to, about when his parents will die?

The woman with the fringed shawl, one chair over from Mario, is rocking in her seat and gesturing at the stage, as if she's trying to signal the monkey. Obviously she's insane. A man in front of her turns around, but she's not quite disruptive enough—not yet—for someone to call an usher. What is she doing here, alone at a children's matinee? Like me, Mario can't help thinking. But who would give *her* free tickets? She calms down when the Jimson kids prance out and yank Mister Monkey around.

Mister Monkey lets himself be yanked, though there's an unsettling moment when Mister Monkey's teenage siblings seem to have discovered something disgusting on their hands. They're kids, but they're professional enough to get past it and go on. Or perhaps it's happened before.

Finally the song ends. Mister Monkey exits stage left, and the focus shifts to the Jimsons.

Mr. Jimson is being played by a handsome but oafish-looking young actor. Still panting from their monkey dance, his teenage son and daughter look stricken.

Mr. Jimson's girlfriend, Janice, a confident, plucky redhead, clicks her long red talons like castanets. She sings the first verse of her song about how much she loves her fingernails. Biting them, chewing them, scratching her back. For a woman who is singing a love song to fingernails and who by the end of the play will go to jail for falsely accusing a monkey, Janice, in her little black frock, projects a calm assertiveness that Mario finds appealing.

Given Mister Monkey's explosive edge, Mario tenses when a cop goose-steps onstage to arrest him. Mario recognizes the Indian girl who handed out the theater programs, only now she's wearing a red clown nose and giant yellow shoes. The kids in the crowd think she's hilarious, so she has to let the laughter subside before she grabs the monkey's arm. The monkey high-fives the policewoman, who high-fives him back, and they skip off arm in arm. Whoever this monkey is angry at, it's not the girl playing the cop.

The actress in the fright wig and the purple suit has been offstage since "Monkey Tango," but now Portia is at her desk with the weak spotlight frothing around her. Looking pretty in her maid's uniform, the actress playing Carmen knocks on the lawyer's door. Carmen's beauty makes Portia look older and more deeply in distress. But Carmen isn't here to be pretty, except insofar as she needs to charm Portia, whom she tells—along with the audience—about Mister Monkey's legal difficulties.

Carmen's magic works. She makes Portia pity Mister Monkey, or at least feel outraged on his behalf. These two good women can't believe how evil Janice could try to break up a family and hurt well-intentioned people who have enough on their plate, raising two motherless kids and a feisty hormonal monkey.

Carmen says, "What can you expect from a woman with these"—she curls her fingers, miming claws—"and a Hermès bag." The children laugh at the claws and their parents laugh obediently at the unfunny fashion joke.

The actresses swing into the salsa number that Mario remembers from previous *Mister Monkey* productions. It's pleasant enough, a fun break from whatever weirdness has infected this production.

Now the grizzled guy who collected the tickets appears, wearing a judge's wig and not saying much as Portia delivers her courtroom speech pleading Mister Monkey's innocence. She's talking fast, triple time, making sense, more or less, but she seems unstable, volatile, veering rapidly and histrionically between tough and fragile. Mario respects her for rising to the challenge of being sincere, forceful, and persuasive in a Harpo wig and a purple suit that emphasizes her worst features.

She says, "The quality of mercy is not strained—not even for a monkey. It droppeth as the gentle rain from heaven."

The others stare at her, and Mario gets the sense that she's jumped her line: delivered it too early. Meanwhile her reference to gentle rain makes it impossible not to notice that Portia's forehead is beaded with sweat. She moves like a woman wearing heels twice as high and a skirt twice as tight as she is. Oh, dear God, that soul in hell! That poor woman never dreamed that one day she would be playing Portia in this abysmal production! Mario's heart fills not only with sympathy but also with awe for the faith with which she is channeling her private desperation into Portia, making something complicated, moving, and grown-up from the raw material of a bizarrely costumed character in a musical about a monkey.

The judge bangs down his gavel. Blam! Case dismissed! Mister Monkey is innocent. Massive jubilation!

Portia says, "I *told* you the quality of mercy is not strained—not even for a monkey!" A lot's going on, onstage. But Mario can't take his eyes off Portia, cowering behind the actor playing Mr. Jimson. It's lucky that Mister Monkey has been exonerated, because how would it look to the judge—a lawyer in such obvious terror of her client?

From the wings Mister Monkey takes a flying leap that lands him halfway across the stage. He rushes at Portia and traps her behind Mr. Jimson. Visibly trembling, Portia presses her forehead into the back of Mister Monkey's human dad. Is Portia acting, or is this real? Mario hasn't a clue. Glancing down the row, he sees that the madwoman in the scarves and shawls has covered her eyes with her hands.

Mister Monkey's silent physical bullying of Portia continues. The kids are practically levitating out of their seats, powered by pure joy. Mister Monkey is doing exactly what they have always wanted to do to countless women like Portia, maybe not in a clown wig but nonetheless bossy, all dressed up, and important. It's what they want to do to Mom sometimes, though it scares them to think about that. The parents sense this strange and terrible play getting even more pecu-

liar, but it's holding their interest, *and* the kids are having
fun, and *that* hardly ever happens.

Finally Mister Money backs away from Portia, either because he's been told to, or because he's bored. Leaving the
stage, the monkey fake-lunges at the other actors and at one
of the stagehands. And now the lady cop marches back out
and arrests Janice for bringing false charges against our favorite chimpanzee.

The curtain sways shut and, after an unsettlingly long
pause, opens on Portia and Mr. Jimson with their phones
pressed against their ears. Portia looks traumatized, as if she's
still peering around the edge of something to make sure it's
safe to come out.

Mario knows what's coming. The distasteful cell phone
duet. The song has always irritated him, and he knows it
annoys Ray Ortiz—and he wrote the damn book. Once Ray
ate at Enzo's twice in a week, before and after Mario went to
see an earlier production of *Mister Monkey*. He'd asked Mario
how he'd enjoyed the play, and naturally Mario said he'd enjoyed it very much. One of Ray's marriages was coming apart.
He was drinking more than usual, and he'd asked Mario how
anyone but a fucking moron could enjoy that fucking idiotic
bullshit with the cell phones, which wasn't in his book because Ray fucking hates cell phones, and he wrote the book
before they existed. Then, just this week, as if God had set
out to prove Ray right, he and Lauren and Mario and many
other customers at Enzo's had witnessed the cell phone disaster ignited when the guy beside Ray texted his date by
mistake.

Mario would like to forget that guy and his sad little kindergarten teacher. He's thought about them enough. But the
song has brought it all back. He too has always hated cell

phones, and now he will hate them forever. And he's meant to think that the spectacle of Mister Jimson and Portia declaring their love on phones that keep cutting out is supposed to be cute—or romantic? Is he meant to see cell phones as the buzzing-bee Cupids of love?

It's the absolute low point in an outrageously bad play. At least Mario hopes it's the low point. He closes his eyes and waits for the scene to end. But this time, in the midst of the song, something unexpected occurs. He hears a loud bang and opens his eyes. Portia has dropped her phone. Portia watches it bounce slightly and skitter, but she doesn't move. The audience falls silent, though a few of the younger kids babble anxious gibberish at their parents.

Portia skips across the stage, then draws back her foot and kicks the phone as hard as she can. Wham! She punts it into the wings. Watching Mr. Jimson, who seems unsurprised, Mario can tell that this apparently improvisational moment has been written into the production. Maybe the first time Portia did it by accident, and it worked, and she did it again.

After a few stunned seconds the audience cheers. And though Mario knows it's just stage business, he too wants to applaud. He feels as if he has participated in some collective ritual of release and redemption, a sacrament more liberating than whatever transpired with the priest in the church. Everyone wants to see their devices get what they deserve, to watch the buzzing implacable demons kicked to the curb for the cunning and deceit with which they've made us unable to live without them and stolen our freedom and our ability to be silent and alone. The audience has seen the forces of good vanquish the fire-breathing dragon in our pockets, the microzombie that eats our brains. Their eyes have seen the glory of St. George in a rainbow wig.

A giddiness starts at the back of Mario's throat and stays with him through the curtain calls, even when the monkey reappears and everyone scatters. The actress in the wig gets a standing ovation. The cast leaves the stage. The audience seems thrilled to be released. Suddenly children are everywhere, hunting under their seats for the sweaters the grownups made them bring in case the air-conditioning was too cold, which it wasn't. The woman beside Mario rockets out of her seat, fringes flying behind her as she clambers onto the stage and disappears into the wings.

As he steps into the warm September afternoon, Mario considers waiting outside the theater. He imagines the woman who played Portia—Margot Leland, according to the program, which he has saved—rushing off to a romantic tryst or simply trying to avoid the thuggish little monkey. She will notice Mario and hold his eye just long enough for him to feel encouraged and go up to her and tell her how brilliant she was, how she'd brought such dignity, complexity—and humor!—to a part that was so far beneath her. How her beauty and spirit shone through that absurd disguise. Best not to say *beneath her.* No creative artist likes to hear that. Best not to criticize her costume, on the chance that she chose it herself. Mario worries that he'll say the wrong thing no matter what, that something about him will tip the scale, alter her perception of him from admiring fan to stalker. Portia—Margot!—is afraid of so much. The last thing he wants is to spook her.

And yet the idea of turning and walking away without seeing her again causes Mario such pain that he knows: this must be about something more than an actress doing an unexpected and original turn in *Mister Monkey.* He wants to talk to her, just talk to her. He wants to tell her about the

production of *Uncle Vanya* that made him fall in love with
the theater. He wants to find out who she is, to hear about
her dreams and hopes for the future, where she has been,
where she wants to go, her memories of childhood. He wants
to put his arms around her and tell her that everything will
be all right, that together they can live a life of simple happiness, that later they will look back on this suffering—and
smile. He knows that's how a stalker thinks, but that's not
what Mario is. He doesn't want to alarm her. He wants to be
kind to her. He has seen so many plays about love, and only
now, after all this time, he thinks: maybe this is what love
feels like.

Mario is a sensible guy, steady, a creature of habit. How
many men have held the same job for almost thirty years?
He is an excellent waiter, which requires a cool head, a good
memory, and plenty of common sense. But there is nothing
reasonable or cool about conceiving a passion for a woman
you don't know, whom you've watched struggling not to
drown with a theater full of children watching, then bobbing
to the surface, her brave face shining above the waves of mediocrity, failure, and public disgrace. Some men fall in love
with movie stars, some with hookers, some with their best
friend's wife. But Mario seems to have fallen for an artist,
an actress playing a lawyer who successfully defends a so-
ciopathic chimpanzee. The yearning inside him feels like a
sob about to well up from deep in his chest. He will never be
happy without her. And he doesn't even know what she really
looks like!

All he needs is the courage to wait for her, to tell her how
good she was. Maybe she'll be impressed by his effort to understand what she was doing. By *any* effort, given the play
and the theater.

But what if she's already seeing someone? What if she's married? Mario feels certain that she is single and alone, that the performance he observed was not within the range of a happily married woman. Not even the most gifted actress could fake the loneliness and desperation that Mario saw—and that he feels himself, that only now *he* lets himself feel, now that he's seen it in her. Mario could sell his parents' house, they could move in together. He knows he is rushing things. He should go home and write her a letter. It would let him say exactly what he means in the most reassuring and least alarming way. If he tries to talk to her now, he will lose her forever.

Jesus help me, have mercy, Mario prays, as he was unable to pray in church. And God recognizes the sound of a heartfelt prayer, of a soul in mortal peril. The despair of the distance from God vanishes when Mario sees Portia—Margot— leaving the theater.

It takes him a moment to recognize her without the rainbow wig. He probably wouldn't know who it was if he hadn't been sitting so close, and if her image hadn't been branded on his heart.

The woman who played the police officer has walked her to the door, and she and Margot chat while the police girl smokes. Margot is wearing blue jeans and a white T-shirt, and, despite the heat, a black leather jacket. The woman in the uniform is coughing, possibly from the smoke and Margot is—tenderly, tenderly—patting her on the back.

Mario can't get over Margot's orange-red hair, exploding like the spiky crown of a gorgeous punk Wonder Woman Medusa. Mario is deeply touched by the message that Margot's hair seems calculated to deliver: outside I'm a prickly cactus. Inside is the cool refreshing water that will save your life if you are lost in the desert.

Margot takes off in the direction of Eleventh Avenue. Mario's not going to follow her. He just wants to see where she's going. He stays half a block behind her. If the light changes too fast and he loses her, it will be a sign.

She walks into one of those tiny Cuban-Chinese places you used to see in Chelsea. A historical relic left over from the time when those places still existed: The Cup of Asia, The Star of Heaven, the Jewel of the Antilles, The Shower of Gold, the Caribbean Breeze—they had such poetic names until they sank like Atlantis under the previous mayor.

Mario walks up and down the block. Then he goes into La Isla des Perlas, the Island of Pearls, a family restaurant with eight tables.

Margot sits at a table facing the far wall. Mario can't believe he is doing this. He finds a seat that's as far from her as possible. He looks at her back, her fragile shoulders, like bird wings. Her amazing auburn hair. He can watch her without bothering her, without letting go of the hope that somehow he will find the nerve to approach her. Meanwhile he just has to stay calm, do a little acting himself, act the part of an ordinary guy ordering an ordinary dinner.

Is there some way to pass her and pause and start a conversation? Mario's not bad-looking, despite his somewhat longish head. Years ago, when he started at Enzo's, the line chefs called him Frankie, for Frankenstein, but the fun of that soon wore off. He doesn't look like a crazy person. He looks like a working man: a waiter in a fancy place. What if he explained that he got the tickets from Ray Ortiz? The author of *Mister Monkey*. It might reassure her and make her pay attention. Famous names work on everyone, no matter how above it you think you are.

He'll apologize for interrupting her meal. He just wants to

say how much he liked her performance. Men pick up women every day in places much sketchier than the Island of Pearls.

The glossy laminated menu, half the size of his chest, is perfect to hide behind. How could anyone cook so many delicious-looking dishes? Piercing one page is a small, charred hole, as if someone put a cigarette out in a steak. Mario pauses on a column of golden, breaded cutlets, each arranged with a lemon wedge, a lettuce leaf, a slice of tomato.

He watches the waitress bring Margot a platter of shiny brown tubes and glistening greens. When the waitress comes over to Mario, he orders a Corona, okay, a Tecate, and gestures at Margot's food. I'll have what the senora's having.

The waitress shrugs. No problem. It's easier for the kitchen, doing the same thing twice.

Excuse me for interrupting, Mario repeats in his mind, until it becomes a prayer that does the opposite of what prayer is supposed to do. Each time Mario says it, a sizzle of terror pins him to his seat. He is a middle-aged man, but he might as well be in junior high.

Soon his food will arrive. He should go over now. Excuse me, but aren't you the star of *Mister Monkey*? Aren't you the actress who played the best Portia I've ever seen, and I've seen the play many times. Margot will be staring at him. He'll have just seconds to explain that he gets tickets from the guy who wrote the book. All he has to do is stand up and take one step and then the next. The rest of his life can begin now: the reward for one moment of courage. And if he fails? A woman will tell him to get lost. It happens to men every day. He makes himself stand. He walks a few steps toward Margot. He's tiptoeing, but so what?

In the aisle he passes the waitress bringing his food. He can hardly tell her to leave it on his table while he bothers a stranger. There would be a shit storm if some creep tried that at Enzo's. Mario can't even bring himself to pretend he's going to the men's room. The waitress will see him stop at Margot's table. She'll watch him be rejected.

It's too late. He's waited too long. His heart can stop pounding. Maybe some protein will help. Languid with relief, he returns to his table. He and the waitress arrive at the same moment.

Mario's food, Margot's food, turns out to be squid and bitter greens in some rich, delicious, mildly spicy brown sauce. Beneath is a mound of fluffy white rice with sweet plantains on the side. This is nothing like Enzo's. Why bother to compare? He is here with Margot. Something could yet happen. The beer, then maybe another beer, might give him the nerve. He feels braver than his normal self, more generous and open. Is Enzo's better than this? More expensive, certainly, more exclusive—but better? The waitress must have her moment like the one he loves best, just before the restaurant opens when all the tables are set, and the lights are coming up. The play is about to begin. Though this place, unlike Enzo's, is probably open all day.

The squid is fresh and tender, perfectly cooked. The greens are silky and just salty enough, with bits of something crusty, ham or bacon. He's fallen into the habit of eating with the staff at Enzo's, but now he sees, or remembers, that there is a world of food all over the city. He could do this on weekends, before or after the theater. He could find simple delicious restaurants and have dinner or lunch. He could do it with Margot, who must like it too. She has come here by herself. All he has to do is go over and start talking.

He has only to cross a small restaurant and say a few words. It would be easier to walk a tightrope between skyscrapers.

He will never begin the life that waits on the other side of that conversation. He has lost the habit of conversation unless it's about someone's dinner or why he isn't married or (if he's talking to a priest) his petty resentments and jealousies of the customers at Enzo's.

He swallows. Get ready. Now. He takes another bite. His chest hurts. It's hard to swallow, and yet he needs to keep eating. If he stops he has to leave. What if he's having a heart attack? That will get Margot's attention. And the joke will be on him because he will be dead.

Margot catches the waitress's eye and scribbles on the air. Mario staves off panic. It would scare her to learn that her "fan" had eaten dinner and watched her and only spoken to her as she was leaving. She passes so close that he could touch her. Mario wants to cry out, Look at me!

And then she is gone. Nothing worse has ever happened. Maybe something will still work out. He could send her a letter in care of the theater. He could see the play again next weekend, and this time . . . What was it that the priest said? There is infinite hope.

He will leave her a note. He will choose his words carefully. Something that will flatter her and touch her heart. It calms him to imagine this. He only has to cross the desert between now and when he sees her again. It helps that he has things to do. He has to pay for his meal. He has to leave a large collegial tip and thank the waitress. He has to walk a couple of blocks until he's breathing normally. He has to go home and go to sleep and go to work tomorrow.

He isn't ready to go home. He concentrates on walking, on not bumping into anyone and not getting run over. After a while he's surprised to find himself in the subway station.

Mario's waiting for the train to Queens when he looks

down the platform and sees the young woman who gave out the programs and played a cop in *Mister Monkey*. She's still wearing her costume with the big yellow shoes, but minus the red clown nose.

Maybe God is rewarding Mario for going to confession. Giving him a second chance—to do what? To make contact with Margot through this woman. Her friend.

Mario moves down the platform so he's not crowding the police girl, but close enough so they could get on the same car, which she might even appreciate if she goes far enough into Queens so the train empties out. Mario looks safe. Reassuring, he hopes.

When the train arrives the young woman enters and sits near the door. Mario heads to the opposite side, from where he can watch her without being too close. Perhaps he will move nearer and find some way to start a conversation. It would be easier than talking to Margot: less fraught. From halfway down the car, he could call out, very genially, Didn't I just see you in that terrific production of *Mister Monkey*? What a coincidence! They could begin with a casual chat. A friend gave him tickets. Well, a little more than a friend. The author of *Mister Monkey*.

That actress who played Portia was great. Truly brilliant. Doesn't Police Girl agree?

The train heads into the tunnel. Mario stares into the blackness beyond the glass. He will wait a few moments more. Then he'll get up and walk down the car.

LAKSHMI PLANS TO write a one-act drama about a talented, compassionate, hardworking, underappreciated costume designer who gets a walk-on part as a cop in a sweet but basically retarded musical for children. Her play will begin at the theater, with the young woman straightening up the costume racks and saying good-bye to the cast members whose (recorded) voices can be heard from offstage.

No need to hire extra actors, or to slow the opening by including her conversations with the depressed deranged stage mom and her son, the deranged depressed boy-actor whose hormones have turned him into a psycho who deserves a tragedy of his own that Lakshmi's not going to write. No need to dramatize how the boy monkey is bullying certain members of the cast, a potentially explosive situation, which the director has decided to ignore. Everyone knows about it, but no one has the time or money or energy—or the courage—to hire a lawyer to lodge a complaint against Adam or the theater, which would be expensive and could ruin their careers. The run has two weeks left. It's better for everyone if they finish out their contract.

Our heroine (Lakshmi will call her Devi) stays behind to neaten the costumes, not only because she *is* the wardrobe department, but also because with everyone gone she can leave without having to explain why she's wearing her stage outfit home. Only Roger the director (no need to change names and identifying details until her play is produced, and for now using real names makes it easier to visualize her characters) has caught her leaving the theater in costume. Lakshmi explained that dressing as a cop makes her feel safer on the subway and on the streets of her Queens neighborhood, which still has some rough edges. Roger has probably never been to Queens, so Lakshmi can make it sound like whatever Roger fears most.

Unlike Roger, Lakshmi's audience will know that no one in their right minds could believe that a woman would feel more secure in a jokey imitation (nightstick! handcuffs! floppy ears! outsize yellow shoes!) police uniform you can buy in a Halloween shop, or online, which is where Lakshmi got it. It's a fashion choice that signals: this woman is drunk or insane, or an old-school club kid zombie back from hell, or a discount hooker catering to special tastes. So why is Devi dressed that way? That is one question that will run throughout the play and which will, Lakshmi hopes, keep the audience on the edge of their seats.

In the play (as in life) Devi's outfit will combine a police uniform and a clown suit, more creative and liberating in terms of what she can do onstage and say in her work. In the play (unlike life) she will wear her red nose and floppy ears, even on the subway.

Most (or maybe all?) of the play will be set on the train. The various ways in which strangers react to Devi—looking, not looking, staring, moving closer or farther away—will generate physical comedy as passengers notice that they are sitting across the aisle from a policewoman in a costume more appropriate for a Disney World employee than for one of New York's finest. The clown who blows a whistle and arrests the clowns in the clown car. The humor will disarm the audience and make them more vulnerable and open to the personal revelations that Lakshmi is saving for later.

The clown idea came from the outfit that Roger is making Margot wear in *Mister Monkey*. It's humiliating for Margot, but, to be honest, Lakshmi finds it useful for dramatic inspiration. She'd supported Margot when Margot volunteered a vintage Armani suit that would have been fun to work with and way more in character for Portia. After all the commotion and tears, Lakshmi had to agree with Margot: Roger is punishing her for being a middle-aged woman.

Lakshmi is fond of Margot. Sometimes she wants to put her arms around her and hold her until Margot's brain and heart stop batting around like crazed birds trapped in Margot's fragile house of a body. At first she'd liked hearing Margot's stories about being the star of her class at Yale and touring in the road company of *Wicked* and about all her insanely bad romantic choices and marriages to gay or otherwise unsuitable husbands. Margot can be funny when she's trashing Roger and the cast and the collective nightmare of *Mister Monkey*.

But Margot's bad-husband stories and the pain she's suffering because she isn't famous began to make Lakshmi feel gloomy. Lakshmi believes that it's better to respect your co-workers than to pity them, and Margot (along with most of the cast and crew) have made this guiding life principle a bit of a challenge to follow. If Lakshmi makes money on her play—or, as is statistically more likely, on her second play—she plans to find some secret, pride-preserving way to channel part of her new fortunes into Margot's bank account, if she has one.

Lately Margot's been telling Lakshmi that Adam's a little perv, that he sexually aggresses her and rubs his penis against her. Margot has tattled on Adam to Roger, who won't fire Adam with such a short time left in the run and risk destroying the remains of his own future as a director. Lakshmi believes Margot. *Something's* wrong with Adam. He's started playing Mister Monkey like some coked-up gangsta rapper. Young as she is, Lakshmi has already learned from experience (specifically, her experience with her boyfriend Mal) that unruly sexual feelings and thwarted love can make people do things that no one who knew you could ever imagine you doing. In Lakshmi's opinion, Adam has a crush on Margot, and that's how this whole mess started. When Lakshmi wants to feel sympathy for Adam (which she does sometimes, though not often) she tries to imagine Mal when he was Adam's age, and her heart hurts for them both.

Is it morally sketchy for an artist to use the sufferings of real people as a source for her art? On the scale of suffering, an unflattering wig and an ugly purple suit are *nothing* compared to what people endure every day in Syria and Gaza, or to the horrors her fathers witnessed before they left India, which they have told Lakshmi about so many times and in such detail that she feels she's seen them herself. Which she did, though she was a baby, too young to remember.

Sometimes, at gloomy moments, Lakshmi considers finding a hypnotist to take her back to the Hindu-Muslim riots in which her parents were killed and from which she was rescued by a cousin, a distant relative of her Hindu dad's, who adopted her and brought her to this country. Thank God Roger doesn't know about that, or he would have used it to try and make the cast feel sorry for real-life orphan Lakshmi, and he would have exhorted them to let their sympathy spill over onto Mister Monkey.

Lakshmi doesn't want anyone feeling sorry for her. So she hasn't told that part of her story to anyone except Mal. How free—how almost weightless—she felt when Mal made it clear that he wasn't impressed. His dad died in a drunken car wreck.

When she was younger, her fathers' stories made her cry. She knows that her dads have asked each other, Please don't tell those stories to Lakshmi! A few times she heard them argue about it. But early on she understood they *had* to tell them over and over, even to a little girl. That was the only way in which her dads were less than terrific parents, but on the scale of the fucked-up things parents do, telling your adopted daughter about what you survived—two men, one Muslim, one Hindu, both in medical school during the communal riots—hardly counts as child abuse.

In the play, the experience of riding the subway with Devi will inspire her fellow passengers to volunteer impassioned confessional monologues. Lakshmi has yet to figure out why this would be. For now she hopes that the audience will get so involved in the passengers' stories that they forget to wonder why they are telling them to Devi. Lakshmi will use the language of the play, metaphors or whatever, to convey the idea that, for a wide range of New York subway riders, a lady clown cop can function like a priest in a confessional. You don't even have to be Catholic!

After each speech, the actor/passenger will exit the stage/train, and another actor will enter/get on. And he or she will tell another story—and so on. Lakshmi hasn't decided how many stories she will include, and now each time she rides the train she looks for a passenger whose narrative she can turn into the missing piece of the patchwork she will craft into her play. Set entirely on one car of the train, and with a minimal cast, all wearing their own clothes, the play will be cheap to produce: a fraction of the Scrooge-like budget for *Mister Monkey*.

It would be impossible to set a play on the 7 train and not deal with the immigrant experience. So the first passenger who sits across from Devi and stares with frank curiosity at the Indian clown cop is himself Indian: a sparrow-like elderly gentleman whose thin arms stick out of the short sleeves of his white business shirt. He looks at Devi as if he is trying to calculate her family's origins and caste, but all those surface indicators have been erased by Devi's life in Queens and in the theater. None of the signs are legible in her round face, her clown nose, and the black braid beneath the police hat. So he asks, in English, where she is from.

"Queens," says Devi. "And you?"

"Bombay," says the old man. "Mumbai."

The spotlight finds him and he turns, so that he is in theory facing Devi but is in fact facing the audience. Slowly and in a sorrowful tone he begins to tell his story about having been a *paanwallah*, custom-making betel-leaf chews for his customers near the Strand Cinema, in Colaba, and how he saved every penny and bought a sweet shop and then a café and saved and scrimped to send his son to college and then medical school. The son went to America and married for love (an Indian lady obstetrician, at least) and had two daughters and brought the old man to the United States and bought him a small co-op apartment in Queens, where the old man started over and built up a business, importing Indian toothpaste and a special holiday kind of sweet dried saffron noodle.

By now the old man's wife has passed, and he is a widower preparing to enter the final stage, which in India might
have meant leaving home and taking up begging or doing
charitable work, but which here means assisted living and
babysitting the grandkids. His son and daughter-in-law are
in Delaware and have never once suggested that he join
them. After selling the importing business, he was at a loss
until an old friend from Bombay got in touch to say that he
was starting a sort of theme-park Indian market, like Eataly,
only South Asian, in Queens. Would he like to design and run
a *paan* stall: a trendier, more sanitary version of his shop in
Bombay? More sanitary! He'd resented that, but he'd wanted
to try something new. He imported Indian goods based on
how elaborate and exotic the packaging was. He'd created a
kind of art-piece retail shop with the premium ingredients
for *paan*.

He had plenty of customers, nostalgic grandpas, the fathers of doctors and lawyers, young Indian-identity types,
South Asian lesbians, and Brooklyn hipsters who enjoy chewing through bursts of sweet and salty and sour and then
spitting a red spume that looks like blood. He hired two
pharmacology graduates to work extended hours. He trained
them to combine the betel and areca with coconut, herbs, and
various pastes based on signs they read in a customer's skin
tone, face, and eyes—and on something less tangible. There
were write-ups in health magazines and online naturopathic
forums about the digestive and psychoactive benefits of betel,
and about *paan*'s efficacy against psoriasis and rheumatoid
arthritis.

Then, just when business was booming, his doctor son
called to say that he'd read in a scientific journal that, after
decades of speculation and anecdotal evidence, it had been

conclusively proven that *paan* increases the risk of oral cancer
by more than 30 percent. Not only oral but also cancers of the
esophagus, lungs, stomach, and even the brain.

The old man was too shocked to answer, too amazed to
learn that he had spent his life depriving himself and his
wife to raise a viper who would grow up to call him a poi-
soner and a killer. Anyway, he doesn't believe it. Who cares
what the doctors say? He has had customers who have lost all
their teeth to *paan* (he admits its unhealthful dental effects,
but modern dentistry can fix that) and lived to 120.

So he would like the clown cop to tell him: What should
he do now? Sell his business and give away everything and
put on a mendicant's robes and go from door to door, begging
for stale hot dog rolls and forgiveness?

Devi says nothing. The spotlight finds her sitting motionless, her palms upturned in her lap, like some stern Hindu
clown goddess. The light rises over her head and projects a
bright circle on the black sky/backdrop above the stage set/
subway car.

The old man asks her, though really he is asking the audience, if she wants to know a secret. He tells her that whenever there is a full moon, he goes up to the roof of his house
in Queens and pretends that the moon is the same moon (as
indeed it is) that he used to see from the roof of his house
when he was a small boy living in India with his parents. He
looks at the moon and asks his parents where they have gone,
and if, wherever they are, they can hear him. Lakshmi is reasonably certain that by changing some key details—Africa
to India, monkey to human—she will prevent anyone from
realizing she's borrowed a few tiny touches from the deserv-
edly obscure children's musical *Mister Monkey.*

Devi says, "We are also an immigrant family, and my

father is a doctor." She will save the information that both her fathers are doctors till later in the play. Besides, telling this old man that she has two dads will make him doubt that she is anything like him, that she can understand him and feel his pain.

Devi looks down at her outfit. "Costume party," she says. For now it's easier than telling the truth, which she'll also save for later in the play.

The old man is disappointed by Devi's failure to give him comfort or helpful advice. The train stops, and he gets off, passing a middle-aged woman with spiky red hair, wearing a vintage Armani suit. When Lakshmi's play is produced, she will offer Margot this part, unless the producers insist on a marquee name. She will let Margot wear whatever she wants because she will be playing a lady judge, an even bigger wreck than Margot. Wobbling on heels so high that just looking at them makes Devi's feet hurt, the woman makes several loopy circuits around the subway car before plunking herself down opposite Devi, crossing her legs, leaning forward, and saying, "Can I tell you something?"

It is, she explains, a story that no one will believe. She herself wouldn't believe it, if a case like hers came before her court.

In this way Lakshmi plans to build up interest in the woman's confession and at the same time cover herself because the story she's about to tell is really very unlikely. Lakshmi herself wouldn't believe it if it hadn't happened to a friend of a woman who lives in Mal's mother's building.

Lakshmi has decided to call her lady judge Portia. It's the perfect name, nothing else seems right, and nobody's going to notice if she steals another detail from *Mister Monkey*, which actually stole this one from *The Merchant of Venice*.

Besides, plagiarism is so old-school. Lakshmi calls it sampling. Incorporation.

Lakshmi's Portia, the lady judge on the train, has been married for twenty-four years, a close supportive marriage. Her husband, Bill, is a lawyer, and if he ever resented her being a judge, he never let on. He has always been loyal and proud of her. Or anyway, so she thought. He specializes in estate and property cases that require him to travel. He always calls when he's gone. He tells her that he misses her and can't wait to come home.

Then one day the mailman brings a letter for her husband, from a doctor's office, though not her husband's doctor. It's marked PERSONAL and CONFIDENTIAL. Actually, it's addressed to someone with her husband's name who lives across the street. A coincidence, though not such a crazy one when your name is William Smith.

"There are no coincidences," Devi says. "Everything happens for a reason."

"Oh, yes there are," insists the lady judge, a less spiritual person than Devi. "The world is senseless chaos."

If Portia had been thinking, she would have asked the mailman to give the letter to the proper addressee. But she wasn't thinking. Or maybe she was thinking more clearly than she knew. She crossed the street to the brownstone and pushed the button that said O'LEARY (not her name) and SMITH. When the buzzer rang, she said into the speaker, "I have a doctor's letter addressed to a Mr. William Smith."

Someone buzzed her in. Maybe someone was expecting an important doctor's letter. Portia climbed three flights of stairs and reached the end of the hall just as a woman opened her door. The woman (Ms. O'Leary, Portia assumed) looked enough like Portia—similar body type, features, even the same red spiky hair—that both women noticed the resemblance and laughed, a little nervously. Possibly that was why the woman invited Portia in, instead of just thanking her for the letter and closing the door.

The first thing Portia saw, on a little round table in the fake "colonial" style that she would never have had in her own home, were several framed vacation photos of her husband and this woman. Why did a stranger have so many pictures of Portia and Bill? But wait. They were pictures of Bill and this woman. Her husband and this woman in Paris, in Vienna, squinting up at the statue of Marcus Aurelius in Rome. All places he'd been with *her*. Could this woman have Photoshopped her face onto photos of Portia and Bill? No, it seemed. She hadn't. This woman had *been* to these places with Bill. Or, as she said, *my husband Bill*.

Portia was glad she'd brought her phone. She showed the woman photos of herself and Bill in the same spots. Of course the photos of Portia looked worse, that is, Portia looked worse, because they were taken with the phone, and some of them were selfies, a bad idea over forty. But mainly Portia looked less happy to be in the same places with the same husband.

If Lakshmi directs as well as writes, she will have to think of something besides pacing and crossing and uncrossing her legs for Margot to do, to signal Portia's agitation. This is what a director does—though unfortunately not Roger, who seems to have left his brain in some regional theater somewhere.

Portia's husband had been a bigamist for a decade. The street he worked both sides of was not wide Upper Broadway but narrow Bank Street in the West Village. How could someone get away with that for so long and not slip up and get caught?

Devi will tell Portia not to blame herself, because we all

have inner lives, secret selves. And it sometimes happens that the inner kernel takes over the outer husk, like a pod from outer space. The words *outer space* make the bigamist's wife give Devi a quick suspicious look and jump up and get off the subway, though it's not even clear if this is her stop.

Lakshmi needs another story to insert either before or after the story of the bigamist's wife. Why are all her stories about lying and betrayal? She would like it to be a story about a monkey, maybe because she has been working on *Mister Monkey*, and because she's proud of the monkey costume she sewed from a brown bedspread they practically paid her to take from Goodwill.

If her play has a decent producer, and it doesn't jack up the cost of the production too much, which it probably would, she would like to bring an actual monkey onstage, perhaps a rescue monkey kidnapped from the set of a children's movie or horror film that paid the monkey wrangler extra to drug the chimp and make it even more hyper than normal.

Maybe she'll put the bigamist story before her own true story, because she likes how the idea of an "inner life" segues into the story she wants to tell about her own history—that is, Devi's history. Devi's monologue will be the emotional climax of the play.

Lakshmi-Devi's story could just as easily go after the monkey story, if she finds the right monkey story. Because both of her fathers have told her about troops of monkeys in Lucknow stealing the lunches of picnicking medical students. The part she likes best is the part about how they met. Devi's Muslim dad, Hussein, heard the siren song of the cheap CD player on which Devi's Hindu dad, Prakash, played Stephen Sondheim in his dorm room. How happy they were to have found each other until their affair was discovered by their fellow students, and they were beaten and expelled from medical school and might have gone to jail for being gay had the Hindu-Muslim riots not broken out and ironically saved them by killing thousands of innocent people, including their parents and many close family members.

They had nothing left. Nothing more to lose. They applied for student visas. Allah or Ganesh or both must have wanted them to come to the United States. They landed in Detroit, where Lakshmi's Muslim dad (future dad, at that point) had rich, exceedingly modern, and liberal-minded relatives who took pity on them. After overcoming many setbacks, both dads completed their medical training and moved to Queens, where together they opened their urology practice and became community heroes during the AIDS epidemic. They adopted Lakshmi, the child of her Hindu dad's niece— who had been killed in yet another, later outbreak of sectarian violence.

How could she not love the musicals that had brought her fathers together? *Company*! *Into the Woods*! She'd learned the songs as a child. She still knew the lyrics. Her dads would be so proud if Lakshmi wrote a play that was produced. They are concerned but supportive about her career choice. They are much more worried about Mal, but they know that forbidding her to see him would only strengthen her love.

Naturally she's inherited her fathers' passion for the theater. That was why she'd applied to NYU and gotten involved with *Mister Monkey*, the saddest show on earth. She should have known from the handwritten notice on the drama department bulletin board: from the fact that the notice was there at all. Internships and low-paying theater jobs are in such demand that students remove the announcements of jobs for which they plan to apply.

Her Hindu dad, Prakash, was so delighted that Lakshmi was in a play about a monkey that he took it upon himself to pick her up at the theater after an early rehearsal. He asked Roger if he had a minute, which turned into twenty minutes, during which her dad lectured Roger about Hanuman, the Hindu monkey god.

He listed the god's holy attributes, explained that Hanuman was the smartest, the strongest, the most in control, the god who resembles a golden mountain. He described how the god tried to eat the sun, which he mistook for a mango. How he lifted a mountain to find the herb that healed the god Rama's wounded brother. How he set fire to an island because his enemies tied a burning branch to his tail. How his courage, speed, and strength helped reunite Rama with his beloved Sita.

The other gods were so jealous of Hanuman's superpowers that they cursed him with the inability to remember the fact that he *has* superpowers—unless he is reminded.

Unless someone or something reminds him.

Roger said, "Is that a good thing? I suppose that not knowing that you have superpowers would make you more modest. But I'm not sure that modesty would be a fabulously useful quality for a god. Don't you agree?"

Lakshmi had never heard Roger talk that way. He was flirting with her dad!

Roger couldn't see, or maybe he did, how happy it had made Lakshmi's dad to lose himself in those beautiful childhood stories. It hurt her to watch how quickly Roger got bored and in his boredom began to fantasize that her dad was cruising him. She watched Roger become simultaneously huffy and kittenishly seductive. She has never forgiven him. Some part of Roger knows that, which is partly why he is going to fire her and blame it on the producers.

Roger told her dad, "We have a beautiful line in the play. In fact it's one of my favorites. I'm sure you heard it. 'Mister Monkey is the smartest, cutest, nicest, strongest, most powerful chimp of all!' "

"Excellent," her dad had said. He'd thanked Roger again and collected Lakshmi and taken her all the way home to Queens by taxi.

Whenever Roger didn't listen to her, or talked over her, or disagreed with her, which was practically always, Lakshmi wanted to quit the play. But she liked the costume job, the tiny acting job, and it's made her fathers proud. Both dads commented on the wonders that Lakshmi achieved with Mister Monkey's costume. They were sorry to hear that *Mister Monkey* is about to sink and take everyone down with in it, except for Jason and Danielle, who are so light they'll bob to the surface. Everyone except Eleanor, who, amazingly, has been able to turn in a stellar performance as Janice and then go on to her day job as an ER nurse.

Lakshmi has a tiny girl crush on Eleanor, who is strong and hopeful about the future and therefore a positive role model for a young woman planning a life in the theater. Roger likes Eleanor too, and Roger hates everyone else. Even Adam gives Eleanor a pass when he's on the warpath. Only Margot is jealous of Eleanor, which is sad. Eleanor could have been Margot's friend and ally, and Margot needs a friend and ally.

In Lakshmi's opinion, *Mister Monkey* is a nasty piece of imperialist propaganda justifying human trafficking, which you would know if you were smart enough to substitute a person for a monkey. The white man kidnaps the savage chimp and gives him an Upper East Side apartment and a super-straight snooty new family. It is not a fair trade for his freedom and his idyllic life in the jungle. Lakshmi is still deciding whether or not she'll have Devi give a little speech—nothing too didactic or off-putting—about monkey and human trafficking.

Better to end it with Devi's story about her two dads and about her memories of being a beloved, blessed child sitting in the dark theater before the lights came up on *Into the Woods.* Better to leave out the politics, just as it's better to save the details of her relationship with Mal for her second play.

Maybe Devi should tell the audience about her—that is, Lakshmi's—conversation with Roger. If she does she'll change the production they've been working on together. She'll make it a more successful and popular play than *Mister Monkey.*

Roger comes to inform Devi—Lakshmi—that he is going to fire her because the producers are cutting back and have decided to save the pennies they pay her, barely enough to cover her subway fare, a salary on which she couldn't survive, not even in Queens, were she not living half the time with Mal and half the time with her dads. It will seem more important and tragic if Devi is being let go from a Broadway hit and not from a miserably failing production of *Mister Monkey.* The audience will understand and sympathize with her inability to speak up in her own defense because she wants the director to recommend her when someone asks for a good inexpensive costume designer.

At least (in real life) Roger had the decency to apologize. He was sorry. It wasn't his decision. It was all the producers' fault.

Roger has zero interest in Lakshmi's outer or inner life. He knows nothing about the play she plans to write. She hasn't decided if, in her play, he will say he's sorry.

Devi faces the audience. Signal lights scatter like fireflies in the subway tunnel behind her. She tells the audience that, at the end of the conversation, her former boss, Roger the director, felt around in his pocket. He grew increasingly frantic in search of something he appeared to have lost, something he'd wanted to give her . . . Lakshmi waited for him to tell her what it was, but he didn't, and she didn't ask.

Lakshmi is not entirely sure where the play will go after that. That's why now, whenever she rides the subway, she studies her fellow passengers for something she can steal.

Tonight a guy with a weirdly long head and a lantern jaw, like Frankenstein or Lurch, is sitting down the car from her and across the aisle.

He can't stop looking at her, which she understands, because she's still wearing her clown-cop costume. But he's not giving her anything, not a scrap of information, let alone a monologue that would work onstage. Useless, completely useless! Besides which, the intensity of his stare is starting to make her nervous.

When she was in junior high there so many more perverts around on the subway and in the streets. She hardly ever took the train without glancing up from her book to find herself looking straight into the winking eye of some icky stranger's penis. Has their number really decreased, or do they just prefer junior high girls? Does not seeing them mean that she's old? Dear God, where did her youth go? She's spent too much time around Margot, and now she's caught Margot's ill and desperate way of thinking.

The long-faced guy almost seems as if he want to talk to

her, as if he's about to speak but doesn't know how to begin. Lakshmi is plotting how she'll outsmart him if he gets off at her stop and tries to grab or grope her en route to Mal's.

If only she could call Mal and ask him to meet her at the station. But that would ruin everything they do together later. And Mal will be grouchy all night.

The young woman clown-cop and Frankenstein facing off on the subway car, both on the edge of speech. Could this be the end of the play?

The train stops. Lakshmi waits till the last possible second, jumps up and rushes out the door too fast for the man to follow. In fact he doesn't even get up. Maybe he was harmless. She was just being paranoid.

He watches her until the subway pulls out of the station and he can no longer see her.

It's the perfect place to end the play. Lights out. No sound except the thumping of human hearts rising into human throats. Wild applause. Straight to Broadway. Lakshmi's name in lights.

LAKSHMI'S NIGHT ENDS somewhat differently.

By the time she walks the ten blocks to Mal's apartment, she's begun to sweat. But Mal likes her better sweaty, so she doesn't worry. Of course she worries, but she's worried about so many things aside from being sweaty that it makes more sense not to worry at all.

One might think a person would never forget something like that, but Lakshmi can't remember how exactly it began. A lot of *what if*s. What if you wore your uniform home? What if you knocked on the door? What if we had sex like that? Nor can Lakshmi remember how it gradually became apparent that Mal wouldn't have sex with her or even be nice to her any other way.

She is the daughter of scientists, so she experimented. But the results were depressingly clear. If Lakshmi changed at the theater and came home in her street clothes Mal would frown and turn his back and sleep on the couch, even though it was his apartment. The same thing happened if she didn't pound on the door but simply let herself in with her key.

After a while the *what if*s grew more specific, more precise. What if I'd done something wrong? What if you were the cop who'd come to arrest me? What if I resisted arrest? What if you did this with your nightstick? At first it was a shock, and a humiliation, but the shame faded along with the shock, and now it's just her relationship with Mal. It's not what she would have chosen, but a woman in love can't always choose.

So she *is* like a specialty hooker, except that a hooker gets paid, and Lakshmi is doing this for love. For love, whatever that means. She believes, with her whole heart, that she is in love with Mal. She thinks of him when he's not there. She thinks of him when she's fixing a costume or knocking on an actor's door.

And of course she thought of Mal whenever she marched out to arrest Mister Monkey. Could Adam have somehow sensed that a fake arrest is Lakshmi's principal means of real-life foreplay? If Adam picked up on that, maybe that was why . . . she can't let herself think that. She is not responsible for Adam's roiling hormones!

She wants to be with Mal, she wants Mal in her life. He is the person she wants to see when she gets home from the theater.

Lakshmi pounds on Mal's door.

"Who is it?" Mal says, through the door.

Lakshmi says, "Police. May I come in?"

Mal says, "If you must."

Mal opens the door. He is lank and bleached and indefinite-looking, like a watercolor of a person. He can't stand without bending slightly, sagging at the knees, though he's not very tall.

He says, "Good evening, officer. Is there some sort of problem?"

He backs away as Lakshmi walks in. He looks guilty and afraid.

"Am I under suspicion?" Mal asks.

"Stay where you are," Lakshmi says.

CHAPTER 9

ELEANOR AND THE CHILDREN

OF GOD

PORTIA AND MR. JIMSON have nearly finished the scene which got minimally more interesting when Margot accidentally dropped her phone and persuaded Roger to let her incorporate this "mistake" in her performance.

Portia's phone hits the floor. As always, the audience falls silent and watches her pause before drop-kicking her prop phone behind the curtain.

Adam jumps out of the wings, vaults halfway across the stage, and lands on both feet, crouched, his arms hanging limply, knuckles dragging the floor. Wham! Mister Monkey body-blocks Portia, who has moved toward her phone in preparation for the crowd-pleasing penalty kick.

What the hell is Mister Monkey even doing in this scene? He isn't supposed to be present at this love duet between his human dad and his future stepmom.

Margot scrambles away from him, then inches back. It's awkward, squeezing past Adam, who stays close behind her, imitating her wobbly walk. Margot is a professional, Eleanor will give her that. During these last weeks, she's soldiered on, playing Portia, undaunted by the fact that she is being sexually harassed by her underage monkey client.

When Portia gets a clear shot at the phone and raises her leg to kick it, Adam lunges forward and grabs her foot and holds it in the air, a few inches off the ground.

This is way beyond off-script. Nothing like this has ever happened.

They square off, staring, mongoose-cobra, Margot cork-screwed around and tottering on one high heel, the frayed hem of her purple skirt riding dangerously up her poor little chicken thigh. Adam could break her leg! Does the audience have any idea how rogue and psychotic this is? Do they think that violent assault is acceptable children's musical theater?

A few seconds more and Eleanor will have to run out and grab the monkey she just tried to put in jail. The monkey she *should* have put in jail.

Eric, she's glad to see, is on high alert. He's watchful, but he too is waiting before he wades in and pulls Adam off Margot.

The disaster they've all feared is finally happening, though each has pictured a different disaster, or near disaster. Now all they can do is watch from across the gap between the reality and whatever they'd imagined even as they convinced themselves that, if they were lucky, nothing would happen.

EARLIER THIS AFTERNOON Roger called a meeting to tell the cast what they already knew. *Mister Monkey* is terminal: the production has two weeks. Everyone's sorry. They want the play to go on; it's a job, it's work in the theater, it's not being unemployed.

Everyone is sorry but Eleanor, who only auditions for shows that she knows won't run for long. Not that she wants to jinx things, but from the start it was clear that *Mister Monkey* was unlikely to move to Broadway or become a perennial off-off-Broadway hit.

The hospital lets her work half-time and is flexible about her hours. She can start her shift after the play. But she can't expect them to be patient forever.

That could be one reason why she's the only one in the cast who has been having fun. She's the only one who isn't concerned about her future.

It's taken focus to play Janice, plotting to ruin everyone's life, when in fact Eleanor is so often worried about her colleagues. Margot has every right to panic. What could be more scary than the prospect of middle age in a clown wig trashing *The Merchant of Venice* to save an abusive preteen chimp you legally represent? Roger is running on empty. Eric and Rita are in love with each other and with other people. Adam is darkness, darkness, terror, and rage building toward a volcanic eruption inside a monkey suit, and Giselle, poor Giselle, is nearly out of her wits.

How ironic that Eleanor should play the villain when she is the only one with compassion for the others, with sympathy for all of them, hapless children of God. Though—she's only human—she does have a problem with Margot.

Maybe there's some special mood-altering chemical in the adhesive, but whenever Eleanor puts on Janice's press-on nails, she feels the bubbly onslaught of bliss. She's exactly where she wants to be, doing what she wants to do.

When she sings her gross, crowd-pleasing, chorus-girl high-kicking song about how she adores her nails—biting them, chewing them, scratching herself with them—she means every disgusting word. She loves peeling off her nails like a stripper and flipping them into the crowd and seeing the well-behaved audience turn into a grade-school mosh pit. Eleanor loves *Mister Monkey* and everything about it. After being a saint at the hospital, it's not just a release but also a blessing to play a lying, scheming, heartless, gold-digging bitch.

Eleanor has enjoyed it, or most of it, but it will seem like a vacation—not to go to the hospital directly from the theater.

When he'd given them the bad news, Roger, lately grown so detached, rallied enough to exhort them to keep pushing their limits, giving the play their best shot, to remember that they are artists telling the stories of the tribe.

For the second time, Roger told them to do it for the Fat Lady, which Eleanor feels is a private message for her, whether or not Roger knows it. Except perhaps for Margot, she is the only one who might get the reference to *Franny and Zooey*, the book that changed her life, the book that woke her up to the fact that she and other beings have precious living souls, the book that made her begin to understand that everyone has a Buddha nature, which we can see if we only look hard and patiently enough.

She has never mentioned this coincidence, if that's what it is. The subject is way more personal than she wants to get with Roger, who has always liked her, and certainly way more spiritual than anything she wants to discuss with Margot, who has never liked Eleanor and who never will.

From the first day of rehearsals, Roger treated Margot badly. He's more impatient with her than with anyone, even Giselle. That's another reason why he's resisted scolding Adam or even firing him, as Eleanor has suggested to him during more than one maddening conversation.

Roger went deaf when Eleanor talked about the production being sued, a word that in her experience usually sharpens people's hearing. He claimed to be in control.

Just between the two of them, he said, Eleanor had to admit: this is definitely *the most* interesting thing to have

ever come out of *Mister Monkey*. They're watching male adolescence *happen*! In real time! Onstage!

Roger pretended not to hear her ask, What if someone gets
hurt?

When Roger announced that the run was ending, his re-
stored attentiveness and momentary zeal were so unexpected
and touching that not one person snickered at the idea of
Mister Monkey as the story of any tribe, anywhere. Besides,
they knew Roger wasn't talking to them. He was aiming
his Hail Mary–pass pep talk at Adam's heart, or whatever
organ governs his behavior. Roger preached at Adam, as if
his speech about theater and art might somehow tamp down
the hormones (Eleanor hopes it's hormones) that has made it
tricky to work with him.

Margot calls Adam an embryonic sexual freak, and Eleanor believes her, though he has never gotten funny with her
or Rita, or Lakshmi, before she got fired. If Adam wandered
into Eleanor's ER, she'd suggest a psych workup. She'd page
the best guy in psychiatric and, if necessary, the beefiest,
kindliest orderly who's handy with a syringe.

ADAM HOLDS ON to Margot's foot. The audience waits,
silent, motionless, like the dead in *Our Town*. *What are they
waiting for?* After an eternity, Adam releases Margot and
lopes offstage. Portia totters a little, then gives the phone a
girlish punt beneath the edge of the backdrop. The audience
applauds, but this time with less jubilation than relief. At
least he didn't flip Margot off the edge of the stage, which is
what Eleanor has feared. What she was prepared to prevent.

Standing nearby Eleanor, watching from the wings, Rita
refuses to look at her. Except for Roger and (possibly) Adam,
the cast doesn't like her. They've confused her with Janice,

the witch. How could they, of all people, not understand that she's chosen to stay in character when she's in the theater? And why couldn't she tell them? Janice never would.

The moment she peels off the press-on nails—ta da!—she morphs back into Eleanor, the only person in Crazy Town who knows that someone is going to have to talk to Adam before someone else gets hurt.

Officially, that's Roger's job. But Roger's not going to do it.

And now it's happened, or almost. Adam needs to be helped. Or stopped.

Eleanor is good with people. She can figure out what's wrong and what to do about it. It's her job in the hospital, and it's fallen to her here. She's the one who steps in when no one else will step up. She has become the go-to person for cases that not even the social workers will touch.

Not long before the *Mister Monkey* rehearsals began, an old man came in to the ER, having just murdered his cat, which he'd brought with him in a black plastic trash bag. He'd killed it because his wife was dead, and he was alone. He was afraid of dying, but he was more afraid of his cat eating him after his death.

No one wanted to touch this. They'd called Eleanor, who bypassed the curtained cubicles and put the elderly gentleman in the one consultation room where the magazines hadn't been stolen. She was the person who paged the psych guy and the orderly she would call, if she had to, for Adam. Everyone knows what Eleanor does, which is why the folks in administration have been flexible about shifting her hours to make time for *Mister Monkey*.

Compared with the old man and his cat, Adam will be a breeze, though Eleanor has no idea what she'll say. It's easier in the ER. Just being there means that you're asking for help.

Adam hasn't asked Eleanor for anything. Though isn't grabbing Margot's foot a plea for *someone* to pay attention?

As Adam muscles past Eleanor on his way offstage, she grabs his arm and says, "Adam, I need to talk to you later. Let's go get a cup of coffee after the show."

Weeks ago Eleanor would never have done that. Mister Monkey and Janice are arch enemies and rivals. And back then Adam had still seemed like a normal kid, on the grumpy side, but at the age when boys are either enraged or unattractively eager to please the adults.

The situation has deteriorated and now has reached the point at which Eleanor must weigh safety and common sense against *Mister Monkey the Musical*'s paper-thin resemblance to art.

Adam shrugs off her hand, but the tilt of his monkey chin tells her that he likes the idea. A grown-up woman is asking him out for a grown-up drink.

He knows he's in trouble for what he just did to Margot. But even if Eleanor yells at him, it will be more interesting than sitting around and waiting for his gaga mom to quit bothering *gaga* Roger.

When the curtain drops, Eleanor waits until Giselle rushes backstage to *get a note from* Roger. Shouldn't the *note* be about Adam's twisting Margot's leg? *Shouldn't* someone talk to Adam? Shouldn't it be *his mother*? Or failing that, the director? Giselle and Roger will find a way to avoid the subject. This is how murders happen with lots of people around. Eleanor should find Margot and make sure she's okay. But someone else, Eric or Rita, will have to do that.

Slumped against the wall outside Roger's office, in an orange T-shirt with white bleach blossoms and baggy lemon-yellow satin basketball shorts, Adam could be any sad guilty kid waiting for his mom to emerge from a parent-principal conference. Eleanor has changed out of Janice's little black dress and slipped into the faded green scrubs that will save her time when she gets to work.

Maybe not being Janice will make it easier to get through to Adam. Wrong! When he sees what Eleanor's wearing, he scowls. His immediate future has gone from cool to embarrassing: coffee with a nurse. At the same time he can't quite believe that Eleanor has actually come to find him.

"Ready?" Eleanor says.

Adam shuts his eyes and shakes his head. His cheeks wobble like a baby's. Even though he's a gymnast he's going soft in that way boys do just before they turn into men. He can't look at her when he says, "You need to ask my mom."

Eleanor opens Roger's door without knocking. Roger has his back to the wall. Giselle sits demurely in a chair, Adam's monkey suit neatly folded in her lap. Giselle has told Eleanor that she hand-washes the costume every night, because she doesn't trust the dry cleaners not to soak it in poison, and because she's read how dust mites can damage Adam's respiratory system. Has Eleanor heard about this in her work as a health professional? Eleanor said no, she hadn't, and when Giselle looked crushed, she'd said she'd ask; new information comes down the pipeline, all the time.

Eleanor doesn't want to know what Giselle and Roger are discussing. She asks Giselle if she can borrow Adam for fifteen minutes and go get a cup of coffee.

Giselle's face goes slack with horror. Why is Eleanor doing this to her? Perhaps because her son just grabbed an actress's foot and almost flipped her? That may be why Eleanor might want to talk to him now.

In fact Giselle is grateful, but her fragile pride in her mothering skills won't let her admit it.

"Adam doesn't drink coffee."

"Of course," says Eleanor. "A soda." She should have said *juice*.

Even Eleanor tortures Giselle, though she tries hard not to. Giselle squinches her eyes and shakes her head. It's where Adam got the gesture. It would kill him to know that.

"Bullshit, Mom," says Adam, who has wedged behind Eleanor in the half-open door. "I fucking drink Red Bull."

"Adam!" says Giselle.

"Juice?" says Eleanor. "Orange juice?"

"Organic?" Giselle pleads.

"And an order of General Tsao's chicken," says Adam. "For one. Right, Mom?"

"Please, Adam, please don't." Giselle is practically whimpering.

"Back in fifteen minutes!" trills Eleanor, ignoring Roger's expression: the kidnap victim whose rescuer is leaving without hearing the cries from the basement. Roger and Giselle should be *thanking* Eleanor for doing their job.

Adam follows Eleanor out of the theater. The audience has fled. The only person around is a man with a long sad face who looks like Boris Karloff and seems to be waiting for someone.

"See ya, Frankenstein," Adam says, halfway down the block. "That freak is here every day."

How could Eleanor not have noticed? Because she's always running off to the hospital. She reminds herself to text Betsy, the head nurse, and say she'll be late.

Talking to Adam will be hard enough without having to

watch the clock. Eleanor takes Adam's arm, to hurry him. It's a shock to feel skin instead of nubbly chenille. She'd forgotten how short he is. His anger has made him seem taller. No wonder he's unhappy. Adam pulls away and follows her down the block to the café that says We're French by serving thin bitter coffee in awkward soup bowls.

Adam stands in front of the bakery counter and gapes at the croissants, apple tarts, macaroons.

"You've been here, right?" asks Eleanor. Wrong again.

"A billion times," lies Adam.

"What would you like, Adam?" Eleanor has learned, in her work in the ER, that it's helpful to say the patient's first name as often as she can without it seeming peculiar. In TV detective procedurals, the cops keep repeating first names— sometimes to comfort the victim, sometimes to extract a confession from the perp.

Most of the other nurses use surnames with adults, but Eleanor thinks it's a mistake. The Jamaican nurses say *honey* and *dear*, but Eleanor can't. And certainly not with Adam.

Adam says, "I'll take two of those almond thing-ies. And a large coffee. Black."

It's madness to let a testosterone-poisoned twelve-year-old stoke up on sugar and caffeine. He'll tell Giselle, if he thinks it might upset her. So what? One cup of coffee won't hurt. Let the kid feel grown-up.

"We only have one size ," says the barista, her white toque rakishly bobby-pinned to her jaggedly cropped ice-blue hair. Eleanor thinks, I used to be you, or a version of you. I used to be worse off than you. My dad was so cheap I had to clean up little-kid vomit from the rides at the local amusement park so I could have money to go to the movies.

Adam says, "Then I'll take whatever fucking size coffee you fucking have."

"Bad words!" says Eleanor.

Now the young woman looks at them. She sees a boy and a nurse. She raises her eyebrows, one more slowly than the other because of the piercings. By the time Eleanor has paid a shocking sum for their coffee and croissants, Adam has taken his bowl and plate to a table and is sitting with his back against the window. He has already eaten most of one pastry. He's got almonds and sugar all over his mouth. He looks defiantly at Eleanor.

"Hungry," she says.

"Fuck yeah. You try climbing around that theater like a tweaking chimpanzee when every second you know some cheap-ass construction could break and paralyze you forever. Did you know that chimpanzees fall from really high up in the jungle? And die?"

Sir, where does it hurt, sir? When did the pain begin? Honey, can you rate your pain on a scale of one to ten? In the ER, Eleanor would know what to say, but here, surrounded by strangers focused on trying to keep their coffee from dripping into their laptops, she doesn't know where to begin.

She has never looked at Adam this closely. Not even during "Monkey Tango." She always turned away, flashing the audience with her smile, belting out the lyrics. Mister Monkey is the smartest, cutest, nicest, strongest, most powerful chimp of all. Wasn't that enough for Mister Monkey? No. As it turned out, no.

Adam's skin is smooth, almost waxy, but the circles under his eyes give him the look of an aging, Satan-worshipping rock star. He's put on weight. He used to jump into Margot's

arms. Margot used to catch him. Gone forever, those innocent days.

Adam says, "Did you know that monkeys and humans
share ninety-eight percent of the same DNA? Do you know
that lots of monkeys can sing, and the male monkeys with the
best voices attract the most fertile females? Do you know
that male chimpanzees don't enter puberty until they're fifteen and that they sometimes eat infant baboons? Do you
know that chimpanzees have wars, and that a mother and
daughter chimp turned into serial psycho killers, murdering and eating babies? When I read that, I wanted . . . I just
wanted to just give up. Do you know that practically every
monkey in the wild, everywhere in the world, is in danger of
extinction because their habitats are disappearing? Do you
know that some monkey breeds will become extinct before
humans get a chance to even *see* them? Do you know that
when a chimpanzee is happy, his eyes sparkle like a human's?
Do you——"

"Interesting!" interrupts Eleanor. It suddenly seems possible that Adam could go on reciting monkey fun facts until
it's time to bring him back to Giselle. "No, I did not know any
of that. How do you know so much about monkeys, Adam?
Are you studying monkeys in school?"

"I don't go to school. I was kicked out. My private school
hated me so much they wouldn't take my dad's thirty-five
grand a year."

Eleanor would like to know why, but asking might further dampen Adam's mood. Giselle never mentioned Adam's
school. Usually that's the first thing New York parents tell
you, even in the ER, where you'd think it wouldn't matter.

"Me and my best friend Derek set the gym on fire. So
I'm being homeschooled." Finger-quotes around *schooled.*

Adam's got confectioners' sugar all over his plump little hands. Shouldn't a gymnast have calluses? The monkey suit, thinks Eleanor.

Adam's exaggerating. But *something* happened. Eleanor needs to stay focused on what he just did to Margot. She needs to gain his trust in order to get him talking. In that way, he's like a small grown man: he'll only listen if he's talking.

"Homeschooling . . . meaning you and your mom?" Eleanor takes a bite of croissant to chase away the tragic Old Master painting that's appeared, like a hologram, in her head: Adam and Giselle alone, at night, a dimly lit table covered with books. Adam is sleeping, or pretending to. Giselle sits there, sad and mystified, watching her son. A religious painting in an abandoned church.

"Right. Just me and mom. Plus of course Wikipedia to fill Mom's gaps. My mother has a lot of gaps, in case you haven't noticed."

"So what are you studying?"

"Monkeys," Adam says sourly. "Darwin." Adam looks at Eleanor to see how she's reacting.

Eleanor cannot think of one thing to say about Darwin. How stupid she's become! She needs to cut herself some slack. It's a lot: the hospital, *Mister Monkey*, and now trying to fix Adam for long enough to get through the final performances.

Adam says, "Want to know some interesting facts about bonobos?"

Eleanor knows where this is going. Once a famous opera singer came into the ER with tonsillitis; his doctor was in the Hamptons. He tricked Eleanor into agreeing that tonsils were a vestigial organ, so he could say, as he must have said to countless women: what about the clitoris, isn't that a vestigial organ? Eleanor had asked him to rate his pain on a scale of one to ten. "Six," he said, "sixty-nine," and laughed. Let Adam talk about bonobos. Talking is better than silence.

He takes a giant swallow of coffee and chokes, his brimming eyes trapped and mortified behind the scarlet face of a breathless boy.

Finally he says, "Little known fact. Bonobos are the only species besides human to have missionary sex. It's how they say hello. Welcome home. They let bonobo children hook up as soon as they figure out what goes where. Why couldn't Mister Monkey be a bonobo? Who would you rather live with, a bunch of bonobos feeling good? Or chimpanzees eating each other's babies? Or humans waterboarding each other and destroying the planet?"

"That's harsh," Eleanor says. "That's not all humans do." In the ER, this would be the moment when she'd quietly ask Adam, or his appropriate adult, if he was taking any medications . . . for example, for depression.

"What else?" demands Adam. "Build bridges? Fly drones? What do we do that's worth doing?"

"We write children's musicals about pickpocket chimpanzees."

One corner of Adam's mouth twitches. Coffee foam clings to his lower lip. He wipes his mouth with his paper napkin.

Eleanor says, as gently as she can, "Adam, what you've been doing onstage—you think that's how bonobos act?"

Adam stares into his coffee. "Okay. Maybe not. I was trying to work in some hip-hop moves I've been teaching myself in the gym where I work out."

"How often do you work out?"

"Not as often as I used to." He pokes both thumbs at his stomach, then pinches the roll of baby fat under his shirt.

Eleanor says, "Your body's constantly changing. In seven years you won't have one cell you have now." That's not exactly true, but it's the kind of thing kids like to believe. They can still turn into a whole new person.

"Change for the worse." Adam bites into his second pastry. "Can I ask you something? Do you have a boyfriend?"

"Not at the moment," Eleanor says. "To be honest with you, Adam, I've had plenty of boyfriends. I haven't had one for three, four years. And you know what? I'm working two jobs. I'm busy. I don't miss it. Maybe I'll have another boyfriend sometime. But why are we talking about *me*?"

Adam says, "Do you know that once this orangutan practically raped a human female? And that young male orangutans are practically constantly gang-raping female orangutans?"

Eleanor says, "Adam, you're not an orangutan. You're a human. And you can't keep doing what you're doing to Margot. Someone's going to get hurt."

Adam recoils, as if from a slap. It's the first time they've mentioned Margot. He turns and looks out the window for so long that Eleanor is losing hope of ever restarting the conversation when he turns back and says, "How old is she?"

"Who?" Eleanor knows who.

"Margot." Adam shuts his eyes when he says her name.

"Hard to tell. Early forties, maybe."

"That's what I figured," Adam says. "I Googled her and added five years."

"Why do you ask?" says Eleanor, though she knows that too.

"I think I love her," mumbles Adam so softly that Eleanor has to lean forward to hear. "Does that make me a totally sick person? She's like thirty years older than me."

"Not at all," says Eleanor. "When I was your age, I was in love with my science teacher and my drama teacher. That's why I'm doing what I'm doing today."

There was no science teacher, there was no drama teacher. Eleanor is saying whatever she thinks will make Adam feel less alone.

"I hate being a kid," says Adam.

"Try not to," says Eleanor. "You won't be a kid much longer. You won't be living with your mom all your life. Nothing stays the same."

"Whatever," Adam says. Then even more dubiously, "I'll try." He's heard what she has to say.

Eleanor should let it go, but she can't. There's one more clause in the treaty they need to hammer out together. "You can't keep sliming Jason and Danielle with spit or snot or whatnot."

"How do you even *know* about that? Did those bitches tell you?"

"We watch each other. We watch people. We're actors. That's what we do."

"I guess." Adam likes her calling him an actor.

At the table beside them are two elderly women, old friends. Eleanor wishes she could be having coffee with them. She wishes she was at work. She *is* at work. She's just supposed to be somewhere else.

It's a law of nature: at the worst possible moment, her phone chirps. At first she thinks it's Giselle, demanding she return Adam. But Giselle doesn't have her number. Eleanor declines the call, and when it buzzes back as a text, she sees that it's Betsy, from the hospital.

"My day job," she tells Adam.

Adam says, "You could make a fortune consulting for a

TV medical show. My mom met a woman who does that and is going to get me an audition."

"That's wonderful," Eleanor says.

"So could I ask you one more thing?"

"Depends." Eleanor braces herself.

"Why do you bother? You waste all that time and energy getting them breathing again or starting their hearts up when you know the polar ice caps are melting, and the city will be flooded or burn to a crisp, and the monkeys are disappearing forever, and everyone will either drown or die of thirst or both. So what the fuck?"

"Bad word," says Eleanor. "How's that going to play out? I'm sorry, sir, I'd like to help you with your gunshot wound, or your toddler who's eaten all the Tylenol, or Grandma's broken leg, but the world's going to end pretty soon so we can just do nothing and wait for the apocalypse."

Adam says, "I wasn't going to hurt Margot."

"I know that," Eleanor says. "But you could have broken her ankle."

She wishes she could forget the look on Margot's face when Adam grabbed her foot. She looked like someone remembering some past hurt and fear. Eleanor has seen a YouTube clip of Frances Farmer, the beautiful lobotomized actress, on the 1950s TV show *This Is Your Life*. You could watch her wondering how to arrange her face, how she was supposed to feel about the most important people in her life.

Early in rehearsals, Margot asked Eleanor out for coffee and got on the subject of some drama school production of *Uncle Vanya*. Right in this café, Margot did Sonya's final speech.

Embarrassing! Eleanor had always loved that speech, but Margot made it sound like bullshit. A life of service? *Meaning what*? Chekhov was a doctor, he'd worked through a cholera plague. He knew, and Eleanor knows, what service is.

Margot is a child of God, Eleanor reminds herself.

"Margot hates me now," Adam says. "I don't know why I'm so mean to her."

Eleanor says, "Sometimes we treat the people we love worse—" She stops in midsentence, appalled by the platitude burbling out of her mouth.

Adam looks as if a gunman has just burst in the door, but Eleanor knows the danger isn't in front of his eyes but behind them. His horror grows as tears well up, slowly at first, then faster, gelid and fat. Giselle would blame Eleanor for making him cry. Giselle should be having this conversation.

Eleanor wants to put her arm around Adam's shoulders, but her job in the ER has taught her how to tell who wants to be touched and who doesn't. Adam doesn't. He stops crying and drags his arm across his face.

He says, "At least you got to have your lives. You got to grow up. Every night I look out our window, at that view my mom is so crazy about, and I *see* the flood, like in some cheesy disaster movie where the dad tries to get his family to higher ground. If my dad saves anyone, it'll be Heidi and baby Arturo. But Dad won't even save *them*. He's not smart enough or brave enough or—"

Eleanor says, "My dad was the miser in the fairy tale. He made me work in an amusement park mopping up toddler puke."

Adam says, "Gross. Coney Island will go first. My dad isn't *that* bad. He gives me a twenty whenever I see him. Which isn't that often."

"I used to be like you," Eleanor says.

"I doubt it," Adam says. And he's right. She *was* angry. But she didn't grab someone's foot onstage. She didn't think the world was ending. The world didn't end.

"Want to see something?"

"Sure," Adam says uncertainly.

Eleanor stands and turns her back to him, raises the blouse of her scrubs, lowers the waistband slightly. Adam makes sure that the two women beside them are deep in conversation, then looks more closely at Eleanor's tattoo: a shattered bleeding heart encircled by a crown of thorns.

"That's a statement," Adam says.

"It was meant to be. That was my heart."

"So what happened?"

"Time passed. I like my life. I like the people I know. Even Roger. Even you."

"Even Margot?"

Eleanor wishes he weren't making her lie. She wishes he didn't know it.

"Margot too." A child of God. But she's not going to say that.

"There's so much time between now and when I'm grown up."

"It goes fast."

"And what do I do until then?"

Adam thinks there's so much time, but there's no time at all. Eleanor needs to be at work. She tries not to look at her phone.

She says, "You're an actor,"

"I guess," says Adam. "My friend Derek says I'm a poseur."

"Then he's jealous of you. And he's not your friend."

"That's what my mom says," says Adam.

"She's not wrong about everything. Give her some credit."

"The play's closing," Adam says. "So much for my acting career."

"It's not just this play. It's your life. Act like you don't think the world is ending. Act like you think it can be fixed." Eleanor wants to say: do it for the Fat Lady. But Adam would think she meant Giselle and, even if she could explain, it would deafen him to the rest.

Eleanor says, "You've got talent. You can have a fun life."

"Where? Underwater? Blue and with gills?"

"On planet Earth. Breathing oxygen."

Adam doesn't answer. They look down. The table is covered with crumbs. Eleanor looks Adam in the eye and flicks, or tries to flick, a crumb at him. The crumb sticks to the table.

"Goddammit," Eleanor says.

"You need the press-on nails," says Adam.

"That I do," says Eleanor.

In this café full of strangers, the nails are the secret that she and Adam share. The secret is that they are actors. Less than an hour ago Eleanor had long red nails and was scheming to put an innocent monkey in jail.

The story of Janice's fingernails is the story of their tribe. Eleanor and Adam have been doing something together, creating a world, the illusion of a world, the world that is *Mister Monkey*. That world has music and color, song and dance, villains and lovers and heroes. It transcends Roger's tyranny and vagueness, transcends Adam's feelings for Margot; transcends the group nervous breakdown occurring backstage. It is the consolation and the reward for what Adam is suffering at home. Janice's fingernails and Adam's monkey suit are all they need to make them, and the people who watch them, feel less alone.

Adam doesn't need to be punished or medicated. He needs to have faith and grow up and be less sad. Eleanor looks across the table at Adam, whose eyes are shining. With tears? With hope? With chimpanzee happiness?

"You'll be happy, I promise," Eleanor says.

"Okay, fine," says Adam. "I'll try to be more boring. Mom's got to be finished driving Roger nuts."

Eleanor says, "Roger's already nuts. I've got to go to work. You want me to walk you back to the theater?"

"Jesus Christ," Adam says. "I'm twelve. I can walk down the fucking block."

"Bad word," Eleanor says. "You promise you'll keep your shit together?"

Adam says, "I promise."

They get up and walk to the door. Eleanor leans down to kiss Adam's cheek, and Adam, his sad chubby face clenched tight, tilts his chin so she can reach.

ELEANOR MISSES THE crosstown bus and chases it to Seventh Avenue, where it pulls ahead. She runs the rest of the way to the hospital, rethinking her conversation with Adam, adding to it, improving upon it, telling him all the things she didn't think of, things she didn't have the time to say and probably wouldn't and shouldn't have said, if she'd had forever. Should she have told him that she understood something about him and his family because, on the night *Mister Monkey* opened, she'd seen his dad's brittle trophy wife kneel and pretend-hug Adam just to torture Giselle? Eleanor's glad she didn't say that. It would have made Adam feel worse.

Maybe she should have told him how her high school English teacher, whom she'd always despised, had assigned the class to read *Franny and Zooey*. She'd read and reread the section in which Franny repeats the Jesus prayer from the book in which a Russian pilgrim learns that constant repetition can synchronize the prayer with your heartbeat.

Eleanor wasn't going to waste her senior year repeating, Lord Jesus Christ, have mercy. But she'd liked the idea of something in tune with her heart.

That was what Roger was quoting when he'd told the cast to do it for the Fat Lady. Do your best, act your heart out for the Holy Spirit or Jesus or the Buddha or whoever you want to imagine is out there in the audience, watching the performance and caring what you do. For the one person out there for whom it is making a difference. That was something Adam could think about. Something he could try.

Eleanor doesn't believe in God, but she does believe that every living creature has a soul like a sparkler throwing off shards of light. She believes that everyone is a child of God, though she can't remember where she first heard that expression. She's afraid it might have been some horror film about a cult, or a Joni Mitchell song. But so what? She's made it her own, a cult of one, a cult in which she is the leader and the leader's only disciple.

It was almost like a science experiment she performed on herself. Whenever someone annoyed her, she would think, That person is a child of God. The algebra teacher who failed her was a child of God. The cop who nearly busted her and her friends for smoking pot in the park and made her friend give him a blow job, he was a child of God. Her miserly, mean, alcoholic father was a child of God. Her sad, delusional mother was a child of God.

Eleanor whispered it under her breath until she no longer had to think or say it, because it was always there, synchronized with her heartbeat. Child of God, Child of God. All of them children of God. It got her through college and drama school, and then, when it became apparent that the theater might not be the best place for someone who wants to keep believing that the world is populated by God's children, she'd decided to go to nursing school. That she can work in the ER and still find time to act, that she can put in the days and nights she puts in, is a sign that her beliefs have not only made her a better person but also have magically enabled her to have her cake and eat it.

How much could she have told Adam? It was better to keep it simple, to say what she said. Eleanor thinks she got through to him, but she's been wrong before. Almost exactly a year ago a Columbia freshman staggered into the ER. They got his blood alcohol level down and sent him back to his dorm, and a few days later his body washed up against the Morton Street pier.

It's bad luck to think about that, especially now that she's almost at work. But it's important to remember and never let happen again. One difference between the ER and the theater is: in the ER, mistakes matter more. You don't ask the director if you can incorporate them in your performance.

THE EMERGENCY ROOM has seasons that change with the weather and time and day of the week. In the fall and on Halloween and St. Patrick's Day, it's alcohol-poisoned college kids. In the winter more fractures; more overdoses and suicide attempts in early spring. Since St. Vincent's was razed to make room for condos, their territory has expanded. Now they see elderly tubercular bachelors from Chinatown, and West Village line chefs with lopped-off fingertips wrapped in dish towels. They don't get as many stabbings and gunshots as they do in the boroughs, but enough taxi and bicycle accidents, enough heart attacks and strokes to remind them of why they are there.

Eleanor's mood bumps up a notch when she walks past the guard desk. Cranky Clarence is on duty, but even he gives her a nod.

She loves the smell of the ER the way a farmer loves the smell of the earth, the sailor the salt of the sea. The sweet and sour bite of alcohol, floor soap, disinfectant, and something more organic, faintly rotten underneath. She loves the chemistry of panic overlaid with the hard-won patience and calm. The hospital is Eleanor's life. The theater is recreation. Outsiders talk about the adrenaline rush of working at the ER, but they're being reductive, distilling it down to one hormone.

Cure sometimes, heal frequently, comfort always. They've all heard that saying at some point during their first week of medical or nursing school. It's always seemed so much more useful than the curt, judgmental, unforgiving "First do no harm." How do you know you've harmed someone until it's too late? If Eleanor ever gets another tattoo, which she won't, it will say "Cure sometimes, heal frequently, comfort always," and she'll ask that the words be arranged in a rainbow arc above her shattered, bleeding tattoo heart.

The ER has jerks and egomaniacs, like everywhere else, but you meet fewer of them here than you do in the theater. Eleanor likes the people she works with. She's heard about nurses bullying other nurses, but she's never seen it.

Everyone loves Betsy, the intake nurse. Even people in pain, even the loved ones of people in pain, respond to the steady warmth with which Betsy looks at them, to her soothing, musical, islands accent, to how clear it is that she's listening and understanding and not just waiting for her turn to speak.

Betsy brings Eleanor up to speed. It's been a quiet Saturday afternoon, a welcome break before the circus of Saturday night. One playground fall, three stitches. Little League softball in the eye. Guy with asthma left his rescue inhaler at his girlfriend's house in Boston. A guy with kidney stones sobbed until they hooked him up to a morphine drip, and now he's on a gurney in the corridor telling everyone he loves them and how good at their jobs they are. Elderly dementia patient overdosed on Ambien, but not seriously. Eight-year-old boy with strep. College girl drank too much and couldn't get her hard contact lens out of one eye, but it was just a panic attack; the nice ophthalmology resident still here from the softball kid found the lens in no time. She gave him her phone number. Nobody died. No one was badly hurt.

Betsy asks how the play went.

Eleanor says, "Pretty crazy."

Betsy has seen the show. Eleanor got tickets for Betsy and her kids. She's gotten tickets for everyone on the staff who has kids. Knowing her coworkers were in the house made Eleanor self-conscious, but she got into being Janice, and everyone—or anyway, the kids—greatly enjoyed *Mister Monkey*.

"Chimpanzees can get crazy," Betsy says.

"Did you read my mind?" asks Eleanor.

"Just saying," Betsy says. "Remember that story about the chimp ripping his handler's face off over some birthday cake?"

"How could I forget?" Eleanor considers telling Betsy about Adam, asking her advice. But Betsy has enough to do without listening to Eleanor worry about a troubled child actor.

Betsy hands Eleanor a chart.

Leonard Marber, 67, chest pains. No previous cardiac history. Eleanor knows who he is: the distinguished-looking older gentleman in the waiting room who, not wanting to seem impatient, tried not to look too yearningly at her as she passed. She asks who did Mr. Marber's EKG, the bad technician or the good one?

"The good one," Betsy says.

Eleanor calls Mr. Marber, who gets up and follows her to her office.

He hoists himself onto the table with some effort but with the pride of a man who until lately was confident and strong. Eleanor listens to his chest with a stethoscope, but it's theater.

Most of what she needs to know is in the printout: a minor coronary hiccup. But he's at risk of something more serious in the not-so-distant future. She takes his blood pressure. It's 140 over 90, not great, and his pulse, which is racing.

Mr. Marber gratefully hops down when Eleanor suggests he'd be more comfortable in a chair.

"I read a quote from Sophia Loren," he says. "Someone asked her how she manages to seem so young, and she said the way to seem young was not to groan when you stand up."

"I'll remember that," says Eleanor. "Okay, let's see, Leonard. May I call you Leonard? Your blood work's mostly within the normal range. And this little thing—see this?—on your EKG?"

"Yes?" says Mr. Marber.

"An irregularity." She'll tell him what he needs to know, a little at a time. She doesn't want to scare him out of seeing a doctor. Men are so easily spooked. He needs a cardiology consult. Sooner rather than later.

"Nothing major," Eleanor says. "But I need to ask you some questions, Leonard, just to be on the safe side. We need to make sure we're not missing something, and regardless,

you'd probably be smart to make an appointment with a car-
diologist. Just to be on the safe side."

"On the safe side," Mr. Marber says. "You said that twice."

Eleanor says, "I guess I mean: just to be on the safe side."
She leans forward until their knees are almost touching.
"Leonard, do you remember when the chest pains began?"

"It must have been more than two weeks ago. I took my
grandson to the theater. That evening, at my daughter's
house, I had some . . . discomfort. Actually, now that I think
of it, that wasn't the first time, so it must have begun before.
I've had a hard few years. My wife died, I retired. By which I
mean they retired me."

"I'm sorry."

There's a pause.

Eleanor can't help asking, "What play did you and your
grandson see?"

"Do you have kids?"

"No," says Eleanor. "Not so far." Not ever.

"Then I don't imagine you would have heard of it. Maybe
even if you *did* have kids. A small neighborhood production
for children. Very modest, very low-key. A musical."

Which musical? Did he like it? Eleanor can't do this. They
need to get back to Mr. Marber's heart.

"It was called *Mister Monkey*." Mr. Marber laughs.

"Cool title, Leonard," says Eleanor. Of all the children's
musicals and all the emergency rooms in this enormous
city! What are the chances? Maybe Eleanor doesn't believe
in God, but she pictures a cosmic playwright with a weird
sense of humor setting up scenes like this one: unlikely coincidences, improbable events, good and bad surprises. What
are the odds of her patient's taking his grandson to see *Mister
Monkey* and not *The Lion King*?

It feels not merely unprofessional but dangerous to continue this line of questioning, and yet Eleanor asks, "Was it good? Did you and your grandson enjoy it?"

The old man sighs. "What can I tell you? Everybody was doing their best."

This is the moment to tell him, before he says something about the play that will make it awkward for her to admit that she was in it. She'll say, Believe it or not . . . I was Janice! She'll sing a few lines of her fingernail song. He'll be amazed by the coincidence. Unlike her fellow actors, he'll understand that she's not the character she plays. And he'll have an interesting story to tell his grandchild.

"And since then?" she says. "The pain?"

"Since then and before then," Mr. Marber says. "Want to hear a funny story about my grandson?"

"Sure!" Eleanor takes his wrist again. Just the idea of a funny story about his grandson has slowed his pulse, ever so slightly.

"It's about that play. *Mister Monkey*. Like I said, the cast was trying. The actors had some strikes against them. And I think even my grandson knew that the production had something . . . something *sad* about it. The actors were grinning like maniacs. The costumes were falling apart. And there were a couple of times when the lighting guy was . . ." Mr. Marber walks two fingers across the examining table, imitating the spotlight looking for the actors. Eleanor is supposed to laugh, but she can only fake a stiff-lipped monkey grimace.

"Anyhow my grandson, who by the way is the world's most polite and well behaved and thoughtful human being, I know I sound like just another proud grandpa, but you wouldn't believe how *conscious* a little kid can be . . . Anyway, one of the actresses drops her phone, and everyone is waiting to see what she'll do. And my grandson asks me, loud and clear, 'Grandpa, are you interested in this?'

"I know he didn't expect it to come out so loud. I don't think he noticed that the theater had gone silent. Maybe the acoustics were . . . I don't know. Everybody heard. The poor kid was mortified. I felt awful for the actors."

Mr. Marber laughs ruefully, but it's a laugh nonetheless.

What exactly did this old guy think would be *funny* about this story? Little Jesus blowing the whistle on a pathetic production? Is this meant to amuse people who haven't been to the play, who haven't been *in* the play, who haven't put *everything they have, their hearts and souls* into their performance? Is his little anecdote intended to give people a chuckle because an innocent child told the truth about a group of underpaid, brave, disappointed actors? How can he not understand that this "sad" production is part of these people's *lives*?

She presses the lever on the metal canister that releases a cotton ball. She squeezes the cotton, worries it between her fingers. She rubs her fingertips with her thumb and tries to recover the feeling of putting on her press-on nails. Poor Margot. Poor Roger. Poor Leonard. Poor Lakshmi. Poor Leonard Marber's grandson. Poor everyone. Cure sometimes, heal frequently, comfort always.

Children of God. Leonard Marber is a child of God. Leonard and his grandson are the Fat Ladies for whom they were performing.

"What did you tell him?" Eleanor asks. "*Were* you interested in the play?"

"I said yes. I was. Very. But maybe not for the usual reasons. Maybe not for the reasons the cast would have preferred."

Eleanor pretends to have to write something on Mr. Marber's chart. He thinks that *Mister Monkey* . . . he thinks *the whole show* was about some adorable thing his grandson said.

Strangely, or not so strangely, she remembers that afternoon. How unnerving the child's outburst was. They all heard his question. It threw everyone off.

Actually, come to think of it . . . things went downhill from there. Adam got more rambunctious, Margot more fearful and depressed. It all began at that show. Would Mr. Marber like to know *that*? Would that put a new spin on his *funny story*?

Or maybe he would like to know how much time she just spent talking to the sad little boy who plays Mister Monkey, reconciling him to the end of a childhood and to a future no sane person would choose. Grandpa, are you interested in this? What if Adam was your grandson?

What would it do to Mr. Marber's heart rate if she said that she was in the musical that he just insulted with his patronizing and oh-so-thoughtful and gently humorous bad review? She cannot let that happen. Eleanor closes her eyes. She is not here to care what this man thought of a play she was in. She is here to help this child of God.

She takes Mr. Marber's forearm and looks into his eyes. He's not used to it, and it startles him, but after a moment he likes it. Eleanor works to communicate what she actually feels, which is warmth and goodwill. She's not insulted. She means him no harm.

She just wants to tell him how strange this is.

If this becomes another one of his funny stories, or a funny coda to the funny story about his grandson at the theater, it will remind him of where (the hospital!) this part of the story happened and of what Eleanor (a nurse!) advised him to do. Like those pillboxes with alarms that remind the elderly when to take their meds.

Eleanor says, "Okay. This is crazy. A crazy coincidence. You're not going to believe this. And I need to tell you that this is not about what you thought of the play. That's not my point."

"Now I'm scared," says Mr. Marber. Is there a microflirtation in this? Mr. Marber hears it too, and is more shocked by this than he could possibly be by whatever Eleanor is going to tell him.

"When I'm not doing this, I'm an actress. I was in that play. I played Janice, the evil girlfriend . . ."

Mr. Marber looks hard at her. "Wait. You're right. Minus the fingernails. A crazy coincidence. Like you say. How amazing. That was you. You did a wonderful job! Really, I mean it. The thing I didn't say was that you were fun to watch, the way a good actress is fun to watch.

"The kids and the grown-ups liked you. I'm sorry for what I said about the play. But my grandson didn't mean *you*. I'm sure even he knew you were good."

"Thank you," she says uncertainly. She lets go of his hand but manages to make it feel like he's let go of hers.

He says, "I read about you in the program. You know, the program kind of surprised me. In my day the actors' program bios were lists of credits. But these were award ceremony speeches. Thanks and a big shout-out to my vocal coach and my mom and dad."

Eleanor's bio in the program has none of that, and is, she'd thought, the most professional and impressive. A lot of small productions. Brief but interesting projects. The longest run she'd had was as Pirate Jenny in a hip, critically successful off-off-Broadway revival of *The Threepenny Opera*.

Mr. Marber says, "That actress who played the lawyer. Her performance was very . . . unusual, in that purple suit and that wig . . ."

Another fan of Margot's. What appeal does Margot have for these guys, one twelve, one sixty-seven? There's nothing enviable about Margot's life, yet Eleanor feels a dispiriting twinge of something like sexual competition.

"How could something like this happen?" Mr. Marber says. "First I take my grandson to your play and then I have chests pains and come here instead of——"

"Stranger things happen," Eleanor says. "They happen all the time. New York's a small town. You know what? You should take a photo of us. On your phone. For your grandson."

"A selfie," says Mr. Marber. "I don't know . . ."

"I'll take it," says Eleanor. "On your phone. And you can show him. *If* you promise you'll go right out to the reception desk and make an appointment for more tests."

"I promise," says Mr. Marber.

Eleanor believes him. The coincidence is a good omen. The snapshot of himself with evil girlfriend Janice/friendly Nurse Eleanor will be a lucky charm, protecting him from harm. Nothing bad can happen to a man who has, on his phone, a picture of himself with a nurse-actress from a play he saw with his grandson.

"I can't wait to show Edward," he says. "Can I ask you something?"

Eleanor likes Mr. Marber, but if this is going to be about the grandson, she's beginning to wonder how many patients are out in the waiting room.

"I've been worried about my grandson." That Mr. Marber has no one else he can talk to is information that should go into his chart.

"Worried how, Leonard?"

"Something happened at his school. His class got into

a discussion about evolution. Some parents got upset. His teacher, whom he loves, almost got fired, but the principal stood up for her, and the fuss died down. My grandson blames himself. Some things he's said . . . I know. His parents have no idea. He's been throwing up a lot, but the doctors say nothing's wrong.

"The strange thing is, he blames his dinosaurs. He used to be crazy about dinosaurs. You know how kids can be."

Eleanor says, "They're big, and they're dead."

"Exactly," says Mr. Marber. "Edward knew everything about them. He'd say, Ask me one thing I don't know about dinosaurs. He had a big collection we kept in my apartment. In my late wife's jewelry box. But last week he came over and dumped the dinosaurs in the garbage and turned on the TV. The dinosaurs were dead to him. Extinct. First the dinosaurs, then the humans."

His chuckle means: we're doomed.

"Kids outgrow things." Eleanor hopes no one's waiting outside.

It's been quite a day. First Adam attacking Margot, then the heart-to-heart with Adam, then this, and everybody talking about the end of the world. She doesn't want children. A person only has so much to give. It's better to know your limits. If she regrets her decision later, she'll deal with it then. Worrying about the future—the way children make you worry—will compromise her ability to be useful right now. Cure sometimes, heal frequently, comfort always. Play Janice in *Mister Monkey*.

"He's the love of my life," the grandfather says. "He'll never love me as much as I love him. He's my unhappy love affair. My first. I guess you're never too old."

"Children heal quickly." When did Eleanor go from sitting to standing up? She looks down at her hand, which seems to have alighted on the grandfather's shoulder.

She says, "Whatever happened at school, with the dinosaurs, he'll get over it. Or he won't. It could be one of those things he'll never forget."

"That's what I'm afraid of," Mr. Marber says.

Eleanor says, "Don't be afraid."

[C H A P T E R   1 0]

T H E   M O N K E Y   G O D   (M I S T E R

M O N K E Y)   D R E A M S   T H E   F U T U R E

JUST BECAUSE MISTER MONKEY is a chimpanzee and a
celestial being doesn't mean that there aren't things he likes
and doesn't like about himself. He likes the story about him
eating the sun because he mistook it for a mango, though to
be perfectly honest he would have preferred a mango. He
likes the story about him setting the island on fire because
his enemies were stupid enough to tie a burning branch to
his tail.

He likes the story about how he reunited the god Rama
with his beloved Sita, but he's not sure he likes the part where
he opened his chest to show the world that he *literally* had
the god and goddess, Rama and Sita, inside his heart. When
it comes to the heart, three's a crowd, and his monkey heart
has enough trouble containing the human emotions inside it,
always brimming over and threatening to overspill. Only the
heart of the monkey god is large enough to contain the hearts
and souls of all the monkeys, all the humans, the gods, every
shining thread that connects them.

He doesn't like the story about the curse that makes him
forget his superpowers until someone reminds him. He
doesn't like how dependent it makes him on other peoples'

memories. What if no one remembers? Will his powers be lost forever? And he won't even know it.

In his opinion this is the absolute worst part of being a monkey god: not to know what kind of god you are, or that you are a god, until you are reminded by someone else.

But there's nothing he can do to remove the curse—the curse that all the other gods have conspired to put on him. Forever.

He also doesn't like the story about his biting a human's face off, over a piece of birthday cake. He doesn't like being negatively compared to the happy sexy bonobos. And he *really* doesn't like *Mister Monkey the Musical*.

Except, that is, for one beautiful line, a line that is like a prayer.

In his experience, the children in the audience cannot make any sense of the play. None whatsoever. It's okay to steal wallets as a party trick? But it's not okay to steal them for real? Except that Mister Monkey didn't really steal a wallet. The woman with the fingernails made that up.

And when the truth comes out, everything's fine, and everybody goes right back to happy-funny monkey-human life, except that the pretty redhead goes to jail. Any kid in the audience who pretends to be interested is faking it, he's lying, and Mister Monkey hates lies, perhaps because in his monkey-god trickster career he has been forced to tell so many.

Nor does he like the part about Mr. Jimson and his kids. Why couldn't the antimonkey genius who wrote the play have given him monkey brothers and sisters? He's seen a play about monkeys in Japan in which every primate had loving siblings.

He hates the part about being taken from his home, about his parents' murder. In real life they prosecute people who keep monkeys as pets. The authorities take the monkeys away and send them to live on refuges funded by wealthy American universities. He's supposed to "get over" being orphaned and kidnapped, "healed" by singing one bullshit song about the moon. He should eat the fucking moon like a fucking mango.

And he's supposed to believe that Mr. Jimson and the kids are great, his heroes, his saviors, his adoptive family, how cute and chic to have a monkey. They must have a special variance passed by the city of New York, to say nothing of permission from their co-op board. They might as well be in league with the poachers. A maid taking care of him means what? Does the sexy Carmen comb his fur for nits as gently as his monkey mom did? Meanwhile around the world his cousins, if he has any cousins left, are being slaughtered and starved and forced out of their disappearing habitats and sent into lifelong incarceration and exile.

Mister Monkey tries not to think about that, just as he tries not to think about the ridiculous lie that humans are more highly evolved than monkeys. He can fly through the air, he can swing from the trees, he can survive in the jungle. And what can humans do? Hold bogus trials and put on plays and kill monkeys so other humans can drill for oil and destroy the planet.

There is so much that Mister Monkey doesn't want in his mind: the sufferings of the confused and frightened child actor Adam, who is his current iteration on earth. The sadness of Adam's mother and of the actress he torments onstage.

Mister Monkey imagines the teacher Miss Sonya taking a sleeping pill, and (supposedly unevolved creature that he is!) he sees so deeply into Miss Sonya's mind that it's as if he has taken the pill himself, and he falls asleep.

Mister Monkey loves to sleep. Because he dreams about the future.

He sees Ray and Lauren at breakfast in their sunny kitchen. Lauren is pregnant, and though Mister Monkey considers himself a rebel, he is glad to see that Lauren and Ray are wearing wedding rings.

He is alarmed to see Miss Sonya with cats. But there is a child, Miss Sonya's child, squeezing the cat until Miss Sonya rescues the cat, and then he sees her in a classroom full of children who adore her.

He barely recognizes Adam in the tomato juice commercial. He's older, he is more like his true self, doing midair somersaults in the sneaker commercial, taking circus classes in drama school.

Giselle marries a widower she meets at a Battery Park City neighborhood Christmas party, and stays married long after Adam's dad has left Heidi and Arturo.

Mister Monkey loses track of Mr. Marber in the dead of night, in the bed he used to share with his wife. But he sees the grandson Edward receiving a high school science award on a stage and thanking his late grandfather for introducing him to dinosaurs and monkeys. The mention of the grandfather brings tears to the eyes of the grandson's parents, and to the eyes of many people in the audience. Mister Monkey (the Monkey God) likes that. It gives him a hopeful feeling about the future, even in the sort of dream in which he is watchful because he doesn't know what comes next.

He sees Lakshmi sewing, surrounded by clothes, pooled rich fabrics and silks. The Monkey God would like to think that she is making costumes for a spectacular extravaganza about a monkey. He has a vision of Eleanor in the emergency room, onstage, until the sound of applause turns into the rustling of plant stalks outside a Buddhist temple where she has gone to pray.

For some reason Roger, Margot, and Mario refuse to visit Mister Monkey, to enter his dream. He doesn't care. His dream is crowded enough. Perhaps he will catch sight of them when he falls asleep tomorrow. He will find out about them later.

What he wants is to wake up now, so that he can think about *Mister Monkey the Musical.*

With his head tilted back on his jeweled gold throne, he goes over the scenes in his head. The lyrics, the dances, the songs, all of which are garbage.

But there is one line that he listens for, one sentence shouted by the whole cast at the end of the first big dance number that he waits for. He listens for it, so excited that he can hardly breathe until he hears it.

"Mister Monkey is the smartest, cutest, nicest, strongest, most powerful chimp of all."

That is the single greatest line in the play. In any play. It is like a prayer.

Mister Monkey is the smartest, cutest, nicest, strongest, most powerful chimp of all.

When he hears that, it breaks the spell.

He remembers his superpowers.

CHAPTER 11

ROGER THE DIRECTOR

A BISHOP IS sailing from Archangel to the Solovetsky Monastery.

He sees a tiny island in the distance and asks the ship's captain about it. The captain tells him that the island is inhabited by three hermits: bearded, filthy, ragged, silent, devoted to saving their souls.

Against the captain's advice, the bishop hires a boatman to ferry him to the island, where he finds the hermits just as described. When he asks how they are saving their souls, the oldest hermit replies that they work and pray. And how do they pray?

Three are we. Three are thee. Have mercy.

The bishop realizes that they know something about the Holy Trinity, but they are praying all wrong. He offers to teach them how to say the Lord's Prayer correctly. Our Father who art in heaven hallowed be thy name. And so on. First one, then the second, then the third make many stupid mistakes. A whole day passes before the hermits get it right. But finally they can say it. Night has fallen by the time the bishop returns to his boat.

Standing on deck, he's gazing over the water, feeling good about a day well spent, when suddenly he sees a speck of light, glowing over the sea. The light grows brighter and larger and is rapidly approaching.

It's the three hermits, hand in hand, radiant, running over the surface of the water. They've forgotten the Lord's Prayer! As long as they kept repeating it, everything was fine. But they lost one word, then another . . .

The bishop replies that their prayer will reach God; it's not for him to teach them. He says, "Pray for us sinners," and bows low before the hermits, who turn and fly back across the sea. And a light shines until dawn at the spot where they disappeared from sight.

TOLSTOY'S "THE THREE HERMITS" is Roger's morning prayer. Everywhere Muslims are bowing toward Mecca, Jews going to temple, Catholics to confession. The Carmelite nuns and the Buddhist monks have been up for hours, chanting.

The story lifts Roger in its arms and carries him back to his childhood in Brooklyn, to his Russian grandmother, whom he loved above all the world. He has never loved anyone so much. His grandmother who made pickles in the family washing machine, and cherry brandy in summer, until one day the family found her lying on her back on the basement floor, beside the washer, her mouth to the hose from which dark brandy dripped. The grandmother who every Easter filled the kitchen with sweet cheese puddings made in flower pots, with flaky dough crescents covered in powdered sugar, who every Sunday took him to the Orthodox church in Brownsville or Bushwick before it was Bushwick, where you prayed standing up, listening to the deep low chanting of the men's choir in the stall high above the altar.

The worshipers were all taller than Roger, and as it got hotter, acolytes ran around with ice water and smelling salts for the ones who fainted. One summer morning Roger passed out. Just before he slumped to the floor, overwhelmed with sleep, he saw the church and everyone in it covered with glittering mirrors and light and the edge of a white bird's wing, reflected kaleidoscopically, an infinite number of times. He looked up to find himself surrounded by adults looking down.

Roger sits up in his bed, in his small but sunny and miraculously rent-controlled apartment on West 11th Street, with his pug Ilya on his lap, and a cup of excellent coffee, and tells himself the story of the three hermits. It's like one of those vocal warm-ups that, to tell the truth, he's never liked hearing actors do: all those embarrassingly visceral grunts and howls. The story of the three hermits is Roger's prayer and his workout, his daily affirmation. Unsurprising that a story about repetition should derive its power from repetition. Three are we. Three are thee. Have mercy.

The story of the three hermits is his kale salad, his lemon juice and warm water: more effective than the faddish crap his actors swear by because they read about it when they're getting their hair styled. It's his *ritual*, though he hates that word, along with *custom* and *tradition*: hocus-pocus designed to speed us into the grave.

Such a simple story, but how generous with its consolations. When he forgets something, which has been happening so often that, he knows, the cast thinks he's losing his mind, he comforts himself by thinking of the trouble that the hermits have with the Lord's Prayer. His brain has begun the process of sifting the gold from the straw. The story of the three hermits is better for Roger's blood pressure than for his work in the theater, but the story is the sweet spot in his day before he must leave his apartment and go to his job breathing life into the cold dead corpse of *Mister Monkey*.

The production was cursed, the way theater people believe *Macbeth* to be cursed. *Mister Monkey Macbeth*. When Linda, who is producing along with her husband, Dave, called and asked him to direct, Roger didn't bother asking who had been fired or quit. Nor did he try to find out. He'd done *Mister Monkey* once before, so he was the logical choice, whereas he can't afford to be choosy.

The last time he did *Mister Monkey* he had asked the cast how many of them had read the book when they were kids. No one had, and he'd learned his lesson. This time he asked a harder question so that it would be less disappointing when no one knew.

How many of them had heard of Raymond Ortiz? Not one hand went up. Roger explained that Raymond Ortiz was a Vietnam vet from the Bronx, who didn't set out to write a book for kids, but the god of children's musical theater had other plans for *Mister Monkey*. Possibly only Rita had ever been to the Bronx, and even she was wondering where Roger was going with this.

Recalling those early rehearsals, Roger feels something like the chagrin with which he remembers desperately loving young men who turned out to be not worth his love, social climbers and geishas who saw Roger, during his brief golden moment, as a step up the ladder toward someone more successful and famous.

His life (by which he is afraid he means *his pride*) depends on doing his best, even with this silly children's musical. How hard he'd tried to make the cast sympathize with Mister Monkey or at least have strong feelings. Perhaps if they'd liked Adam more . . . He'd shown them a film about poachers killing gorillas, and a video about animals trained to help the elderly and the crippled. *That* went over their heads. They don't have pets, they live in small apartments. Pets urinate in their hallways and defecate on their doorsteps. Roger's the one with the beloved dog, and no one ever asks, How's Ilya?

In those first days his throat hurt, and his fingers ached from snapping them at the cast. He preached about the power of words, about hard work, about telling the stories of the tribe. He exhorted them to push themselves harder. Do it for the Fat Lady. He was referring to *Franny and Zooey*, of course, with its stirring explanation of the reason, the only reason, to go out there and act your heart out.

No one caught the reference, and Roger lost the will to explain after dumb-ox Eric told the others that he was referring to *The Catcher in the Rye*. During the first weeks Roger so wanted the play to do well that he'd gone into the lobby after the show and shaken the audience members' hands and thanked them for having come. But so few people could look him in the eye, and when they did he was so unnerved by what he saw that he gave up. Now he cowers in his office until Giselle arrives.

Every so often Roger needs to step back and get his bearings, to remind himself of who he is and of everything that he's accomplished. Instead he swims like a salmon upstream against the current of his own better judgment, against the wisdom of bad and good experience. He has denied the obvious all through those early rehearsals, determined to wring something real and new out of this troupe of the walking dead that rose from the ashes of open auditions for *Mister Monkey*.

In desperation, he told them about the dog tried by jury and hung in England, a century ago. If Mister Monkey had been a Victorian . . . Roger should have quit right then when

Danielle screamed, and Giselle covered Adam's ears and whined about euthanizing puppies.

Only Eleanor seems to have some feeling for Mister Monkey—or perhaps for Adam—though she is the one who's supposed to be trying to send him to jail. Doubtless her day job in the ER has helped Eleanor develop more compassion. In Roger's opinion Eleanor is from a higher species. She is a saver of lives. Nothing they do can approach the good she does. Some days they are artists, some days they are entertainers.

Some days, not even that. Some days the stage swarms with soulless, monkey-tango-dancing zombies. Roger has had to detach himself, to wean himself from the warm milky breast of hope, and to pretend (at least to himself) that there is some higher purpose to this communal sabotage of a moronic text and a tuneless score. Roger's no stranger to failure. But during this production he's become newly acquainted with guilt, remorse, and a new set of weights on his conscience.

One of those weights is Lakshmi. Roger wants to believe that there was nothing more he could have done to save her job or persuade her to stay and work for free and a great recommendation, which he'll give her anyway. When Linda and Dave told him they were shutting down the play, they told him to slash the final weeks' budget. Quit giving the kids free booster seats, let them sit on Mom's lap. When Roger said there wasn't one more cent he could trim, they asked to see the spread sheets. Tipped with a nail that cost as much as Lakshmi's weekly stipend (no one could call it a salary), Linda's finger skimmed down the columns and stabbed the line that said "costume department."

Linda and Dave had never seen the need to have a costume department for a production in which everyone but

Margot and Adam could just wear their own clothes. From the moment Roger hired Lakshmi, even as she was excitedly designing Mister Monkey's nubbly suit, Roger has been preparing for the day when he would have to fire her.

Roger worries about Lakshmi. When one of her musical-loving dads came backstage for a casual chat (actually, a lecture) about Hanuman, the Hindu monkey god, Roger had the distinct impression that the guy was cruising him. Twice Roger has met Lakshmi's boyfriend, who—even allowing for Roger's diminished ability to understand the young—seems like a grifter, a pervert, and a creep.

One night Roger saw Lakshmi leaving the theater in her police uniform. She claimed that wearing a clown-cop suit made her feel safe on the subway. Roger caught the musky scent of some sexual weirdness involving the boyfriend. After Lakshmi left the show, the intern who filled in for her couldn't find the police outfit. Roger wasn't surprised to learn that Lakshmi had taken it with her.

The heavier drag on his conscience is Margot. Roger knows he's been unfair. He's ashamed of the satisfaction he gets from ignoring her suggestions, from not trying to hide his contempt. There is no excuse for his bad behavior. He is honestly baffled by his impulse to make her unhappy. He's spent enough years in therapy to suspect that he can't forgive her for being a dark mirror of his own worst fears about, and for, himself—loneliness, mediocrity, age, failure—and for what he and Margot share in common: their undignified refusal to go gently into that good night of children's musical theater.

Margot enlisted Lakshmi in her case against Roger for making her wear that costume, but he stands by that decision: it loosens up the crowd. The audience response is more welcoming and jollier than any she would have gotten in her vintage Armani pants suit and her butch-cut red hair.

Roger can feel his shoulders tense every time Margot walks onstage. Why can't she see her outfit as Beckett-inspired children's theater avant-garde with a nod to Dada, instead of through the microlens of her vanity and self-involvement?

Even Eleanor believes that Roger's failure to control Adam—who has gotten somewhat aggressive since the start of the show—is because Roger doesn't care about Margot or about what Adam does to Margot. But that's not true. Roger knows that Adam has gone off the rails, and he's made at least one concession for the general good of the cast: banning Adam from doing his acrobatics during Margot and Eric's cell phone duet, though the audience had been grateful for something to watch while Margot and Eric sang.

The truth is that Roger has been fascinated by what Adam is doing with the paradoxically predictable and implausible role of the orphaned chimp. As Roger told Eleanor, they were watching adolescence happen in real time. Onstage. Who would have imagined that something so rich and complex could be mined from tapped-out *Mister Monkey*? Roger hasn't asked Adam to dial it down, because he doesn't want to know if what Adam's doing is the result of hormonal madness or a considered artistic choice.

If Adam's gone mad, it's Giselle's fault, though Roger knows that it's no longer socially permissible to blame the overburdened single mom. Why is Roger so intimidated by tragic, powerless Giselle? His fear of her has intensified along with Adam's testing behavior. Maybe it isn't fear at all, but a frightening sort of pity, as if he and Giselle are complicitous in a crime. Roger is guilty of not persuading her and Adam to turn themselves in. Roger can't bear to be in the same room with her, and yet they are often together, in his office, so Giselle can administer an extra dose of pain after each performance. Does he have a minute? Could she get a few notes about Adam? How can Roger refuse that suffering human being? The Fat Lady made flesh.

ON THE DAY that Adam grabs Margot's foot and makes them all aware of how recklessly they are flirting with disaster, Giselle again asks Roger if he has a minute. Good. She is finally going to ask for help with her son. Roger wishes she wouldn't bring him into this, and yet he can't say no.

Giselle takes the only chair. She's got something folded under her arm that she drapes carefully across her lap. Adam's monkey costume. Roger thinks of the knife-pleated Stars and Stripes they give the families of dead soldiers. Who would believe that a monkey suit could be folded with such precision?

Seeing the costume causes Roger a pang of grief over Lakshmi. How inspired to have fashioned the costume out of a brown chenille bedspread! Roger should have offered to pay her out of his own puny wages.

Giselle looks at Roger expectantly. If there was ever a moment to suggest counseling, this is it. Someone to talk to, an outsider, a professional specializing in early adolescence. Roger has heard Giselle disparage the therapist in whom Margot places such faith. Roger should tell Giselle that in the past he himself has been greatly helped by therapeutic intervention.

That's what a responsible person would say. But Roger is not a responsible person. He is a man who is getting old and tired and wants to get through the next two weeks with minimal offstage drama. Let Giselle deal with Adam. Let *Mister Monkey* die a merciful death.

Whenever Giselle is in his office, he shrinks as far from her as he can, until he's backed into a corner. Of course, she notices, and Roger feels badly about it. But his retreat is a reflex. Self-protective. He and Giselle are repelled by reverse animal magnetism.

The door flies open, and lovely energetic Eleanor bursts in, wearing her hospital scrubs. She's come to cart Giselle and Adam away to a mental ward!

Eleanor asks Giselle if she can please borrow Adam and go get a cup of coffee.

That lucky bastard Adam! What did *he* do to deserve this, except almost hurt another actor onstage? Why couldn't Roger be going out with Eleanor to drink coffee and talk about the play and Roger's career and Eleanor's life in the ER? That would be so much more fun than remaining prisoner to Giselle's delusional plans for Adam. Now he'll be stuck here with Giselle until Adam returns.

Giselle looks as if Eleanor is pointing a gun at her son. She's too shocked to think of one good reason why Eleanor can't take Adam out for coffee.

No coffee! Okay, juice. Organic juice, Eleanor promises, with a parting look at Roger, a blank beat of holding his gaze that functions like an eye roll.

The door slams shut. His rescuer has departed and left him to his captor's mercy.

What is Giselle saying? Roger finds it hard to think when there so many things that he is trying not to think about. For example, his life. His teachers, the lectures he went to, the plays he saw performed by talented actors in people's living rooms. Stella Adler, Sanford Meisner, Uta Hagen. He took classes with them or at least heard them speak. There's no one like them now. The technique. The exercises. The inspiring talks about art and the body, about breath, about every word having meaning. About letting the words do the work. What exactly are the hard-working words? Mister Monkey is innocent. Mister Monkey is the smartest, cutest, nicest, strongest, most powerful chimp of all!

Everything used to be about *the work*, on which Roger still places great value. He believes that every production has a spark that can be fanned into life. But he has grown too shortsighted or exhausted or lazy to see the flicker in this one, except for the hellish runway lights along the catwalk Adam is strutting. Roger is the only one thinking about the play— the only one who has ever thought about the play. The others are already planning their getaway, the next step. Where in God's vast universe can they go after *Mister Monkey*?

There's been work to do, and Roger has done it. Musical numbers had to be staged, on a *very* minimal budget. Spark or no spark, it's proceeded more or less smoothly. No one has fallen or gotten hurt, the cast has delivered their lines, and mostly the spotlight has found them, though sometimes it's taken a couple of tries. Adam's become a loose cannon, but the run is almost over. Maybe Eleanor will figure out some temporary fix that will allow them to make it through until the end.

Giselle is mumbling about how New York audiences would be *fascinated*, theatergoers all over the world would flock to see the amazing results when two young gymnasts, one American, one Chinese, threw themselves into a music, dance, and acrobatic spectacle based on *Monkey*, the Chinese folk classic that she has been studying with Adam. What Giselle has in mind is *a much bigger production*, more like a Lincoln Center kind of thing. They could partner with a Chinese cultural foundation. Adam and his Chinese counterpart could alternate scenes in an "unforgettable" spectacle about the monkey god.

Roger says, "Great idea, Giselle. But don't the Chinese already do this? Don't they have companies that come over here every so often and play Lincoln Center? They have ads all over the subway and even on TV."

"This would be different," says Giselle. "That's my point. This would be a partnership: an American-Chinese project. *Monkey: Bridging the Gap.*

"And here's the beauty part, Roger. We gather up all those brilliant Chinese musicians you see playing *in* the subway. And we put them in an orchestra along with musicians we've brought over from China. Bridging the gap. Am I right?"

Giselle is watching columns of acrobats spinning and twirling ribbons, rope dancers twisting in midair, choruses crooning Chinese lullabies as Adam cartwheels onto the stage in a magnificent embroidered monkey costume and a mask fit for an emperor's New Year's party. He does more handsprings and midair somersaults on his way to meet his Chinese counterpart . . .

After an eternity there's a knock.

"Come in," Roger says belatedly. No one ever knocks.

The door opens, and Adam walks in.

"Hi, Mom. Hi, Roger," he says.

Giselle and Roger stare at him as if he's made some shocking announcement. Something's changed in his face, something's shifted, a slight alteration most people wouldn't register unless they'd been monitoring the scowl that's been darkening daily. He looks less enraged, more boyish—more *normally* aggrieved—than he has since the first rehearsals when he sighed and rolled his eyes when Giselle complained about the imaginary dust mite infestation.

Bless you, Eleanor, thinks Roger.

"Where's Eleanor?" Giselle demands. The flake who's abandoned her son.

The saint who healed him, thinks Roger. For now.

"She had to go to work," Adam says.

"She works in the ER," Roger says.

"Everyone knows that, Roger," says Giselle. "Anyway, think about it, Roger. Will you think about what I said?"

"Yes," say Roger. "Of course."

Giselle gives her son's monkey costume one more loving fold and slides it into her fringed bag.

"See you tomorrow," says Giselle.

As he allows his mother to steer him out of Roger's office, Adam looks back and says, "See you tomorrow, Roger."

By the time Roger leaves, a short while later, he assumes the coast will be clear, that the cast will be long gone. So he's surprised to see Margot talking animatedly to a man, standing on the sidewalk not far from the theater.

Roger stifles the impulse to rush off in the other direction. Instead he stops and watches Margot and the man, at whom she is smiling. She is gesturing with both hands, making half twists in the air.

Margot's wearing jeans and a sweatshirt. Her red hair stands up in tufts that make her look like a child just awoken from sleep. Like a girl, Roger thinks. Though maybe he just thinks that because the man is so much taller, with the long sorrowful face of a saint in an El Greco painting.

Margot sees Roger and smiles and waves him over. There is no way out.

She says, "This is Mario. We've just met. He's a fan. He's seen the show three times. Mario's the guy who sent me that letter you gave me backstage. That letter in the envelope. Remember?"

The tall man—Mario—looks at Roger, pleadingly. Mario has no idea what letter Margot is talking about. But if Roger knows, and if he knows that Mario is not the person who sent it, Mario's begging Roger: please don't tell.

Obviously this letter means a lot to Margot. She wants to think that this guy wrote it. And he's interested in Margot. That much Roger can see. Later the two of them can sort out the truth and correct the misunderstanding.

Roger remembers the letter. Of course he does.

ROGER WROTE IT.

All that week, he'd been lying awake at night, thinking of how to tell Lakshmi, when it came time, that he'd have to let her go. Finally he remembered how, near the start of his career, he'd been fired from a summer stock production of *The Seagull*. He'd been doing fine as assistant stage manager. He still doesn't know why he lost the job. Someone didn't like him.

The producers were sorry. One of them, a grand old lady of the theater by the name of Ruth Peabody—Roger will never forget her—gave him a note on which she'd typed the quote from Chekhov. "Failures and disappointments make time go by so fast that you fail to notice your real life, and the past when I was so free seems to belong to someone else, not myself."

Roger has never forgotten how that quotation had taken away the sting. Like those sticks one rubs on insect bites. And it had occurred to him that he could do Lakshmi the same favor.

He typed out the quotation from Chekhov and folded the paper and put it in an envelope. He'd carried it in his pocket until the time came when he'd have to give it to Lakshmi.

Then one afternoon he passed Margot in the corridor backstage. The sight of Margot, in her fright wig, stumbling on her high heels, in that cruelly short purple skirt, her ravaged white face and the helpless rage with which she pointed to the ragged hem of her skirt, it had affected Roger like a punch, not that he's ever been punched. How could he, Roger, a good person, a decent human being, how could he have done this to a fellow creature who had begun her career, just as he had, with dreams that didn't involve doing *Mister Monkey* in a soon-to-be-replaced-by-condos theater beneath the High Line?

Dear God, how sorry he was. Forgive this miserable penitent sinner, now and forever.

He'd wanted to beg Margot's forgiveness. To touch her cheek, to run his fingertips down the side of her face, to ruffle her curly wig, to kiss her on the forehead, to do any one of many things that would have mortified them both.

He'd looked at the envelope that contained the letter to Lakshmi, and he knew that it was never meant for Lakshmi. Lakshmi would be fine.

Without knowing it, he had typed out the quote for Margot. She was the one who needed the kindness, the sympathy, the consolation.

A sudden inspiration had guided Roger to pretend that the note had been left for Margot by an anonymous male fan.

It's fine with him, it's better, for Margot to think that Mario wrote it. It's a way of Roger making amends for what a prick he's been.

"Good to meet you," Roger tells Mario. "It's always nice to meet a theater lover."

"It's quite a show," says Mario. *"Mister Monkey.* I know Raymond Ortiz—"

"You *know* him?" Roger says.

"I've known him for years," Mario says. "He gives me tickets to the plays. I've seen the play many times. And your production was the best I've ever seen. Portia was . . . amazing."

"Thank you," Roger says.

Margot kisses Roger on both cheeks. Mario shakes Roger's hand. His warm neutral handshake is neither too tight nor too sweaty.

"We're having an early dinner," Margot says. "Right down the block. Want to join us?"

Roger knows where they are headed. The Isle of Pearls. Roger has seen Margot eating there and walked by very fast. Roger imagines Margot and Mario in the restaurant. He sees their faces shine with the light of how much they have in common. Mario is a theater lover! Margot is an actress! Roger pictures the start of their romance, like some sparkly Noël Coward play, some 1930s screwball comedy, or, going back, like Cyrano. Like Frankie and Johnny, but without the whining.

Their whole understanding will be based on a misunderstanding. And when at last the truth emerges, and Mario tells Margot that really and truly he didn't send that letter, she will still think he is teasing. By then it won't matter. It's how they met. The first sentence of their love story. It might as well be true.

Roger wishes them well. If Margot and Mario fall in love, *Mister Monkey* will have been worth it.

He sees, as if from a great height, the three of them standing awkwardly, shuffling from foot to foot, on the sidewalk. Waiting for something. *What are they waiting for?*

Are they waiting for *him* to do something? To offer up some sort of prayer or give them some sort of blessing? Why *him*?

Roger looks up. A charcoal smudge has darkened the white cotton of the clouds. A storm is coming. Then autumn. Then something worse. A gleaming white bird plummets straight down through the cloud cover, leaving a hole through which a shaft of light pours all the way down to the pavement. The bird hovers, suspended in the thickening pillar of light. Of course the light intensifies. Of course it grows closer and larger.

Roger takes Margot's and Mario's hands in his, in that overly effusive manner that theater people affect, until it becomes who they are. Mario flinches, then surrenders. Margot winds her fingers around Roger's. They could be the candy bride and groom on a cake, except for the difference in height, except for Margot's red hair, except for their shining faces.

Now Roger remembers the prayer, and in just a moment he will remember the names of the bride and groom standing before him. For now he only needs the prayer. He hears the distant chanting, the drone of monks praying for their salvation. There's an explosion of fireworks. Each word is a pinpoint of light, a shooting star growing brighter. It's night. The water and wind are rising. A comet has entered our orbit. There is rain and heat, fire and ice.

Roger sees the prayer in marquee lights.

Three are we. Three are thee. Have mercy.

About the Author

FRANCINE PROSE is the author of twenty-one works of fiction, including the *New York Times* best-selling novel *Lovers at the Chameleon Club, Paris 1932*; *A Changed Man*, which won the Dayton Literary Peace Prize; and *Blue Angel*, which was a finalist for the National Book Award. Her most recent works of nonfiction include the highly acclaimed *Anne Frank: The Book, the Life, the Afterlife*, and the *New York Times* bestseller *Reading Like a Writer*. She is a former president of PEN American Center, and a member of the American Academy of Arts and Letters and the American Academy of Arts and Sciences. She lives in New York City and is a Distinguished Visiting Writer at Bard College.

ALSO BY
FRANCINE PROSE

LOVERS AT THE CHAMELON CLUB: A Novel
Available in Paperback, E-book, and Digital Audio

MY NEW AMERICAN LIFE: A Novel
Available in Paperback, E-book, and Digital Audio

GOLDENGROVE: A Novel
Also Available in Hardcover, Paperback, E-book, Digital Audio, and Large Print

A CHANGED MAN: A Novel
Also Available in Paperback, E-book, and Digital Audio

BLUE ANGEL: A Novel
Also Available in Paperback and E-book

PRIMITIVE PEOPLE: A Novel
Available in Paperback

HOUSEHOLD SAINTS: A Novel
Available in Paperback

THE GLORIOUS ONES: A Novel
Available in Paperback

GUIDED TOURS OF HELL: Novellas
Available in Paperback

THE PEACEABLE KINGDOM: Stories
Available in Paperback

WOMEN AND CHILDREN FIRST: Stories
Available in Paperback

READING LIKE A WRITER: A Guide for People Who Love
Books and for Those Who Want to Write Them
Available in Paperback, E-book, and Digital Audio

ANNE FRANK: The Book, The Life, The Afterlife
Available in Paperback, E-book, and Large Print

CARAVAGGIO: Painter of Miracles
Available in Paperback and E-book